Education and Technology

A companion website to accompany this book is available online at:
http://education.selwyn.continuumbooks.com

Please visit the link and register with us to receive your password
and access these downloadable resources.

If you experience any problems accessing the resources, please
contact Continuum at: info@continuumbooks.com

Also available from Bloomsbury

ICT and Literacy, Nikki Gamble and Nick Easingwood
New Technology and Education, Anthony Edwards
Role of ICT, Avril Loveless

Education and Technology

Key Issues and Debates

Neil Selwyn

B L O O M S B U R Y

LONDON • NEW DELHI • NEW YORK • SYDNEY

Bloomsbury Academic
An imprint of Bloomsbury Publishing Plc

50 Bedford Square	1385 Broadway
London	New York
WC1B 3DP	NY 10018
UK	USA

www.bloomsbury.com

Bloomsbury is a registered trade mark of Bloomsbury Publishing Plc

First published in 2011 by the Continuum International Publishing Group Ltd
Reprinted 2012 (twice)
Reprinted by Bloomsbury Academic 2014

British Library Cataloguing-in-Publication Data
A catalogue record for this book is available from the British Library.

ISBN: HB: 978-1-4411-1182-1
      PB: 978-1-4411-5036-3

Library of Congress Cataloging-in-Publication Data
Selwyn, Neil.
Education and technology: key issues and debates / Neil Selwyn.
p. cm.
Includes bibliographical references and index.
ISBN: 978-1-4411-5036-3 (pbk.)
1. Educational technology–Study and teaching–United States.
2. Educational technology–United States–Curricula.   3. Internet in education.
4. Computer-assisted instruction.   I. Title.
LB1028.3.S38883   2011
371.33–dc22
2010028661

Typeset by Newgen Imaging Systems Pvt Ltd, Chennai, India
Printed and bound in Great Britain

Contents

Preface

This book addresses a topic that lies at the heart of contemporary education. The use of technology – and in particular the use of digital technology – is now a feature of most forms of teaching and learning. Yet despite its prominence, technology use continues to be an area of education that only occasionally receives sustained critical attention and thought – especially from those people who are most involved and affected by it. Indeed, educational technology tends to be something that is approached in a routine rather than reflective way by many teachers, students and parents. This is also the case for most policymakers, politicians and industrialists. The benefits of technology use are often taken for granted in education – part of the received wisdom of twenty-first-century teaching and learning.

At best, popular debates concerning education and technology (such as those in news media and political discourse) tend to be reduced to concerns of whether a certain technology is a 'good' or a 'bad' thing. Rarely, if ever, is sufficient attention paid to the contradictions, compromises and conflicts that lie behind the realities of technology use in education. Of course, the failure to think carefully about technology is not unique to education. Because digital technology is now such a familiar feature of most aspects of modern life, people often find it difficult to maintain a discerning and objective perspective on something that they are so close to. In this sense, finding the time to disengage ourselves from our own personal experiences of the digital age and think dispassionately about the role of technology in society is, in Joost van Loon's words, 'something we cannot do often enough' (van Loon 2008, p. 4).

This book has been written for anyone interested in thinking more carefully about the relationship between education and technology. This is deliberately *not* a technical guide concerned with 'how to' make the best use of different educational technologies in the classroom. Instead the book focuses on the people, processes, practices and structures that underlie the implementation of digital technology in education. The next eight chapters address the 'wider picture' of educational technology – that is, the key social issues and debates that underpin the everyday use of technology in education settings. Readers are introduced to theoretical discussions and debates from academic disciplines such as sociology, psychology, media studies and social policy. The book also offers an introduction to five decade's worth of empirical research literature in the area.

With all these thoughts in mind, this book should provide an engaging and provocative 'way in' to the many debates and controversies that underlie the academic study of education and technology. The next eight chapters consider some of the fundamental but often overlooked challenges and conflicts that underpin the implementation of digital technologies in education. While all of the chapters will raise as many difficult questions as they can offer definite answers, the book should help readers to develop a rich understanding of why technology use in education 'is the way it is'. Yet this is not a book that simply describes and dissects the present shortcomings of technology use in education. Each chapter is intended to act as a starting-point for further discussion, debate and possible change. Above all it is hoped that the book inspires readers to look beyond some of the popular (mis)assumptions and received wisdoms that surround the use of technology in education and, instead, begin to think critically about the educational technology of the near future.

Acknowledgements

While this book draws on the work, ideas and arguments of many others, ultimately I remain responsible for writing it, and so any inaccuracies or errors are mine. That said, there are a number of people who deserve acknowledgement in helping the ideas and arguments expressed in this book come to fruition – especially in challenging and refining my own understanding of education and technology over the past 12 years.

In particular I would like to thank colleagues at the Institute of Education's London Knowledge Lab who have helped develop my thinking about education and technology, as well as being kind enough to read over various draft versions of the material in this book. These colleagues include David Buckingham; Carey Jewitt; Diana Laurillard; Harvey Mellar; Ambrose Neville; Richard Noss; Martin Oliver; Kaska Porayska-Pomsta; John Potter; Sara Price; Rebekah Willett and Niall Winters. I would also like to acknowledge the contribution made by all of the undergraduate and postgraduate students who I have discussed these ideas with during the various courses that I have taught in the area of education and digital technologies.

Finally, I am always aware of the hard work that goes into the production of any book. So in terms of the writing and production of this book I would also like to thank all of the production and editorial team at Continuum – notably Ally Baker and Ania Leslie-Wujastyk – as well as the anonymous readers and referees for commenting on earlier drafts of the manuscript.

Neil Selwyn
London – October 2010

What Do We Mean by 'Education' and 'Technology'?

Chapter outline

Introduction

Educational technology is a topic that is often talked about, but less often thought about. This is not to say that intelligent or thoughtful things are never said about education and technology. Yet many people in education now see little need to pay close attention to something that is such a familiar feature of their educational landscape. The use of technology in educational contexts would appear to have become such a commonplace occurrence that, for many people, it has entered the realm of the common-sense. The notion of 'educational technology' is now accepted by the majority of people in education as inevitable and, for the most part, something that is simply 'got on with'.

We are therefore faced with a prevailing sense that the use of technology in education is something that does not merit particular critical scrutiny or thought. A computer in a classroom is now just as much 'part of the furniture' as domestic appliances in a kitchen, or traffic lights, ATMs and security cameras on a high street. Yet all of these technologies are connected directly with issues that are of fundamental importance to contemporary society. Although generally nonplussed by fridges, cookers and washing machines, most people are concerned greatly with matters of energy consumption, sustainable living or gender inequality. Although often oblivious to many of the technologies that overcrowd public spaces such as high streets, most people are also concerned with issues of traffic pollution, banking and finance, crime and surveillance. Paying closer attention to something as mundane as a refrigerator, a CCTV camera or even a classroom computer can provide a powerful 'way in' to engaging with some of the major societal issues and debates of our time.

With these thoughts in mind, it makes good sense to pay close attention to the many technologies that are used throughout education. As will be stressed over the eight chapters of this book, this needs to be done in a careful and considered manner. In particular our primary focus should not be on the actual technological devices, tools and applications *per se*, but the practices and activities that surround them, the meanings that people attach to them, and the social relations and structures that these technologies are linked to. At this early stage of the book these may all appear to be unwieldy and daunting concepts. This opening chapter will therefore lay the foundations for our later discussions of all these serious issues. First, then, it is useful to start with some very basic questions of definition. What exactly do we mean by the terms 'education' and 'technology'?

So what is education?

Perhaps the best way to develop a clear understanding of 'education' is to start by defining another term altogether – that is, that of 'learning'. Despite being a concept that is an integral part of education, many educational writers and academics are surprisingly inconsistent in their basic definitions of 'learning'. As Hodkinson and Macleod (2010, p. 174) have reflected:

> Learning is a conceptual and linguistic construction that is widely used in many societies and cultures, but with very different meanings, which are fiercely

contested and partly contradictory. Learning does not have a clear physical or reified identity in the world.

With this ambiguity in mind, the description offered by Ivan Illich is perhaps as good as any, explaining that 'to learn means to acquire a new skill or insight' (1973, p. 11). In these terms at least, the process of 'learning' refers to an individual's acquisition of new skills, or else new forms of knowledge and understanding. These different aspects of learning are also reflected in Benjamin Bloom's well-known 'taxonomy of educational objectives' (1956). Here Bloom argued that all learning can be described in terms of three over-lapping domains – the psychomotor domain (manual and physical skills – that is, 'doing'); the affective domain (emotions and attitudes – that is, 'feeling'); and the cognitive domain (intellectual capability and knowledge – that is, 'thinking').

One key area of contention among educationalists is whether learning should be seen as a product or a process. Many of the theories of learning that were developed during the first decades of the twentieth century certainly conceptualized learning as an end product or outcome – most often as a distinct change in behaviour. This view of learning is expressed, for example, in the 'behaviourist' conception of learning as a relatively permanent change in behaviour as a result of an individual's experiences. This idea of learning as a product continues to be a popular way of understanding learning – especially among learners themselves. Many learners (and some teachers) continue to see learning consisting largely of 'gaining knowledge' and 'the filling of empty vessels' – ideas that Carl Bereiter (2002) describes as 'folk' theories of learning. These concepts were reflected in Roger Säljö's (1979) research work during the 1970s and 1980s where he questioned large numbers of adult learners to explore their perceptions of what they were doing when engaging with education. The view of learning as a product was certainly apparent in the first three types of answers that Säljö received, that is:

- learning as a quantitative increase in knowledge, learning as acquiring information or 'knowing a lot';
- learning as memorizing, learning as storing information that can be reproduced;
- learning as acquiring facts, skills, and methods that can be retained and used as necessary.

That said, the fourth and fifth categories of answers revealed in Säljö's research could be said to point towards a different notion of learning. In this sense some learners were also found to describe their learning as an ongoing process rather than a finite product, that is:

- learning as making sense or abstracting meaning, learning involves relating parts of the subject matter to each other and to the real world;
- learning as interpreting and understanding reality in a different way, learning involves comprehending the world by reinterpreting knowledge.

These latter descriptions of learning as an ongoing process introduce the idea of the individual learner building upon their previous experiences and, in some instances, then changing their behaviour as a result. As we shall see in Chapter 4, this is certainly a view of learning that most contemporary educationalists and psychologists would concur with. As Jerome Bruner (1996, p. 146) put it, learning 'is not simply a technical business of well managed information processing'. Instead, learning can be seen to involve an individual having to make sense of who they are and develop an understanding of the world in which they live. From this perspective learning can be seen as a continuing process of 'participation' rather than a discrete instance of 'acquisition' (Sfard 1998).

In this respect we should acknowledge that learning can sometimes be an unconscious and unplanned process that individuals are unaware is taking place. Alan Rogers (2003) referred to this type of learning as an ongoing process of 'task-conscious' or 'acquisition learning' that takes place all the time. As Rogers argued, this learning is 'concrete, immediate and confined to a specific activity; it is not concerned with general principles' (Rogers 2003, p. 18). For example, much of the learning involved in parenting or in running a home could be said to fit this description. While some commentators have referred to this kind of learning as unconscious or implicit, Rogers (2003, p. 21) suggests that it might be better to speak of people as having a consciousness of the task. In other words, while the learner may not be conscious of learning they are usually aware of the specific task in hand.

Of course, when asked to describe 'learning' most people would think of forms of activity that are rather more organized and planned. In this sense learning can often be a process that individuals are consciously engaged in. Rogers (2003) labelled this as 'learning-conscious' or 'formalized learning' – that is, learning that is facilitated in some way by someone else. This can be described as 'educative learning' rather than the incidental accumulation of experience just described above. This definition implies a consciousness of learning where individuals are fully aware that the task they are engaged in involves some form of learning. As Rogers put it, this process usually involves guided episodes of learning – in other words, 'learning itself is the task. What formalized learning does is to make learning more conscious in order to enhance it' (2003, p. 27).

In these terms, then, the processes and practices of what we understand as 'education' are most obviously related to Roger's 'learning-conscious' or 'formalized' descriptions of learning. When most people talk about 'education' they are referring to the institutionally sponsored provision of formalized learning – that is, learning that is structured and often assessed and credentialized. *Formal education* is perhaps the easiest form of education to identify and by far the most discussed in the academic literature. A wide range of institutionally provided educational opportunities exist – most obviously the compulsory forms of school-based learning for children and young people. Similar forms of continuous post-compulsory education also exist in the shape of colleges, universities and different types of distance education. Formal education can also be found outside of settings such as the school and university. For instance, adult education institutions offer a range of full-time and part-time opportunities on a face-to-face or distance basis. Work-based training also represents a major source of adult formal education – including health and safety training, work-related evening classes as well as more complex forms of professional development. These latter forms are increasingly relevant to the broad concept of 'lifelong learning' – that is, the notion that education embraces not only the compulsory phases of schooling but also education and training throughout the life-course.

In contrast to these examples of formal education, Roger's notion of task-conscious or acquisition learning relates mainly to what could be termed *informal education*. In one sense, informal education can be seen to simply be learning 'which we undertake individually or collectively, on our own without externally imposed criteria or the presence of an institutionally authorised instructor' (Livingstone 2000, p. 493). In contrast to all the types of formal education just described, informal education 'is not typically classroom based or highly structured, and control of learning rests primarily in the hands of the learner' (Marsick and Watkins 1990, p. 12). The most common form of informal education is work-based 'learning on the job' – yet informal education also includes a range of learning stimulated by general interests, pursuits and hobbies outside of the workplace.

As a whole, then, the term 'education' can be best understood as the conditions and arrangements where learning takes place. Yet in reaching this definition we should recognize at this early stage of the book that education is not simply a technical matter of facilitating an individual's learning. It is important to acknowledge that much of what takes place in an educational setting has little or nothing to do with learning *per se*. Often the most significant aspects of education lie beyond the immediate instance of the individual engaging in the process of learning. Instead, it is important to also consider what can be termed the social 'milieu' of education. This can include the organizational cultures and micropolitics of educational institutions such as schools, colleges and universities. Similarly, how an individual learner engages with education is also often linked closely with the concerns of contexts such as the household, the workplace and wider community settings. In turn, these contexts are themselves set within a range of even wider social milieu – not least commercial marketplaces, nation-states and global economies. While perhaps not immediately apparent to an observer of a classroom setting, it would be foolhardy to attempt to explain any aspect of education without some consideration of all these wider influences.

It therefore seems appropriate that our discussions of educational technology throughout this book give due acknowledgement to the aspects of education that lie above and beyond the context of the individual learner and their immediate learning environment. This will include acknowledging the linkages between educational systems and the various elements of the 'macro' level of society such as global economics, labour markets and political and cultural institutions. Similarly, we need to understand the act of learning as being entwined with many other stratifications of social life such as family background, socio-economic circumstances, income, gender, race and class. The study of education and technology should therefore be seen in 'social scientific' terms – moving beyond making sense of the 'technical' aspects of learning and also paying close attention to the social world of education.

So what is technology?

Making this distinction between the 'technical' and 'social' aspects of education also relates to how we can define the notion of 'technology'. Unlike learning, there is fairly clear agreement among academics on the definition of 'technology'. At a basic level 'technology' is understood as the process by which humans modify nature to meet their needs and wants. In a (pre)historic sense, the concept of technology therefore refers to humans' ongoing use of tools and crafts to adapt and control their environment. Human use of technology is usually seen as beginning over 2 million years ago with the conversion of natural resources into simple tools. This practice took place for reasons of survival and mastery of the environment (e.g. the development of the spear), as well for more emotional purposes such as decoration and adornment (e.g. the development of cave painting). Technology is therefore one of the features that separate humans from most other animals. As David Nye reasons, 'animals are atechnical; they are content with the simple act of living. Humans in contrast continually redefine their necessities to include more' (2007, p. 2).

As Nye suggests, technologies are not just used to sustain forms of life but also to enhance and improve existing forms of living. Early humans' development of the ability to control fire greatly increased their available sources of food. Similarly the invention of the wheel around 4000 BC greatly helped people of the time to travel around and control their environment. In this sense, very little has changed from the development of the wheel to the development of the computer. Indeed, the notion of using technology as a means of improving previous arrangements certainly lies at the heart of what we would see as more 'modern' technologies. For example, technological advances such as the printing press, the telephone and the internet all lessened physical barriers to communication and allowed people to interact on a global basis. Even the development of technologies such as nuclear weaponry could be said to follow this logic of making things better – albeit from a more contestable perspective. As Volti (1992, p. 4) puts it, 'technologies are developed and applied so that we can do things not otherwise possible, or so that we can do them cheaper, faster and easier'.

This emphasis on 'doing things better' implies that the term 'technology' refers to more than just the material tools and artefacts that are used to do something. This can be seen in the origins of our contemporary use of the word 'technology' in the ancient Greek word 'technología'. The first half of 'technología' relates to the Greek word 'techne', which can be variously translated as skill, art or craft. This itself reflects an earlier Indo-European prefix 'teks-' which refers to the process of weaving or fabricating (as in 'textile'). The second half of 'technología' relates to the Greek suffix '-logía', which can be variously translated as the understanding of something, or as a branch of knowledge. In this sense, the term 'technology' has always referred to the processes and practices of doing things, understanding things and developing knowledge. As Albert Teich succinctly puts it, 'technology is more than just machines' (1997, p. 1).

Indeed, contemporary use of the term 'technology' refers to far more than just machinery and artefacts (i.e. the 'non-human' material aspects of technology). Instead it also refers to the social contexts and social circumstances of the use of these machines and artefacts (i.e. what can be termed the 'human' aspects of technology). How we understand these 'human' aspects of technology involves a number of important distinctions and definitions. For instance, Donald Mackenzie and Judy Wajcman suggest that 'technology' can be seen in three ways: the physical objects themselves; the human activities that take place in conjunction with these physical objects; and as the human knowledge that surrounds these activities – that is, 'what people *know* as well as what they *do*' (Mackenzie and Wajcman 1985, p. 3). From this perspective, technologies must be seen as profoundly 'cultural' objects – part of a body of knowledge shared between people and passed down from generation to generation (Goyder 1997).

This idea of technologies being more than just machines or material artefacts is made clearer if we think of a present-day technology such as the internet. Most people would agree that the internet is more than just the copper wires, fibre-optic cables, wireless connections, keyboards, processors and monitors that constitute the material networks of computers that support the internet. Indeed, when people talk about the internet they are usually referring to the activities that they engage in online, the cultures that can be said to surround these social activities, and the knowledge that results from these activities. As such, it is far more useful to describe the internet in terms of its social 'content' rather than its technical forms (Wessels 2010).

One of the most straightforward ways of conceptualizing the social and the technical aspects of technology is offered by Lievrouw and Livingstone's (2002) description of three distinct – but interconnected – aspects of what 'technology' is:

- *artefacts and devices*: that is, the technology itself and how it is designed and made;
- *activities and practices*: that is, what people do with technologies (including issues of human interaction, organizing, identity, cultural practices);
- *context*: that is, social arrangements and organizational forms that surround the use of technologies (including institutions, social structures and cultures).

We shall return to these different aspects of technology throughout this book. As well as neatly reminding us of the human and non-human aspects of technology, these three categories highlight the fact that technologies are not merely 'neutral' tools that humans can use freely to live their lives with. Instead technologies are an important part of the conditions of social life, often 'providing structure for human activity' as Langdon Winner (1986, p. 6) put it. We have already seen how technologies have been developed and used to enhance the quality of life from the invention of the spear and the wheel onwards. Most commentators would agree that modern-day technologies continue to play similar roles in the distinct improvement of society. Indeed, some people would go further than this, and argue that many modern-day technologies are a profound force for transformative change – not least in enhancing the capacity of individuals to act independently and to make their own free choices.

Yet as we shall discuss throughout this book, it is important to adopt a more objective perspective on the presumed benefits and transformations of technology. In particular, any technology must be seen in terms of the limits and structures that it imposes as well as the opportunities that it may offer for individual action and agency. Even what may appear to be the most 'transformatory' technology can end up limiting the choices and opportunities that some individuals possess. In particular, acknowledging that technology is connected with pre-existing organized structures of human activity can help us develop more detailed understandings of why technologies are used in education in the ways that they are. It is therefore important to recognize that educational technologies do not *always* change things for the better. Technologies do not always allow people to work more efficiently, or support people in doing what they want. Instead, educational technologies can often have unexpected and unintended consequences. Technologies are often linked to a range of other issues far beyond immediate concerns of the individual learner or classroom.

The strengths of conceptualizing technology in this way are illustrated if we consider one of the most familiar educational technologies of the past hundred years or so – the textbook. In one sense, understanding a textbook (like the one that you are reading at the moment) as *artefact* refers to the material book itself – its pages and covers, ink and paper. There are, of course, some very important issues relating to textbooks as artefacts, not least their portability and durability, as well as the environmental issues related to print-ing paper-based books. Yet if we also consider the *activities* and *practices* of using textbooks in education then a number of other issues come to the fore. For example, the activity of reading requires certain skills and literacies that can advantage or disadvantage different individuals. The practice of using text-books can also imply certain modes of teaching and learning – often passive, didactic and instructional, but perhaps learner-driven and imaginative. Textbooks can be used as the starting-point for more discursive forms of learning, or simply as an end in themselves. Indeed, when used in a classroom context some teachers will choose to merely teach 'to the text'. In some class-rooms textbooks will be the sole preserve of the teacher – in others they will be distributed to every student.

Focusing on the *context* of the textbook as an educational technology introduces a set of further issues. For example, the content of textbooks is an especially contentious area. Often the content of a textbook will reflect the notion of a state-defined 'official curriculum'. In countries where there is no official definition of the curriculum then the textbook can itself 'become' the *de facto* curriculum – what can be termed the 'curriculum-as-text'. Often the content of a textbook will imbue certain judgements, assumptions, values and perspectives on what is otherwise presented as 'objective' information – what can be termed the 'politics of the text'. Much has been written, for example, about the selective tradition of textbook content where some voices are silenced and other voices privileged. Concerns exist over the promotion of stereotypes and values, such as the presentation of race, class, gender and disability. These issues are reflected in long-running debates over the tendency of history textbooks to privilege the 'voices of the victorious' – usually the accounts of white, European males. Indeed, there have been long-running debates over the tendency for textbooks to portray male-centred versions of history (derided by some commentators as only telling '*his*-story'). Attempts have therefore been made to produce alternative texts focusing on '*her*-story' – that is, historical accounts that are written from a feminist perspective, that emphasize the role of women, and are told from a woman's point of view.

The wider context of the textbook as educational technology also includes the role of commercial companies in producing and selling the books. Like all aspects of educational technology, textbook production certainly remains a big business. A company such as Pearson Education sells over $4 billion worth of textbooks and curriculum materials each year. From this perspective, the politics of textbook production and sales are a complicated affair. In the United States, for example, some states and large school districts have significant leverage over the editorial decisions of publishers concerning what is printed and not printed in their books. Groups who have sufficient purchasing power to influence publishers' decisions can dictate the inclusion of information on contentious topics such as the theory of evolution or the rights and wrongs of abortion. As Michael Apple (1991) has argued, the textbook should be seen in a profoundly social and political light – often providing 'official knowledge' and commoditizing and commercializing school knowledge.

From 'analogue' to 'digital' technology

The example of the textbook suggests that even the most familiar and ordinary of educational technologies will be linked to a wide range of social issues and factors. This is especially the case with the types of technologies that this book is primarily concerned with – that is, recent forms of *digital* technology. We therefore need to now define what 'the digital' is and consider what wider practices, contexts, issues and factors it may be linked to.

The 'digital' aspects of contemporary life are now so frequently talked about that it is easy to overlook the origins of the term. At a basic level of description 'digital' simply refers to discontinuous data, based on the two distinct states of 'on' or 'off' (or 1 and 0) with no value in-between. Digital computers, for example, are only capable of distinguishing between these two values of 0 and 1, but are able to use binary codes to combine these zeros and ones into large numbers and other practical forms of information. In order to understand the significance of digital data it is important to also understand its opposite – that is, analogue data. 'Analogue' refers to data that can be measured as a continuously varying value. The most commonly cited example of analogue data is the hands of a clock that by moving continuously around the clock-face provide an ongoing measurement of time. A digital clock, in comparison, is only capable of presenting a discontinuous series of numbers denoting time with a gap between each value (every one hundredth of a second, for example).

This distinction between digital and analogue may appear to be a subtle technicality, but is crucial in explaining why digital technologies play such an important role in contemporary society. In particular, it is important to remember that humans generally experience the real world in analogue form. For example, vision is a response to the ever-changing intensity and wavelengths of light. Similarly, sound is made when objects vibrate producing continually fluctuating pressure waves that can be picked up by our ears. Nevertheless, as the example of the digital clock suggests, most analogue events can be simulated through digital information.

So why then do contemporary technologies privilege digital information over analogue? First, digital information is far easier to store and distribute electronically as it is dense and compressible, meaning that a lot of digital data can be stored on a small physical space. Moreover, digital data are easier to manipulate accurately than 'real-world' analogue data. A good comparison of the manipulability of analogue and digital information would be the lengths that you would have to go to alter the appearance of a conventional photograph as opposed to a digital image on screen. Digital data are seen to give the user more control over using, storing and altering data as they see fit. Perhaps most significantly it is much cheaper to distribute and sell large amounts of digital data. Digital technologies make good technological *and* good commercial sense.

All of these technical advantages have led to the idea of 'the digital' being associated with a number of wider qualities and characteristics – not least the general perception that digital technologies are more precise, more accurate and more efficient than analogue machines and methods. Digital technologies are seen to allow processes and activities to take place on far greater scales than before, in far quicker and more powerful ways. Crucially, digital technologies and digital practices are seen to give more control and flexibility to the individuals that use them. Digital technologies are therefore associated with dramatically enhanced and improved ways of doing things. For many people, digital technologies are seen to have underpinned a new and improved era of living – the so-called digital age.

One of the striking characteristics of many recent accounts and analyses of the digital age is the generally transformatory (and often optimistic) ways in which the changes associated with digital technology tend to be imagined. In short, most accounts of the digital age are framed within discourses of progress, transformation and the allure of 'the new'. As Kelli Fuery (2009, p. 9) notes, the perception of 'newness' has been closely associated with the digital technologies of the past 30 years or so. Indeed, many people's perceptions of digital technology appear to be driven by the belief that the digital age represents a 'distinctive rupture with what has preceded it' (Gere 2008, p. 17). In particular, many general discussions of the digital age tend to be informed by a notion that the development of digital technology represents a distinctively new *and* improved set of social arrangements in relation to preceding 'pre-digital' times. As Nicholas Zepke concludes, an assumption underpinning the idea of the 'digital age' is that 'digital technologies will define the way we live, learn, teach and be in the future' (2008, p. 5).

This sense of improvement and change has been described by some academics as the 'digital remediation' of everyday life and social processes (see Bolter and Grusin 1999). This idea of remediation refers to the fact that digital technologies appear to be reconfiguring many – if not all – social processes and practices. This is not to say that 'new' digital forms are believed to be usurping *all* practices and processes that have gone before. Instead digitally based activities are seen to borrow from, refashion and often surpass their earlier pre-digital equivalents. For many commentators, then, the obvious answer to overcoming contemporary social problems is now believed to involve some form of digitally related solution. As Steve Woolgar reflects, 'the implication is that something new, different, and (usually) better is happening' (2002, p. 3). One of the main issues that this book will address is how these digitally related changes and remediations are being experienced in educational settings and contexts. Before this can take place, we need to consider one final set of definitions and descriptions – what exactly do we mean by digital technologies?

Defining digital technologies

As has already been implied, the remainder of this book will focus mainly on digital technologies rather than 'pre-digital' technologies such as the textbook or pen. In this sense much of what we shall go on to discuss relates to what is also diversely referred to as 'information and communications technology', 'computerized technology' and a number of other variations on the 'information technology' label. In a technical sense all of these terms refer to computer-based systems – particularly software applications and computer hardware – that can be used to produce, manipulate, store, communicate and disseminate information. Put simply, then, the umbrella term of 'digital technology' can refer to a range of different aspects of contemporary technology use, that is:

- computing hardware, systems and devices (such as desktop PCs, laptop computers, tablet computers, interactive whiteboards, simulation systems and immersive environments);
- personal computing devices (such as mobile phones, 'smart' phones, personal digital assistants, mp3 players);
- audio-visual devices (such as digital radio, digital television, digital photography, digital video);

- games consoles and hand-held games machines;
- 'content-free' computer software packages (such as word processors, spreadsheets);
- 'content-related' computer software packages (such as simulation programmes, tutorial packages);
- worldwide web content, services and applications (not least web-pages and web-based services);
- other internet applications such as email and 'voice over internet protocol' (such as *Skype* and other web-based telephone services).

Perhaps the most prominent digital technology of the past 20 years – at least in educational terms – has been the mainstream emergence of the last 2 of these categories – that is, internet-based technologies. In turn, perhaps the most prominent internet technology of the past 20 years has been the worldwide web. Worldwide web applications are now a major element of contemporary digital technology use – not least in the form of search engines such as *Google*, hypertext-linked web pages and online tools and services such as 'e-tailing', social networking, content sharing applications, and so on. One of the defining features of all these internet technologies over the past 20 years has been the progression from what Zeynep Tufekci terms 'instrumental' to 'expressive' technology use. While the online applications of the 1990s were used primarily for the instrumental purpose of information seeking and knowledge gathering, the strength of contemporary internet applications is seen to lie in allowing communities of users to 'perform and realize social interactions, self-presentation, public performance, social capital management, social monitoring, and the production, maintenance and furthering of social ties' (Tufekci 2008, pp. 547–548). In this sense, many contemporary online applications, tools and practices are best described as 'social media'.

Indeed, one of the defining characteristics of these technologies is they embody a 'mass socialization' of internet connections and activities based around the collective actions of communities of users rather than individuals. In this sense, much digital technology use can now be seen as 'a hybrid of tool and community' (Shirky 2008, p. 136), referring to services and applications that rely on openly shared digital content that is authored, critiqued and reconfigured by a mass of users. In contrast to the transmissive 'one-to-many' modes of information exchange that characterized internet use during the 1990s, social media applications such as social networking, wiki applications and blogging are seen to be based around an interactive and participatory ethos of what can be described as 'many-to-many' connectivity between and within groups of internet users.

Another defining characteristic of most of the contemporary digital technologies listed above is that they draw upon what can be termed as a 'networking' logic. This is apparent, for example, in the networked connections that digital technologies such as mobile telephones now afford – that is, the interconnection of people, objects, organizations and information regardless of space, place or time. Similarly, many contemporary digital technologies are built around 'interactive' rather than 'broadcast' forms of exchange, with information shared between 'many-to-many' rather than transmitted from 'one-to-many' (O'Reilly 2005). As Kevin Kelly (1995, p. 201) noted at the end of the twentieth century, 'the central act of the coming era is to connect everything to everything . . . all matter, big and small, will be linked into vast webs of networks at many levels'. The subsequent integration of digitally supported connectivity into many aspects of everyday life has prompted popular and political commentators to proclaim networked 'connectedness' as an 'essential feature' of contemporary society (Rifkin 2000).

One further characteristic of all these contemporary technologies is their ongoing 'convergence'. The concept of convergence describes the tendency for different technologies to perform similar tasks, share resources and interlink with each other. In this sense the distinctions between many of the technological artefacts and devices that were listed above are continuously blurring. For example, a device such as the mobile phone now shares many features and capabilities of the laptop computer – not least the ability to access the internet. In terms of 'content', a technology such as the internet now supports a convergence of previously separate media forms – for example, television, radio, newspapers, and so on. As the digital anthropologist Mimi Ito has reasoned, technology use is perhaps best seen as a media 'ecology' where 'more traditional media, such as books, television, and radio, are "converging" with digital media, specifically interactive media and media for social communication' (Ito et al. 2008, p. 8).

All of these characteristics look set to continue through the ongoing development of digital technology over the next ten years or so. For example, current technology development is continuing to see the expanding capacity of digital technology to process data. Over the past few years even non-specialist 'ordinary' users have witnessed their use of data storage progress from talk of 'megabytes' to 'terabytes' of information (or, if you prefer, from millions of bytes to trillions of bytes). This ever-increasing capacity for storage and connectivity means that the built-in capabilities of technologies is becoming less important than their ability to connect to more powerful machines elsewhere. This is often described in terms of 'cloud computing', where the everyday technological infrastructure is abstracted and detached from individual users and machines. As Charles Leadbeater concludes, cloud computing looks set to 'allow much greater personalization and mobility, constant real-time connection and easier collaboration. We could all be connected, more continuously and seamlessly, through a dense cloud of information' (2010, p. 21).

Such advances will continue to be accompanied by the increasingly 'ubiquitous' placement of digital technologies throughout the environment. The advance of flexi-screen technology, for example, is now evident in the embedding of miniature and disposable devices being embedded in everyday objects such as contact lenses and paper. These advances suggest that life in the twenty-first century is being built around interactive and invasive digital technologies in the same way that the twentieth century was built around the broadcast technologies of the television, telegraph and radio. We will return to the future implications of these technological developments for education in Chapter 8. Suffice to say, while it may be relatively easy to foresee the technical shape of the digital artefacts of the next ten years or so, gaining a sense of the associated social practices, activities and wider contexts of use is far more difficult.

Conclusions

It could appear to some readers that this chapter has little direct relevance to the key issues, concerns and debates that they would consider to lie at the heart of education and technology. Indeed, while we have talked much of technology and of education there has deliberately been very little discussion of the two concepts in union. Instead, our discussions so far have taken the necessary step of what the introduction to this book described as 'disengaging ourselves from own our personal experiences of the digital age and thinking dispassionately about the role of technology in society'. Often social scientists refer to this process as 'making the familiar strange' – an awkward but necessary initial stage of any objective analysis.

This chapter has therefore attempted to take a step back from the day-to-day details of technology use in education and develop a solid basis for re-evaluating and re-approaching the topic of educational technology. Thus we have seen how the concept of 'education' actually covers a wide range of issues above and beyond formal learning in a classroom. Similarly, we have seen how the concept of 'technology' refers to more than material artefacts, devices and 'kit'. Finally, despite 2 million years of technology use we have seen how the past 40 years or so have been associated with particularly strong expectations of societal change, improvement and even transformation through digital technologies. On the basis of all these discussions, we are now in a far stronger position than before to construct a detailed working-definition of what educational technology is.

Above all, it should by now be clear that the concept of 'educational technology' does not simply refer to the material technologies and tools that are used in educational settings. It should now be clear that it makes little sense to see digital technologies as simply 'part of the furniture' of educational settings. Indeed, educational technologies are not simply neutral tools that are used in benign ways within educational contexts. Like all other technologies, educational technology is intrinsically linked with the social, cultural, economic and political aspects of society. In particular, this chapter has highlighted the need to understand educational technology both in terms of practice and context. As Robert Muffoletto concludes, 'educational technology is not about devices, machines, computers or other artefacts, but rather it is about systems and processes leading to a desired outcome' (2001, p. 2). From this perspective, it is worthwhile returning to Lievrouw and Livingstone's (2002) framework and thereby defining educational technology in the following terms:

- *artefacts and devices*: the technologies themselves and how they are designed and made before they reach educational settings;
- *activities and practices*: what people then do with the technologies in educational settings and for educational purposes (including issues of human interaction, organizing, identity, cultural practices);
- *context*: the social arrangements and organizational forms that surround the use of the technologies in educational settings and for educational purposes (including institutions, social structures and cultures).

It will be useful to keep these distinctions at the back of one's mind while reading the rest of this book. Similarly, it is worth taking some time to consider the different types of questions about education and technology that these distinctions raise. For example, how can we best understand technology implementation and improvement across a range of educational settings?

How can we best understand individual uses (and non-uses) of technology? What are the intended outcomes of technology use and how do they compare to the unintended outcomes of technology use? What are the linkages between technology use at the 'micro' level of the learner and the wider concerns of education organizations and even wider 'macro' concerns of politics, economy and culture? Perhaps the most important questions that come to mind are that of use and usefulness. Why do we actually *need* digital technology use in education? How exactly are digital technologies seen to be *changing* education? Is this even a correct way of thinking about the relationship between education and digital technology? All of these issues will now be explored in Chapter 2.

Further questions to consider

- What instances of technology use in education can you think of that are not concerned primarily with teaching and learning? What issues and processes do these technologies address? How is technology use reinforcing or altering these issues and processes?
- How do the issues raised in this chapter's discussion of the textbook relate to the emerging technology of the e-book? What *new* issues does the e-book introduce? What existing issues remain, or are even amplified in the shift from using textbooks to e-books in education? Remember to think about the activities, practices and wider contexts of e-book use, as well as the artefact itself.
- Digital technologies are often celebrated in terms of their speed, size, storage capacity, and so on. To what extent are the advantages of digital technologies related to matters of quantity rather than quality? What limitations or even disadvantages can be associated with the 'digitization' of educational practices and processes?

Further reading

Further discussions of the nature of education and learning can be found in the following books:

- Kassem, D. and Garrett, D. (2009) *Exploring Key Issues in Education*, London, Continuum
- Bates, J. and Lewis, S. (2009) *Study of Education*, London, Continuum

David Nye is a well-known historian of technology. In this book he develops a wide-ranging and informative overview of key theories and ideas about technology:

- Nye, D. (2007) *Technology Matters: Questions to Live With*, Cambridge MA, MIT Press

A large number of authors have written about digital technology and the nature of 'the digital'. Perhaps the most authoritative account of the digital age and 'network society' is provided by the sociologist Manuel Castells in his three-volume 'Information Age' series of books:

- Castells, M. (1996, second edition, 2000) *The Rise of the Network Society*, Oxford, Blackwell
- Castells, M. (1997, second edition, 2004) *The Power of Identity*, Oxford, Blackwell
- Castells, M. (1998, second edition, 2000) *End of Millennium*, Oxford, Blackwell

An accessible account of the nature of social media is provided by the technology writer Clay Shirky:

- Shirky, C. (2008) *Here Comes Everybody: The Power of Organising without Organisations*, London, Penguin

2 Does Technology Inevitably Change Education?

Chapter outline

Introduction

Most people would not question the assumption that technology – and in particular digital technology – is essentially a 'good thing' for education. This mirrors the widespread belief that digital technologies are leading to a general improvement and even transformation of most areas of society. As we saw in Chapter 1, many accounts of life in the digital age are based on general expectations of progress and the allure of 'the new'. It therefore makes sense to assume that education will benefit from the increased use of digital technology in similar ways to the rest of society.

Evidence of digitally driven improvement and change seems to be prevalent in nearly every area of contemporary life. For example, digital technologies appear to be supporting a 'flattening out' of hierarchies and introduction of a 'networking logic' to how many aspects of society are organized. These changes are seen to be encouraging an open (re)configuration of social relations and a corresponding 'underdetermination' of organizational structures (see Friedman 2007). Put simply, the massive, top-down, bureaucratic organizations of the twentieth century are believed to be losing much of their significance and power in the face of the fast-paced and fluid nature of 'digital' processes and procedures.

Of course, these transformations are not only taking place on a grand societal scale. Digital technologies are also seen to be introducing a distinctly 'individualized' way of doing things in everyday life. Growing numbers of processes and practices are now seen to be centred on the needs of individual rather than the demands of large institutions and organizations. Some commentators even believe that digital technologies are bringing people together in new ways and allowing individuals to do things for themselves without the involvement of official organizations and institutions. For example, strong claims are often made regarding the role of digital technologies such as the internet in enriching people's personal connections and 'social capital' (Haythornthwaite 2005). Some commentators have even claimed that digital technologies 'can be a natural force drawing people into greater world harmony' (Negroponte 1995, pp. 237–238).

Even if we discount some of the more fanciful and idealistic aspects of these statements, the vast majority of popular and academic opinion could be said to hold an essentially optimistic view of the life-changing power of digital technology. These changes are usually presented in wide-ranging and far-reaching terms. As Nicholas Gane (2005, p. 475) reflects:

> It would seem to me that internet-related technologies have directly altered the patterning of everyday life, including the way we work, access and exchange information, shop, meet people, and maintain and organize existing social ties. These technologies have done more than 'add on' to existing social arrangements; they have radically altered the three main spheres of social life, the spheres of production, consumption and communication.

As Gane implies, these 'direct alterations' of everyday life would certainly appear to be evident across many areas of society. In particular it is often argued that education and learning are particularly relevant areas for digital improvement and change. Indeed, there would seem to be a number of substantial overlaps between the main concerns of education and the main characteristics of digital technology – not least the production and dissemination of knowledge through interaction with others. In many ways, therefore, the central concerns of education and learning could be said to be interlinked closely with some of the main functions and processes of digital technologies. Surely, then, the union of digital technology and education is an inherently 'good thing'?

This seemingly close affiliation between the educational and the digital has certainly led many people to assume education to be one of the leading areas of society where technology-based change and improvement will take place. Indeed, the inevitability of digital change in education is usually justified in a number of different ways. On one hand, digital technology is seen to have a clear capacity if used in particular ways to change many aspects of education for the better. In other words, there is an *internal imperative* for the increased use of digital technology within educational settings. On the other hand, the rise of digital technology elsewhere in society is seen to necessitate change in education. In other words, the general digitization of society acts as an *external imperative* for the increased use of digital technology in education. The next section of this chapter will consider the nature of these reactive and proactive arguments in further detail. Just *why* do we need digital technology in education?

The external imperatives for technology use in education

One of the most immediate imperatives for the educational use of digital technology is seen to be the simple priority of 'keeping up' with the rest of modern life. The relentless and rapid development of digital technology over the past 50 years is well-illustrated by what technologists refer to as 'Moore's Law'. This technical rule-of-thumb describes the long-term exponential trend for the number of transistors that can be placed on a microchip to more or less double approximately every 2 years. As we discussed in Chapter 1, this increasing capacity for technological development has been accompanied by a corresponding growth in the use of digital technologies across most areas of life. Yet many people feel that educators and educational institutions are placed in a position of being noticeably 'behind the times' of technology use in comparison to other sectors of society. This creates an imperative for education to respond to technological advances – what Robert Boody (2001) recognized as the priority of keeping 'running just to keep in place'.

Of course, the imperative for education change is not just based around concerns of remaining 'up to date' with technology for its own sake. Many people would argue that education faces an ongoing societal obligation to keep up to date with the economic and societal changes associated with technology. In particular, digital technologies are now seen as an integral part of maintaining education's relevance to the fast-changing economic world. These concerns are often described in terms of meeting the demands of the 'knowledge economy' and 'information society'. Although contestable, both of these concepts seek to describe the changing 'post-industrial' era in which much of the world now finds itself. In most developed industrialized countries the production, transmission and consumption of information and knowledge is seen to have overtaken the traditional importance of manufacturing and the production of goods. These shifts mean that the most successful countries are those that maintain 'knowledge-based' economies – that is, economic systems where the use and application of knowledge produces the majority of economic benefit and power.

Crucially, many of these shifts are seen to have taken place because of the growth of digital technology – especially information processing and telecommunications technologies. It is therefore felt appropriate that digital technologies are used to support the new forms of education required by the knowledge economy. Of course, success in the knowledge economy does not derive from technology and knowledge alone. Nevertheless, many industrialists and governments see technology-enhanced education as playing an important role in providing sufficient levels of 'human capital' within a society. In this sense, one of the most prominent external imperatives for the increased use of digital technologies in education relates to the technology-related skills required to work in the knowledge economy. Many occupations are now centred on information processing, with workers using digital technology to create and manipulate information-based 'virtual' products. These occupations are dependent on increased flexibility in time and space, as well as requiring flexible, adaptable and technology-orientated types of workers – often referred to in terms such as 'self-programmable' knowledge workers or 'symbolic analysts'. All of these economic shifts now mean that digital technology is a key element in sustaining the long-established links between the needs of a country's economy and the nature of a country's education system.

Aside from issues of national economic success and 'employability', the ability to use digital technology is also considered to be an essential life-skill for individual citizens as they grow up into an 'information society'. Education therefore faces the additional external imperative to provide individuals with the necessary life-skills to survive and hopefully thrive in the information society. From this perspective there is a strong imperative for educational institutions such as schools to introduce even the youngest of learners to technology. Indeed, so-called digital competence and digital literacy are seen to be essential capabilities for contemporary life – some of the 'skills needed to survive and thrive in a complex and connected world' (Trilling and Fadel 2009). These pressures are experienced across all stages of education and all ages of learner – from the young child in kindergarten to the retired person in an adult education centre.

Of course, it is important to recognize that these external pressures for technological change do not come solely from government, industry and the educational 'establishment'. Indeed, these external imperatives for technological change are increasingly expected by other 'consumers' of education. Many academic commentators argue that this is especially the case with the young people who are now entering schools, colleges and universities having been born into the digital age and who have experienced no other way of living – leaving digital technologies to be 'so commonplace as to be unremarkable' (Plowman et al. 2010, p. 135). As a result these 'digital natives' are seen to lead lifestyles that are reliant upon the benefits of digital media and who expect these characteristics to be woven into all aspects of their lives – including the ways in which they learn and are educated (Palfrey and Gasser 2008). These changes could have profound implications for education and educators. As commentators such as Marc Prensky (2001, p. 1) have been warning since the start of the twenty-first century, 'our students have changed radically. Today's students are no longer the people our educational system was designed to teach.' Arguments such as these suggest that education must simply change in order to 'keep up' with the demands of young students. As Jabari Mahiri (2011, p. 209) reasons, 'new media permeates the lives of young people . . . we must define its place for learning in schools or watch it take the place of schools'. Of course, much of the pressure for increased technology use in schools, colleges and universities is also being driven by the personal beliefs and experiences of parents and teachers. Indeed, it could be argued that there is an almost unconscious connection in the minds of many adults between digital technology and the 'quality' of contemporary education.

All of these external imperatives for educational change can be found in developed and developing countries alike. In particular these pressures and demands have prompted considerable political efforts around the world to increase the use of digital technology in education. The past 20 years or so have seen digital technology become a prominent feature of education policy-making around the world. Nearly every developed nation (as well as many developing nations) now has a detailed 'educational ICT strategy' based around the broad aim of guiding educational institutions to use digital technology in their teaching and learning. These strategies and initiatives most commonly involve spending significant amounts of money to ensure that the internet is available in every classroom and that learners and teachers have sufficient access to computers. Much effort is also put into the training of newly qualified and experienced teachers, alongside the adjustment of curricula to include technology-related components. Digital technology has therefore formed a central part of the improvement and modernization of most education systems over the past 15 years or so regardless of a country's social or economic circumstance.

The internal imperatives for technology use in education

As all these examples suggest, many of the justifications for using technology in education derive from 'top-down' pressures and external imperatives that are often only partially related to matters of teaching and learning. Yet, it is important to remember that what takes place in education is not wholly driven by matters of economy, policy and society. Instead, many of the rationales and reasons for using technology in education are also related to what was referred to earlier as 'internal' issues and pressures. As we shall now go on to discuss, these internal issues are not necessarily related to making education more responsive to agendas of policymakers, industrialists or parents. Rather these reasons and motivations often relate to 'bottom-up' concerns of making education provision 'work better'. In particular, many academics and practitioners alike believe that technology is capable of supporting a range of improvements to the core processes of education. Against this background, growing numbers of educationalists are proving keen to harness the potential of digital technologies to overcome some long-existing problems and limitations of education.

These 'internal' benefits and changes tend to be expressed along a number of lines, all of which will be elaborated upon in later chapters. Perhaps the most frequently discussed benefit of digital technology use is its role in supporting and enhancing learners' cognitive processes and thinking skills. The use of digital technology is seen to support a wide range of cognitive benefits. For example, it is argued that digital technologies assist some of the main prerequisites to higher-order thinking, namely, memory and automation of 'lower level' skills such as spelling. Digital technologies are often associated with 'constructivist' forms of learning – allowing learning to take place within collaborative and supportive social contexts. Indeed, digital technologies such as the internet fit neatly with the constructivist view that learning often best takes place as a social process of collective knowledge construction. In this sense digital technology can link learners to other people and tools that may support and mediate effective learning (Scardamalia and Bereiter 1994).

As these claims suggest, a key advantage of technology-based education is seen to be its positioning of the learner at the centre of the learning process. In particular, digital technologies are believed to increase the freedom of learners to choose the information and the people appropriate to their particular needs and circumstances. Digital technologies such as the internet can certainly provide learners with almost instantaneous access to a wealth of information and communication. In particular, digital technology can offer learners a ready means of contact with other learners, teachers and experts at a global as well as local level. Indeed, many academics have been especially enthused by the educative potential of computer-mediated communication. Learning and the exchange of information are felt to lie at the heart of digitally supported 'virtual communities' and the collation of collective knowledge through the formation of 'online brain trusts', 'computer-assisted group minds' and 'crowd sourcing'. Through these means, individuals can learn with and learn from whomever they chose. This increased flexibility and individualized control makes digital technology an especially appropriate means of supporting the forms of 'informal' education and learning outlined in Chapter 1.

Digital technologies have also been welcomed as invaluable tools for teachers as well as learners. With the ability to deliver learning that is directed and differentiated, teachers can concentrate their efforts on the majority of students in a class. As an almost limitless bank of resources from around the world, the internet can allow teachers to present more rigorously researched and engaging lessons to learners. The use of interactive presentation devices such as electronic whiteboards can make educational content 'come alive' for learners. Digital technologies are also portrayed as assisting teachers in the more procedural and bureaucratic elements of their job, enabling teachers in tasks such as marking and producing lesson materials and allowing them to spend time with learners. Computer-mediated communication is also seen as a valuable source of professional support and development, acting as a space for online dialogue and sharing resources between teachers around the world. In short, digital technologies are seen to be a valuable and integral part of the modern-day teacher's repertoire – allowing them to explore and extend their own practice and improve the overall 'learning experience'.

Besides from individual learners and teachers, other 'internal' educational benefits of digital technologies are seen to include the improved organizational effectiveness of educational institutions. As digital technology has grown to become an integral part of the running of organizations in sectors of society such as commerce and industry, the pressure for educational institutions to follow suit has increased. Digital technologies are seen to 'modernize' schools, colleges and universities – instilling businesslike efficiencies in how these education organizations operate. Aside from matters of organizational, managerial and administrative efficiency, another popularly perceived benefit of digital technologies is that they can improve the 'outcomes' of educational institutions, such as increasing standards in the form of reading ages, IQ scores, examination results, retention rates and students' progression to higher levels of learning.

A further organizational benefit of digital technology is the more efficient delivery of education. In particular, one of the most obvious advantages is the use of digital technology to open up education 'beyond the four walls of the classroom' (Gee 2005). In this way digital technologies are popularly seen as widening access to education – supporting a diverse provision of educational opportunities from which learners can choose. Technology-based education is therefore perceived to extend the reach of traditional educational provision (such as schools, colleges and universities) to other organizations such as commercial organizations, community groups and cultural institutions such as museums and libraries. By overcoming practical issues of economy and scale (such as buildings, staffing and other physical resourcing limitations), 'virtual' educational provision allows a diversity of smaller and more specialist organizations to provide learning opportunities. Some commentators have welcomed digital technology as enabling more competitive and effective 'marketplaces' for education to develop (Jones 2010).

All these advantages are seen as having the beneficial effect of allowing greater numbers of people to participate in a wider range of learning than was previously possible. In particular, the increased choice and control for learners associated with technology-based education is believed to encourage the inclusion of social groups who traditionally do not engage in education.

The distribution of educational opportunities via technology, it is suggested, can help overcome the barriers that deter people from taking part in learning. Digital technologies may do this by making learning provision more flexible, bringing costs down, making learning more accessible, offering reliable and accessible information, and allowing people to learn on an 'any place, any pace' basis. This is seen to embody the ideal of 'lifelong learning' that many governments and educators are striving to establish. As Curtis Bonk argues, 'it does not matter if you are a scientist on a ship in Antarctic waters or a young girl in a Philippine village – you can learn when and where you want and from whomever you are interested in learning' (2009, p. 7).

Recognizing the wider significance of technological change in education

All of these claims – and many more – will be examined in detail in later chapters of this book. In the meantime, we should think a little more carefully about the general nature of these claims and arguments. In particular, it is worth developing a critical and questioning approach to all of the assumptions, beliefs and predications outlined so far in this chapter. While they may all appear highly persuasive and commonsensical, none of these claims are necessarily accurate or objective descriptions of the realities of technology use in education. In fact care has been taken throughout the last few sections of this chapter to qualify our descriptions of all of these changes and improvements as 'perceived' or 'argued' rather than being undisputed fact. In moving this book onwards, we need to remain mindful of avoiding what was referred to earlier as an 'unquestioning acceptance' of technology and educational change. The first step in this process is to give further thought to the significance and nature of the changes involved in these claims about education and the 'imperatives' of technology.

Most of the claims and arguments considered so far involve fundamental challenges to existing notions of *what* education is, *why* education is provided and *how* education is carried out. These claims and arguments are certainly not neutral, factual descriptions of inevitable technical adjustments and alterations. Instead they challenge a range of established educational arrangements and assumptions – not least the types of learning and forms of learning opportunities that are currently made available to learners; the role of the learner in the learning process; the role and status of the teacher in the learning process (e.g. issues of pedagogy); the status of knowledge (e.g. issues of curriculum); and the status of the educational institution. As the examples highlighted so far in this chapter suggest, all of these aspects of education are seen to be challenged by the ongoing use of digital technology.

For many academic commentators, the educational imperatives of technology involve a fundamental rethinking of the relationships between learners, knowledge, teachers and educational institutions. As Robert Kozma (2003, p. 5) reasoned, digital technology is implicated in a number of changes to how the nature of education and learning is perceived. These changes include the following:

- re-imagining the role of the teacher: that is, changing from the teacher as initiator of instruction for the whole class to the teacher as a guide who helps students find their appropriate instructional path and evaluate their own learning;
- re-imagining the nature of teaching: that is, changing from teachers working in isolation to teachers collaborating with their colleagues on joint plans and projects;
- re-imagining the role of the student: that is, changing from students as passive individuals to students as active learners working in teams to create new knowledge and solve problems;
- re-imagining the role of the educational institution: that is, changing from educational institutions that are isolated from society, to educational institutions that are integrated into society;
- re-imagining the role of the parent: that is, changing from parents uninvolved in their children's education to parents who are actively involved.

Of course, in suggesting these changes Kozma is assuming the continuation of basic educational institutions and structures such as the school. However, other commentators choose to view the educational changes associated with digital technologies in more drastic terms. With digital technology, it is argued, we do not necessarily need a 'school' or 'university', a 'teacher' or a 'student'. As far as some academic commentators are concerned, many of the learner entitlements and structural shifts suggested above could be best achieved without formal education at all. Arguments such as these lie at the heart of Betty Collis and Lisa Gommer's model of 'different scenarios of change' that outlines the technological future of higher education (see Figure 1). This model outlines the implications of the likely shift from the current arrangement of the institution providing education, to the emerging arrangement of the individual learner seeking out their own learning. This model also highlights

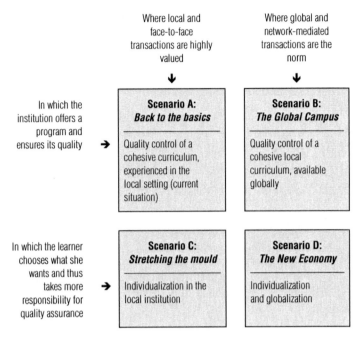

Figure 1 Four scenarios for flexible learning (adapted from Collis and Gommer 2001)

the implications of likely changes to the nature of the learning process – for example, what if learning is technologically mediated on a global scale as opposed to provided through face-to-face methods on a local scale? As these 'different scenarios of change' illustrate, these shifts can lead to different configurations of education provision depending on the respective roles of the individual and the institution.

Using these criteria, Collis and Gommer (2001) offer four broad scenarios of changed provision of education. On one hand, the changes associated with digital technology could involve little more than the continuation of the current institutional arrangements of education coupled with the additional provision of some education through distance provision (what Collis and Gommer term 'back to the basics'). However, this model also highlights the possibility of a shift to 'the new economy' of education where no institution is responsible for the education of the individual *per se*. Interestingly, it is this latter option that Collis and van der Wende (2002, p. 14) described as 'increasingly being seen as the way of the future'.

Collis and Gommer's framework neatly illustrates the far-reaching nature of many of the claims being made about technology and educational change.

As argued earlier, many of the seemingly 'common-sense' claims being made about the changing use of technology in education imply a substantial remoulding of educational provision around the needs of the individual learner. Conversely, they also imply the significant reduction (or even complete replacement) of the educational institution, the teacher and the curriculum. Present discussions of technology and educational change therefore tend to reach one of two possible conclusions. First is the conclusion that educational institutions must make some significant adjustments to their 'traditional' arrangements. As Tony Bates (2004) put it, this view sees educational institutions having to either 'transform or die' in the face of technological progress. Secondly, though, is the more radical conclusion that technology effectively renders many of the present, established arrangements of education provision obsolete and redundant. In other words, educational institutions will soon 'die' whether they change or not.

Both these conclusions imply some very significant changes to education – indeed, arguments such as these should not be taken lightly. Yet it is important to remember that none of these scenarios are as inevitable and cut-and-dried as they may first appear. All of these debates about technology and educational change are not simply matters of discussing *when* these benefits and changes will occur. Instead, we need to think more carefully about *why* these changes should – or should not – occur. In particular, we need to accept that shifts and changes in education are rarely as straightforward and unproblematic as some commentators would have us believe. As Michael Fullan has observed, educational change is not a straightforward process. Not everyone benefits from an educational innovation in the same way and, from a more practical perspective, the consequences of educational change are often difficult to assess. As such, we cannot simply assume that technological change is an inevitable force for good in education. As Fullan (2007, p. 6) concludes, 'change is not necessarily progress'.

It is therefore sensible to approach all of the issues outlined so far in this chapter with a degree of caution and even scepticism. In particular, it is important to recognize that many of the key questions surrounding education and technology are not concerned with issues of technology at all. Instead, they are related to wider questions of what education is, and what we want education to be. The scale of these questions certainly suggests that we should not be seduced by promises of digital technology changing everything for the better. Questions about the future of education are far too important to be left to a blind faith in the 'power' of technology. Instead it is clear that careful, considered and critical thought needs to be given to all of the claims and assumptions that surround the use of technology in education. First and foremost, then, more consideration needs to be given to how we actually go about thinking sensibly about technology, education and change. How can we move beyond common-sense assumptions and exaggerated expectations and, instead, develop a more socially circumspect analysis of education and technology?

Thinking more carefully about education and technology

The first steps towards thinking more carefully about educational technology involve taking nothing for granted, and making no assumptions about either technology or education. From the outset we need to recognize the debatable and contestable nature of all the claims that surround education and technology. None of the descriptions of education and technology presented so far in this chapter are necessarily neutral, objective or empirically grounded. Instead, many of these claims and arguments are most accurately described as value-driven aspirations for the education of the near future. This is most obvious in some of the more exaggerated claims made about technology-related change in education. Take, for instance, the observation that educational technology promises nothing less than 'the creation of a more just, human, inclusive society, where the development and transformation of teaching and learning services social and emotional as well as economic ends' (Sutherland et al. 2008, p. 5). At best, claims of this sort could be seen as enthusiastically ambitious. It could be argued, however, that such rhetoric unrealistically over-extends the capabilities of digital technology to affect change, and distracts attention away from the realities of contemporary education and society.

Although many of these sorts of claims concerning education and technology may be compelling, they should be all treated with a sense of cautious realism. While those who commentate on the possibilities of technology use may often trade in the spectacular, the realities of technology use are often more mundane and compromised. Even the most enthusiastic proponents would concede that the realities of digital technology use in education often fail to match the rhetoric. While the past 20 years may have seen substantial increases in the physical presence of digital technology in schools, colleges and universities, the much promised technology-led 'transformation' of the processes and the practices of education has nevertheless failed to materialize. Although digital technologies and other personalized technologies may well have undoubted potential to support learners, educators and institutions, it seems that this potential is being realized only on occasion. As Diana Laurillard (2008, p. 1) has observed wryly, 'education is on the brink of being transformed through learning technologies; however, it has been on that brink for some decades now'.

This gap between how educational commentators would like technology to be used, and how it actually ends up being used suggests that we need to avoid imagining technology to be a ready solution to existing education problems. Much of the enthusiasm for education and technology covered so far in this chapter appears to be driven by an underlying belief in technology as some sort of 'technical fix'. As Kevin Robins and Frank Webster (1989) observed, the history of education has been characterized by attempts to use the 'power' of technology in order to solve problems that are non-technological in nature. The history of education is also characterized by a tendency to ignore the often ineffective or unsustainable outcomes that arise as a result of technology use. As many of the examples discussed so far in this chapter have illustrated, there is little to suggest that much has changed in the 20 years or so since Robins and Webster made this observation.

Anyone who is studying education and technology therefore needs to steer clear of assuming that any digital technology has the ability to change things for the better. History reminds us that technical fixes tend to produce uneven results – very rarely ending in the same outcomes for all of the population and often just replacing one social problem with another. Even if a technology is seen to 'work' it can be very difficult to understand why, especially when the application of that technology has been accompanied with other non-technological interventions. Often technical fixes will only deal with the surface manifestations of a problem and not its roots. Indeed, the social problems of education are quantitatively and qualitatively different from most of the technical problems of education. They tend to be less specific with many different causes and do not operate within a closed system like many technological problems. In short, we should not assume that the social issues surrounding education are easily 'fixable' via technology.

All of these issues suggest that we need to move beyond thinking in commonsensical ways about education and technology. In particular, some of the most misleading assumptions about education and technology are the deterministic claims that technologies possess inherent qualities and are therefore capable of having predictable 'impacts' or 'effects' on learners, teachers and educational institutions if used in a correct manner. In its simplest form, such 'technological determinism' can be seen as a way of thinking about technology that assumes that technology determines social change. In its most extreme form, 'hard' technological determinism assumes that technology is the only factor in social change. While many people in education would feel uncomfortable in making such a direct association, most would perhaps concur with a 'soft' form of technological determinist thinking which assumes that technology has an influence (and often a strong influence) on social change.

Technological determinism has a long heritage in popular, political and academic discussions of the 'effect' of technology on education. For example, a determinist way of thinking underpins the range of popular claims that various forms of computer-mediated communication have *caused* a decline in traditional literacy standards, or that internet use *leads* to improvements in learning. While appealing to those people who want to construct bounded 'scientific' explanations and models, the dangers of these ways of thinking about the use of technology lie primarily in the simplistic conclusions that they lead towards. In particular, this way of thinking usually reaches conclusions that recommend the overcoming of 'barriers' or impediments within the immediate educational context, so that the inherent beneficial effects of technology may be more fully felt. This logic is illustrated in the frequent 'blaming' of teachers or educational institutions for the failure of digital technologies to be used 'effectively'. Indeed, current discussions and debates about the use of digital technology in educational settings often continue to follow a decidedly externalist logic – 'treating new technologies as autonomous forces that compel society to change' (Nye 2007, p. 27). Many of the claims and arguments presented in this chapter so far have been based around the assumption that digital technology is set inevitably to change various aspects of education. If nothing else, the uneven nature of educational change over the past 40 years or so suggests that this relationship is not as straightforward as some people would like to think.

There are many good reasons to attempt to move beyond a technologically determinist view of education and technology – not least because such thinking often leads to incorrect analyses and conclusions. If the relationships between education and technology are only seen in these 'cause-and-effect' terms, then the main task of anyone studying educational technology is simply to identify the impediments and deficiencies that are delaying and opposing the march of technological progress. This view is implicit, for example, in the increasingly popular proposals to dispense with the educational institutions or classroom teachers that appear to be impeding the benefits of technology in education. Technological determinism of this type leaves little room for manoeuvre, deviation or any other form of social agency in the implementation and use of technology. At best teachers, students and everyone else involved in education are placed in a position of having to respond to technological change by making the 'best use' of the technologies that they are presented with.

The limitations of making determinist assumptions about technological change can be found in all areas of society. Take, for example, the strongly held claims throughout the 1980s and 1990s that computerized technology would lead to the 'paperless office'. With the benefit of hindsight, it is estimated that the use of email in an office-based organization is associated with an increase in paper consumption by around 40 per cent. The interesting question that arises, therefore, is how we can explain this apparent 'failure' of email technology to determine a reduction in paper use. Is it because people in offices are simply failing to use the technology effectively or correctly? Is it because office-based businesses and firms are resistant to change their practices? In fact, as Abigail Sellen and Richard Harper's in-depth study of office life demonstrated, the 'failure' of digital technology to change office practices in the ways that many people expected does not have one simple explanation (2001). Instead, the ever-increasing use of paper in offices is due partially to the complex ways that technologies such as email and paper 'fit' with the existing cultures and structures of business environments. The researchers also found that the continuation of the 'paper-full' office was related to the ways that using paper 'fits' with the wider everyday concerns and priorities of people's lives (think, for instance, about all the reasons you might choose to use a *Post-It* note rather than email to convey a message). Because of all these social and cultural issues, paper looks set to continue to play an important role in office life regardless of the technical efficiencies of email.

Explanations such as these suggest that we should attempt to make sense of education and technology in similarly nuanced terms. As with any office or business environment, the realities of technology use in educational contexts are often complex and not easily predictable. Any technology-driven 'change' is certainly not inevitable or consistent across a whole educational system. In this respect we need to consider the social conditions, social arrangements and social relations that lie behind the use of digital technologies in education – what was referred to in Chapter 1 as the 'social milieu' of technology use. It also makes sense to refer back to the ideas of 'technology as practice' and 'technology as context', and consider how the social and cultural aspects of education processes and practices may influence the use of technology.

Sociologists often refer to this way of understanding technology as taking a 'social shaping' perspective. Following this line of thinking, it is accepted that there can be no predetermined outcomes to the development and implementation of educational technologies. Instead any technological artefact is seen as being subjected continually to a series of interactions and 'negotiations' with the social, economic, political and cultural contexts that it emerges into. As Wiebe Bijker et al. puts it, understanding technology as being 'socially shaped' therefore allows us to 'open up the black box of technology' (1987). This 'black box' analogy recognizes that the use of technology in education is not a hidden process, but one that can be opened up to scrutiny if we ask the right questions. In particular, the social shaping approach suggests that questions are asked about the large number of organizational, political, economic and cultural factors that pattern the design, development, production, marketing, implementation *and* 'end use' of a technological artefact in education. If we wish to gain a full sense of how and why educational technologies are being used in the ways that they are, we therefore need to develop better understandings of how technologies are socially constructed, shaped and negotiated by all of these factors and all of the 'actors' that represent them.

There are many different ways of looking at educational technology from this social shaping perspective. One common approach is to focus on different levels of analysis where social actors and interests may influence the use of technology – what can be termed the 'macro', 'meso' and 'micro' levels of description. Of course, the microlevel of the individual learner or teacher is undeniably important and merits sustained consideration, not least in terms of the continued importance of immediate 'local' contexts in framing learning processes and practices. Yet these microlevel concerns can only be understood fully after having considered what could be termed 'the bigger picture' of educational technology. This includes the mesolevel of the organizational structures and goals of educational institutions, as well as the macrolevel of larger cultural, societal, political and economic values. Many of these issues may be far removed from what one usually finds in discussions about educational technology, but all are important elements of making full sense of education and technology.

So, as the remainder of this book progresses it will be important that we develop an understanding of how all these different concerns work to influence each other. Robert Kozma's (2003) framework for understanding the use of technology in schools offers a good introduction to some of the different influences at play here. At the microlevel, for example, Kozma identifies a range of factors related to the learner and teacher, such as their educational background, experience with technology, socio-economic background and norms. Kozma also considers classroom factors as key elements at the microlevel of analysis – not least issues of classroom organization, class size and the type and arrangement of technology devices. At the mesolevel of Kozma's framework, are people such as school leaders and managers, parents and local business leaders as well as organizations such as educational districts and boards. Here issues such as school type, organization, local culture, technological support and innovation history are seen as influencing the use of technology. Finally, at a macrolevel Kozma points to the influence of education policymakers, business leaders and the IT industry – all associated with wide-ranging issues such as the national curriculum, education funding, economic forces, cultural norms, and so on.

Conclusions

While by no means a definitive list, Kozma's examples highlight the wide range of interests and influences that need to be considered when seeking to explain issues of technology and education change. Even at this early stage of the book, it should be clear that there are many important issues that are usually overlooked or even deliberately ignored in popular discussions of education and technology. One of the key aims for the remaining six chapters of this book, therefore, is to directly address these hidden issues and questions. For example, how is educational technology shaped by the organizational concerns of education administrations that are often responsible for the framing of educational technology practice? How does the 'lived' experience of teachers and students influence their use of technology? What is the influence of commercial and private interests – especially in the production and development of education technological artefacts? While there may be no easy answers to these questions they all deserve consideration and further thought if we are to develop a better understanding of the highly negotiable and unpredictable nature of technology use in education.

Making sense of the socially shaped nature of technology has clear implications for how the study of educational technology is pursued. Above all, this approach suggests that we concentrate mainly on understanding the 'here-and-now' realities of educational technology rather than future possibilities and potentials. As such, the predominant focus of the next six chapters will be on 'unpacking' the ordinary, mundane aspects of education and technology. In particular, much of our discussion will focus on the struggles and conflicts related to educational technology use at individual, institutional and societal levels of analyses. As Gert Biesta and others have argued, making sense of any aspect of contemporary education involves acknowledging the range of issues that lie well 'beyond learning' – not least the political and democratic dimensions of education that are often overlooked in the relentless asking of 'questions about the efficiency and effectiveness of the educational process' (Biesta 2006, p. 22).

With all these thoughts in mind we can now turn to our next set of key issues and debates. If we are not going to look forward to the future of education and technology then where better to turn than the history of education and technology? Chapter 1 has already touched upon the 'long history' of technology development from prehistoric times onwards. Yet if we are to gain a full understanding of the complex relationship between education and technology it is worth paying closer attention to the 'recent history' of educational technology over the past hundred years or so – what can be seen as the development of 'pre-digital' and 'early-digital' technology use. So, what useful lessons can be learnt from the educational implementation of technologies such as film, radio, television and early forms of microcomputing?

Further questions to consider

- Why do we really *need* technology in education? Are digital technologies essential to supporting effective forms of education in the twenty-first century? What do digital technologies allow to happen in education that could not otherwise happen?
- What examples of technological determinism can you identify in popular discussions of education and technology? What 'effects' are digital technologies commonly believed to 'cause' in education? Why could this way of thinking be considered as misleading and reductive? What strengths – if any – does technological determinism have as a way of understanding education and technology?
- What 'actors' at the micro-, meso- or macrolevels have an influence on how technologies are used in education? How is their influence apparent? What links and relationships exist between these different actors?

Further reading

This journal article provides a good overview of the common justifications given for technology use in education over the 1980s, 1990s and 2000s:

- Wellington, J. (2005) 'Has ICT come of age? Recurring debates on the role in education' *Research in Science and Technology Education*, 23, 1, pp. 25–39

These articles provide a good overview of the more recent justifications and debates surrounding technology use in education during the 2010s:

- Collins, A. and Halverson, R. (2010) 'The second educational revolution: rethinking education in the age of technology' *Journal of Computer Assisted Learning*, 26, 1, pp. 18–27
- Njenga, J. and Fourie, L. (2010) 'The myths about e-learning in higher education' *British Journal of Educational Technology*, 41, 2, pp. 199–212

Further discussions of the 'knowledge economy' and 'information society' can be found in this edited collection of key articles:

- Webster, F. (ed.) (2003) *The Information Society Reader*, London, Routledge

A good discussion on the limitations on 'technological determinism' in education thinking can be found in this article. Although it is over 20 years old, it should be available online if you search for it:

- Pannabecker, J. (1991) 'Technological impacts and determinism in technology education: alternate metaphors from social constructivism' *Journal of Technology Education*, 3, 1, pp. 43–54

An authoritative introduction to the social shaping perspective on technology is provided in this journal article:

- Williams, R. and Edge, D. (1996) 'The social shaping of technology' *Research Policy*, 25, 6, pp. 865–899

3 What Can History Tell Us About Education and Technology?

Introduction

When thinking about technology and society there is a natural tendency to look forwards rather than backwards. Like many other areas of life, it is often more compelling to anticipate what is about to happen with technology than attempt to make sense of what has already happened. As the philosopher Andrew Feenberg observes, a recurring feature in popular discussions of technology is a failure to frame arguments about 'new' technologies in a historical context (what can be termed *ahistoricism*). Feenberg also highlights a tendency to assume that society has simply adapted to the technological conditions of the time in order to meet its material needs (what can be termed *substantivism*).

Neither of these perspectives is particularly helpful in developing a good understanding of education and technology. As we saw in Chapter 2, it makes little sense to assume that technology drives human progress, or that education simply adapts to technological 'change'. Instead it is more useful to see technology as influenced by a range of social, cultural, political and economic factors – what was described in Chapter 2 as the 'social shaping' of technology. This chapter continues with a socially focused approach and considers the history of education and technology. In particular it focuses on the 'pre-digital' and 'early-digital' uses of technology in the schools, colleges and universities of the twentieth century. What lessons can we learn from the introduction of various 'new' technologies into classrooms from the 1900s onwards?

Taking an historical perspective on education and technology

Looking back at the history of educational technologies allows us to highlight a number of issues and factors that can only be revealed with the 'benefit of hindsight' (Cassidy 1998). In particular, taking an historical approach has three specific advantages. First, an historical approach frames the development of technology within a long-term perspective, allowing us to understand how one technology may have ramifications for proceeding technologies. This idea of one technology not simply 'replacing' or 'superseding' another was referred to in Chapter 1 as 'technological remediation'. Following this line of thinking we can see how new technologies often pay homage to preceding technologies, drawing upon and refashioning them, as well as challenging and rivalling them. The historical development of technological forms can be seen in terms of continuity as well as change – with 'new' technologies often seeking to both borrow from and surpass earlier forms. In this sense, we can only fully understand the significance of a new technology if we have a good understanding of its predecessors.

Secondly, many historians will argue that the social bearing and significance of a technology is only fully apparent after some time has passed. Only now are we beginning to develop sufficient 'distance' on technologies such as the television or computer to gain a sense of what their influence has been on society. Most people would agree that it is too early to be completely certain of the internet's influence on society or, indeed, its influence on education. Although digital technologies may appear to be developed and thrust upon us in rapid succession, the integration of any technology into a social context is a long-running and iterative process. An historical approach allows us to identify the significant long-term issues and concerns at play as a technology becomes 'embedded' into everyday life.

A third advantage of taking an historical approach relates to 'letting the dust settle' and looking back at the exaggerated enthusiasms and fears that often surround our initial understandings of what a technology is and what it can do. In particular, looking back at the early histories of various educational technologies can remind us of the ways in which 'new' technologies tend to be heavily promoted and 'sold' to educational audiences. Looking at the history of a technology free from the initial exaggerated claims and 'hype' can be a revealing way of understanding how common-sense expectations and assumptions about technologies are formed. For instance, whereas we now assume that computers have the potential to support formal education, this was not always the case. History can therefore provide us with a clear view of the meanings and significances attached to technologies before they become seen to be inevitable, invisible and somehow natural.

All these benefits of hindsight can be achieved in two different ways – what historians of technology refer to as taking either a 'contextualist' approach or an 'internalist' approach. The internalist approach tends to focus on the history of the invention, design and development of technology – charting the progression from one technology to another in a manner similar to describing the history of art. Internalist accounts of the history of technology can be particularly insightful and revealing. As David Nye describes, 'internalists usually find that creativity is no means assured or automatic . . . emphasis[ing] alternative solutions to problems' (2007, p. 57). Contextualist accounts, on the other hand, tend to focus 'on how the larger society shapes and chooses machines. It is impossible to separate technical and cultural factors when accounting for which technology wins the largest market share' (Nye 2007, p. 59).

While an 'internalist' account of the invention, design and development of educational technologies would be of considerable interest, it is perhaps more appropriate for this chapter to take a contextualist perspective. The contextualist approach is especially well suited to examining the social history of educational technology use, thereby shedding light on the present relationships between education and technology. A contextualist approach can provide a useful description of the social and technical issues that shape the use of technology in 'real-life' contexts such as the home or the classroom. As David Nye concludes, if one takes a contextualist approach

> then it appears fundamentally mistaken to think of 'the home' or 'the factory' or
> 'the city' as a passive, solid object that undergoes an involuntary transformation

when a new technology appears. Rather, every institution is a social space that incorporates or doesn't incorporate [new technology] at a certain historical juncture as part of its ongoing development. [New technology] offers a series of choices based only partly on technical considerations. It's meaning must be looked for in the many contexts in which people decide how to use it. (2007, p. 62)

With the benefits of the contextualist approach in mind, the remainder of the chapter will revisit and reconsider four of the major educational technologies of the twentieth century – film, radio, television and microcomputing. These examples will help develop our understanding of how technologies come to find a place in education, and will also help us address a number of wider questions about the relationship between education and technology. For instance, we need to consider the different ways that technologies are implemented into educational settings. What claims tend to be made on behalf of new technologies as they are introduced to education? What meanings get attached to specific technologies – first by proponents of the technology and later by educational users of a technology? It is also useful to explore why technologies are seen to 'work' or 'not work' in education. For example, what 'barriers' and 'enablers' tend to be identified at the time as influencing the 'success' or 'failure' of a technology? What forms of 'evidence' are used to substantiate the educational effectiveness of the implementation of a technology in education? All of these questions will now be explored by going back to the early 1900s and considering the history of educational technologies throughout the twentieth century.

The recent history of education and technology

Our focus on the twentieth century is not meant to imply that the history of education and technology goes back no further than 1901. Over the past five thousand years or so various technologies have been linked closely with the development of educational thinking and reforms. The appearance of the Mesopotamian abacus around 2700 BC serves to remind us of the long history of 'educational' technology. Indeed, technological artefacts and practices played an integral part of the forms of education and learning that were envisaged by the Elder Sophists of the fifth century BC, the medieval scholars and the social reformers of the eighteenth and nineteenth centuries. From the abacus to the chalkboard, and from the written word to the textbook, different educational technologies have played a fundamental role in supporting learning and the development of knowledge across thousands of years.

It should be remembered that some of these early technologies continue to play important roles in contemporary education. Indeed, Comenius' production of the first textbook in the mid-1600s (titled *Orbus Pictus* or *The World in Pictures*) is generally seen as marking the beginning of a long-standing educational dependency on printed text. The implementation of the chalkboard in the 1800s similarly persists in many contemporary classrooms – although usually in 'whiteboard' rather than 'blackboard' form. All of these technologies have had significant bearings on the nature of educational settings and practices, and all have been accompanied by substantial promises of educational change and transformation. The 'new' technology of the chalkboard, for example, was lauded in 1841 by one educational writer in effusive terms when proclaiming that 'the inventor or introducer of the system deserves to be ranked among the best contributors to learning and science, if not among the greatest benefactors of mankind' (cited in Tyack and Hansot 1985, p. 40). As this tribute suggests, the digital technologies of today are by no means the first educational technologies to be 'hyped' up by enthusiastic and excited commentators.

This long history notwithstanding, it is the educational technology of the twentieth century that can perhaps provide the most useful comparative insights into the use of contemporary digital technologies. The twentieth century was a period of intense technological development – from the emergence of audio-visual technologies such as the radio and television to the first digital computers and the early incarnations of the internet and the worldwide web. As we shall soon see, while all these technologies became integral parts of twentieth-century society their use in education was often more compromised. The US educationalist Larry Cuban provides an excellent overview of the difficult history of twentieth-century education technologies in his book *Teachers and Machines: The Classroom Use of Technology since 1920.* Here Cuban looks back over education's long-standing 'fickle romance' with technologies such as film, radio and television, and develops a critical examination of how these technologies were used (and often not used) in twentieth-century classrooms. Tracing the educational implementation of these technologies, Cuban explores the capabilities, claims and uses that characterized people's understandings of 'educational technology' at the time. It makes sense, therefore, to revisit these technologies for the purposes of our own chapter, starting with one of the 'wonder technologies' of the early 1900s – the motion picture.

Educational film

A small number of school teachers in North America and Europe began to experiment with the projection of pictures displayed on film during the second half of the nineteenth century. Besides the use of 'magic lantern' slide projectors and stereograph viewers, the most popular of these technologies was the filmstrip. Here pictures were projected from strips of film, with the teacher responsible for winding on a sequence of images at appropriate intervals accompanied by a narrative text. This use of static pictures was heralded at the time as offering teachers and students a 'window on the world' and prompted a growing enthusiasm for the so-called visual instruction and visual education movements.

Yet it took the development of the motion (as opposed to still) picture in the early 1900s to establish the popularity of visual instruction. On one hand, educational enthusiasm for motion pictures provided an appropriate response to growing political demands at the time for increased educational efficiency – demands that had largely resulted from Taylorist 'time and motion' studies carried out in schools. Of course, educational enthusiasm for film use in education was also driven by interest in the technology itself, particularly as the silent movie industry began to establish itself as a major cultural form in North America and Europe. Accordingly, much of the initial impetus for educational film came from some of the originators of the technology, not least the US inventor Thomas Edison. As Edison predicted at the beginning of the 1920s:

> I believe that the motion picture is destined to revolutionise our educational system and that in a few years it will supplant largely, if not entirely, the use of textbooks . . . The education of the future, as I see it, will be conducted through the medium of the motion picture. (Cited in Cuban 1986, p. 9)

During the first years of the twentieth century Edison invested a great deal of time and money in educational film ventures. From these beginnings, growing numbers of schools began to introduce film into their teaching provision. Classrooms were equipped with black window shades, silver screens and 16mm projectors, all lending a distinct aura of modernity to the teaching process. A range of specifically commissioned content was also produced to cover topics suitable for all levels of teaching and learning. As Paul Saettler (1990) details, films commissioned by Edison for his educational film library included titles such as *Life History of the Silkworm*, *Magnetism* and *Microscopic Pond Life*. By 1910 the *Catalogue of Educational Motion Pictures* listed over one thousand different film titles arranged around 30 different topics and subject disciplines.

This activity was matched by the development of a substantial organizational infrastructure and bureaucracy to accompany the use of film in US schools. Only 20 years after the first school districts had committed themselves to the classroom use of motion pictures, 25 states had established visual education departments and bureaus tasked with overseeing the implementation and use of educational film. Courses to train teachers to use film were run by universities and teacher training colleges, and 5 separate national professional organizations for visual instruction had been established by 1930 (Saettler 1990). All told, the use of motion pictures was an officially endorsed symbol of 'modern' and 'progressive' teaching (Cuban 1986).

Educational enthusiasm for the use of motion pictures in the classroom grew during the first decades of the twentieth century. One popular view was that film provided a powerful means of the mass delivery of public education and enlightenment – as one US Commissioner for Education put it, film offered a 'most valuable weapon for the attack on ignorance the world has ever known' (Tiagert 1923). Many people were especially impressed by the ability of films to 'bring learning to life' – promising a means to represent reality in a visual form and to breathe life and feeling into the spoken and printed word. Indeed, as Charles Hoban et al. argued in *Visualizing the Curriculum* the primary value of visual instruction was its degree of realism (1937). This, in turn, was seen to assist the achievement of at least three main instructional objectives – 'imparting a knowledge of facts, teaching perceptual-motor skills, and influencing motivation, attitudes and opinions' (Allen 1956, p. 125).

Enthusiasm for the educational benefits of motion pictures was supported by a burgeoning body of research and evaluation literature. Early 'experimental' studies, for instance, found that groups of learners using film were 'greatly superior in learning information and concepts' when compared to learners using traditional methods (Allen 1956, p. 132). A number of surveys and evaluations also reported a belief among teachers and other educators that 'a body of factual information such as high-school science could be taught by films alone almost as effectively as by a teacher using conventional classroom procedures, and even better if the films were introduced and supplemented by brief study guides' (Allen 1956, p. 126). Many other studies at times, however, were less certain of the 'effect' of film-based education. As Smith (1962) concluded, any overall findings of learning gains relating to the use of film 'were equivocal'.

Concerns over the lack of tangible effect were later followed by a marked decline in the use of motion pictures. One study of Michigan schools in 1954 found the use of educational film in the classroom to then be 'the equivalent of a one-reel film about every four weeks' (Dale 1958, cited in Cuban 1986, p. 16). By the 1950s it was becoming increasingly apparent that films were not having a major impact on how schools, colleges and universities went about educating students – despite their booming popularity as an entertainment medium. As Larry Cuban describes, 'most teachers used films infrequently in classrooms. Films took up a bare fraction of the instructional day. As a new classroom tool, film may have entered the teacher's repertoire, but, for any number of reasons, teachers used it hardly at all' (1986, p. 17).

Suggested reasons and explanations for this relative failure were varied. A national survey of US teachers at the beginning of the 1950s highlighted four main areas of deficiency. These included the need for 'more time', 'more central coordination' and 'more adapted classrooms', underpinned by the need for 'better support' (cited in Hornbostel 1955). Based on his reading of research findings of the time, Larry Cuban offered four similar reasons for the decline of film use in educational settings. These ranged from teachers' lack of skills in using the equipment and the high cost of the films, equipment and upkeep; to the inaccessibility of equipment when it was needed and the difficulty of finding and fitting the right film to the class. All told, film enjoyed a relatively brief period as a mainstream educational technology, at least in formal classroom settings.

Educational radio

Of course, film was not the only educational 'wonder technology' of the early twentieth century. During the 1920s and 1930s the attention of many educationalists had shifted to the potential uses of radio in the classroom. Again, widespread enthusiasm was expressed for this technology's educational promise almost as soon as it became available to schools, colleges and universities. The first established 'educational radio station' in the United States was at the University of Wisconsin in 1917. Three years later the Radio Division of the US Department of Commerce issued several educational broadcasting licenses that supported the establishment of radio stations to broadcast educational programs for the general public. One celebrated example was the 'RCA Educational Hour' – a successful music program that, at the height of its popularity, reached an estimated 6 million listeners. Alongside the efforts of established broadcasters such as RCA, more than 60 universities and colleges offered some form of radio-based instruction to learners, with some schools districts also developing broadcasting stations and programs that were integrated into everyday school lessons (Cuban 1986). One particularly ambitious educational radio project was the establishment of the 'World Radio University' in 1937, broadcasting classes in 24 languages to 31 countries throughout the world (Saettler 1990, p. 201).

Perhaps the most extensive instance of the educational use of radio were the so-called Schools of the Air. From the 1930s until the 1970s commercial broadcast networks, state universities, colleges of education and local school boards established over a dozen 'School of the Air' initiatives designed to offer remote access to school education. These services offered courses of study in subject areas designed to fit alongside traditional school curricula. In a similar manner to the traditional 'bricks and mortar' school, these Schools of the Air used gradated curricula, followed term-time schedules and even provided learning support materials for classroom use. The CBS-run 'American School of the Air' was launched in 1930 and was soon offering lessons in subjects such as history, literature, art and health. The university-run 'Ohio School of the Air' offered broadcasts that were received regularly by schools across 29 states (Darrow 1932). It is estimated that at the height of their popularity School of the Air radio programmes were used by over 1 million students across the United States – constituting nearly 10 per cent of the nation's school children (Bianchi 2008). In all, the use of radio in education was deemed important enough to merit the US Office of Education to form a dedicated 'Radio Section'.

As with film before it, the educational use of radio was accompanied by considerable excitement and enthusiasm for the new medium. It was argued, for example, that radio had the obvious advantage of allowing high-quality teaching and learning content to be transmitted to a large number of classroom and learners at negligible cost. As the founder of the Ohio School for the Air observed at the time:

> the central and dominant aim of education by radio is to bring the world to the classroom, to make universally available the services of the finest teachers, the inspiration of the greatest leaders . . . and unfolding world events which through the radio may come as a vibrant and challenging textbook of the air. (Darrow 1932)

The intuitive attraction of radio to young learners made some educators believe it could engage learners' interest and increased motivation in their schooling (The Instructor 1928). Other commentators argued that the immediacy of a live radio broadcast allowed teaching to appear more 'real' and relevant to recent events (Morgan 1931). As the above quotation from William Darrow implies, radio was seen as a democratic medium that allowed high-quality education to be experienced regardless of geographic or socio-economic circumstance. As another proponent of education radio was quoted as saying by Larry Cuban, 'with radio, the under-privileged school becomes the privileged one' (unattributed quote in Cuban 1986, p. 23).

As all these examples illustrate, many educationalists held high hopes for the use of radio as an instructional medium in school, college and university education. As the Director of Cleveland public schools radio station reasoned at the end of the Second World War, 'the time may come when the portable radio receiver will be as common in the classroom as the blackboard' (cited in Dreyfus 2001, p. 27). Indeed, the presence of radios in educational settings grew steadily throughout the first half of the twentieth century. In the early years of radio, receivers were scarce due to their high cost. Yet by the late 1930s prices had dropped, and studies conducted in the first years of the 1940s found that over half of schools in Ohio had radio sets, with two-thirds of Californian schools owning one or more sets (Cuban 1986). There was also occasional empirical evidence of the educational effectiveness of radio as a teaching tool. One experimental study in the 1930s, for example, compared students' retention of information from lectures and from radio broadcasts, reporting that radio was an efficient and effective means of imparting information (Matthews 1932).

However, it had become clear by the end of the 1940s that the educational potential of radio was not being realized fully across the US school system. While many schools may have owned sets, studies showed that most teachers made only sporadic use of radio. A survey conducted in 1937 found that 73 per cent of schools used radio programs for 'little or none' of the time (Atkinson 1938). A study of the Wisconsin School of the Air found that teachers who were accessing the service reported only making use of radio programs in their teaching for an average of three times per week. Reviewing the overall national use of educational radio at the end of the Second World War, another study by the US Federal Communications Commission concluded that 'radio has not been accepted as a full-fledged member of the educational family . . . and remains a stepchild of education' (Woelfel and Tyler 1945, p. 85).

Although educational radio continues to be used into the 2010s (especially in developing countries and remote rural regions) the medium had a far more modest impact on formal education in North America and Europe than expected. Again, research studies of the time highlighted a number of contributory factors – typified by a 1941 survey which examined why US high school principals did not make use of radio in their schools (cited in Cuban 1986, p. 25). This survey reported the following logistic, technical and educational issues:

- no radio-receiving equipment – 50 per cent;
- school schedule difficulties – 23 per cent;
- unsatisfactory radio equipment – 19 per cent;
- lack of information – 14 per cent;
- poor radio reception – 11 per cent;
- programmes not related to the curriculum – 11 per cent;
- class work seen as being more valuable – 10 per cent;
- teachers not interested – 7 per cent.

Educational television

The examples of film and radio illustrate a number of recurring themes that can be identified throughout the introduction of 'new' technologies into educational settings during the twentieth century. As Cuban and others have observed, most of the technological developments of the twentieth century – from the x-ray machine to the aeroplane – were singled out at one time or another for their educational potential, with most failing subsequently to disrupt the established classroom 'chalk and talk' model of teaching and learning. Although it is too simplistic to say that education was 'resistant' to film and radio, there were clear discrepancies between the educational rhetoric and the educational realities of these technologies. This apparently compromised nature of educational technology use is perhaps most clearly illustrated with television – one of the defining consumer technologies of the twentieth century.

Experiments in the educational use of closed circuit television can be traced as far back as 1939. The widespread use of broadcast educational television was initiated soon after by the US Federal Communications Commission's decision in 1952 to set aside 242 television channels for educational purposes. As well as prompting the development of public and community television stations, this decision also encouraged some universities and colleges to establish educational television stations (Morehead 1955). Federal funding for these educational television projects was accompanied by support from commercial organizations, in particular the Ford Foundation's $70 million funding for educational television projects. Up until the 1970s, educational television grew in prominence and popularity. While interest may have originated in North

America, other countries were quick to follow suit. In the United Kingdom, for example, each of the three main national TV channels were annually producing around 50 television series for schools and colleges by 1980, with three quarters of schools using TV programmes in some of their lessons.

It would be fair to say that enthusiasm for educational television surpassed even the excitement and hyperbole directed towards film and radio before it. Indeed, some of the most vocal initial proponents of educational television were those who had previously supported these earlier technologies. William Darrow, for example, described television in glowing terms of 'radio with its eyes open', reasoning that 'when the eye and the ear have been remarried in television we shall indeed be challenged to open wide the school door . . . there will be no "blindness" gap to be bridged' (cited in Cuban 1986, p. 26). Even 40 years on from its introduction, proponents of educational television were continuing to enthuse about the medium's ability to provide educators with 'unique teaching resources' – supporting a range of learning 'from the concrete to the abstract' (Bates 1988, p. 215). As with film before it, the visual qualities of television were seen to offer 'a window on the world for our students' coupled with 'the "enjoyment factor" which well-produced television brings to learning' (Bates 1988, p. 214).

Effusive arguments of this sort were advanced regularly from the 1950s onwards. Over 30 years before Bates' claims, similar arguments had been advanced that television could 'provide the closest thing to real experiences for many children' (King 1954, p. 20). As with earlier enthusiasms for film and radio, most supporters considered television to be capable of quantitatively and qualitatively enhancing learning. As Lawrence Conrad reasoned, 'television could well prove to be the power tool of education [. . .] television could certainly increase the effectiveness of teaching, and it might well expand the size of the classroom' (1954, p. 373). All told, most educators welcomed television as a 'quick, efficient, inexpensive means of satisfying the nation's instructional needs' (Hezel 1980, p. 173).

These claims were grounded in some empirical evidence. A number of self-report studies during the 1950s, for example, found the large majority of 'early-adopting' teachers to consider television-based lessons 'valuable enough to continue' (Allen 1956, p. 129). Other educational researchers provided persuasive case-studies of particularly successful television projects and initiatives. Larry Cuban describes some of the more celebrated case-studies of school systems that were making extensive use of educational television. In the Pacific island of American Samoa, for example, a national programme of television-based instruction was introduced to supplement the poorly trained and poorly qualified teaching workforce. Cuban (1986) reports that by 1966, four of every five of school students in America Samoa were spending between one-quarter and one-third of their class time watching televised lessons, which were then supplemented by follow-up exercises and question periods led by teachers. Similar 'immersive' projects in US states suggested that television-viewing students could improve their position in league tables of test scores when compared to national norms.

These instances notwithstanding, educational television was generally seen by the 1980s to have failed to impact on school, college and university education in the ways that its supporters had anticipated – especially when compared to the near ubiquitous use of television in the home. As Larry Cuban describes, by the 1980s it was being reported that 'most teachers seldom use the medium. When teachers do use television, they do so infrequently and for only a tiny fraction of the instructional day' (1986, p. 39). A survey by the UK's Independent Broadcasting Authority in 1990 suggested that a number of reasons could be associated with this failure. These included issues such as the cost of television and video equipment; the general lack of teacher training to use television in teaching; the general incompatibility of television programme content with the school curriculum; and the generally low quality of programming (see Moss et al. 1991).

A further impediment that emerged from some research studies of television use in schools was the suggestion that programme viewing was often felt to be too disruptive to the norms and routines of the classroom. Larry Cuban, for one, observed that television was often inserted into classroom settings without sufficient thought for the nature of the social contexts of schools and schooling. As he argued, 'television was hurled at teachers. The technology and its initial applications to the classroom were conceived, planned, and adopted by non-teachers' (Cuban 1986, p. 36). Other observers of the use of television in the classroom also reasoned that, besides the logistical inconvenience, the 'culture' of television did not necessarily complement the established cultures of teachers, classrooms and schools. As Richard Lewis (1962, p. 564) concluded:

> television is a significant creator of alarm . . . TV, in a dramatic way, cuts sharply across all aspects of an instructional program and prods deeply into the traditionally private classroom life of teachers. Reactions to proposals to use television in instruction include the normal range from uncritical acceptance to automatic rejection.

Microelectronics and the birth of educational computing

The final discrete phase of our overview of twentieth-century educational technologies was also the first phase of digital technology to enter education. The so-called microelectronics revolution involved a number of technologies – not least the pocket calculator and other portable devices such as Texas Instruments' *Speak & Spell* machine (Mably 1980). These technologies were all based around the potential of the silicon chip to offer devices that were miniaturized, relatively cheap and robust, and boasting hitherto unachievable information processing power. Microelectronics devices such as *Speak & Spell* were described in glowing terms as offering educators 'a revolutionary product with electronic voice and brain and not a single moving part to go wrong' (cited in Carter 1979, p. 13).

Perhaps the most enduring – and certainly the most significant – microelectronic device was the non-networked 'standalone' microcomputer. The links between the development of computers and education were long standing. Long before the development of the 'micro', much of the early development of computer technology had taken place in university settings. Subsequently mainframe computers started to be used for teaching and learning rather than research and administrative purposes in universities in the early 1960s. Initially, educators focused on what was termed 'numeric' uses of computers for engineering, maths and computer programming. However, as the 1960s progressed interest grew in so-called non-numeric uses of computers, in particular what was termed 'computer-assisted instruction'. In 1966, the psychologist and philosopher Patrick Suppes heralded the emergence of the 'computer tutor' as an apparent saviour of school and university education, capable of providing education to any child or adult on a flexible and individualized basis. 'Plug-in instruction', we were told, would ensure the equitable future of educational provision, and allow everyone access to top quality teaching and learning (Suppes 1966).

As James Martin and Adrian Norman (1970) described at the time, by the end of the 1960s educational computing had developed into a number of forms. These included the following:

- *tutorial and coaching instruction*: where the computer presents material to the learner and then asks questions about it. A computer-based 'tutor' monitors the interaction between the learner and the system, and decides when and how to intervene;

- *drill-and-practice instruction*: the computer helps the learner acquire skills by repetitive practice (spelling, arithmetic, vocabulary and grammar of foreign languages);
- *problem-solving*: the learner is given a problem and discusses the result with the computer in a conversational style;
- *dialogue systems*: the computer develops elaborate dialogues with the learner to approximate spoken English;
- *simulation/computer-as laboratory*: the computer provides simulated versions of experiments, with learners observing the results of their actions on a screen;
- *database use*: the computer provides large files of instructional information that the learner can browse selectively;
- *educational games*.

The use of all these applications grew across school and university settings during the 1970s and 1980s. By 1983, for example, computers were being used for instructional purposes in more than 40 per cent of all US elementary schools and more than 75 per cent of all US secondary schools. Supported by federal government initiatives and private sector donations from the likes of the new IT firms such as Apple, Tandy and IBM, the proportion of US schools with computers rose from 18 to 98 per cent between 1981 and 1991. Similarly, the ratio of 'students-per-computer' dropped from 125:1 to 18:1 over the same time.

From the early use of the technology in the 1960s onwards, enthusiasm for computers in education was intense, with a wide range of claims and arguments being advanced. In particular, the area of computer-assisted learning attracted considerable (over)enthusiasm. For example, at the beginning of the 1980s the French minister for Education declared the combination of information technology and schooling as nothing less than 'le marriage du siècle' (cited in Hawkridge 1983, p. i). Many of these claims reflected a prevailing awestruck sense of inevitability. As the popular UK technology writer Christopher Evans proclaimed, there was little doubt that 'portable, personal teaching computers . . . will sweep through the education system of the Western world' (1979, pp. 118–120).

One of the major justifications for using microcomputing in education was advanced in terms of 'computer literacy' – echoing the contemporary imperative of 'digital literacy' outlined in Chapter 1. As Howard Besser noted, 'the primary argument given for instituting computer literacy requirements is the 'good citizen' one – that in order to be a productive member of society in the near future, one must know about computers' (1993, p. 63). Much enthusiasm was also directed towards the instructional value of computer-assisted instruction, with commentators highlighting a range of learning-related benefits such as encouraging critical thinking and creativity, as well as matching the learning style and the motivational state of the learner. As Martin and Norman again observed:

> with computer assisted instruction the process is pupil-centred, not instructor-centred and the machine adapts its pace to that of the student. The dull students can ask for endless repetition without embarrassment and the machine will retrace its steps with infinite patience. The quick student or the student who already partially knows the material can skip a segment – with the machine questioning him to check that he does, in fact, know it. (1970, p. 127)

The growth of microcomputing throughout the 1960s, 1970s and 1980s was accompanied by a fast-growing body of supporting evidence for the positive impact on education and learning. One of the first studies of the benefits of computer-assisted instruction took place in 1966 in what was described as a 'deprived' school in Palo Alto, California. Here an extensive programme was run to use computer terminals, light pens and screens to teach reading and arithmetic. As the research team from this initiative concluded, 'the technique was very effective. The children loved playing with the terminals and their teachers had to "peel them off the machines" to get them back to their lessons' (Martin and Norman 1970, p. 123). Claims such as these were repeated regularly over the next 20 years. As this description of a similar Canadian educational computing project also illustrates:

> one the earliest extensive uses of computer-assisted learning occurred in Ontario in the late 1960s. It was designed to help an innumerate group of teenagers fulfil the maths requirement for maths courses. The program was simple drill and practice, but was highly successful. Compared to the more traditional teaching methods, the drop-out rate was reduced by 80 percent, while staff at times dropped to only 10 percent per pupil. Not the least of the successes was the testimony of a girl who stated that the computer was the first maths teacher who had never yelled at her. (Stonier and Conlin 1985, p. 14)

Despite claims for the substantial improvement of teaching and learning, the use of microcomputer technology was generally not sustained across school systems or even within individual schools. Whereas some teachers and students did make use of the technology, the majority of nationally representative studies at the time suggested that educational use of computers was sporadic and often inconsistent (e.g. Becker 1994). School-based studies during this period reported that many computers were only accessible to teachers and learners via dedicated computer rooms and 'labs', and that the most frequent uses of the technology were for the (re)production of work through word-processing packages and the use of drill-and-practice and tutorial software. As Christopher Conte (1997, p. 1) concluded, 'in many schools computers sit idle much of the time or are used for passive rote learning through drill-and-practice routines rather than being used to cultivate higher-order thinking skills like synthesis, analysis, and communication'.

As with film, radio and television before it, the apparent failure of the microcomputer to transform education was linked with several different factors. Issues of teacher expertise and confidence with computers were often highlighted by research studies – issues that were usually reported as being exacerbated by a lack of training. The theme of teacher 'resistance' and 'antipathy' towards computers was also reported regularly. As Martin and Norman (1970, p. 130) lamented, 'most of [the teaching profession] is avidly looking for reasons to hate computer assisted instruction'. A number of technical issues were also highlighted regularly by research studies throughout the 1970s and 1980s – not least the difficulties of accessing computers in educational institutions, a lack of technical support when problems were encountered and the general unreliability of the hardware and software. David Hawkridge's (1983) overview of computer use in UK schools at the beginning of the 1980s identified the following reasons for the relatively low take-up of the technology:

- the restricted quantity, quality and variety of software and courseware;
- perceptions of the overdependence on mediated learning associated with computer use;
- teachers' role changes associated with computer use;
- increased educational elitism;
- concerns over the weakening of public educational systems;
- concerns over commercial bias;
- the overemphasis on IT in government policy to maintain national prestige;
- teachers' ambivalence towards technological innovation;
- concerns over the 'communications effects' gap (e.g. the inequalities introduced by computer 'haves' and computer 'have nots');
- concerns over the social and political bias introduced with information technology.

Learning lessons from the past

All of these 'phases' of educational technology implementation predate the emergence of networked 'online' computing during the 1990s, and the more recent emergence of 'social media' during the 2000s. As such, all of the educational technologies discussed in this chapter are now sufficiently 'in the past' to allow for a detailed and objective reflection on their rise and eventual fall. Indeed, although these technologies were accompanied by the promise of many benefits for education and learning, all failed to meet the substantial expectations for change that surrounded them. Given the considerable impact of film, radio, television and microcomputing in other areas of society it could be reasonably concluded that these failures were linked – in some way – to issues specifically related to education. If this is the case, then it would seem sensible to bear these issues in mind during the remainder of this book's discussions of contemporary digital technologies.

So what can be learnt from the introduction of these various 'new' technologies into educational settings throughout the twentieth century? Certainly all four phases of technology development were surrounded by optimistic hopes of somehow improving education provision and education practice. This is an important point to bear in mind, as how and why technologies are introduced into social settings will have a significant bearing on how they are used. It is clear that technologies like the motion picture were not introduced specifically in response to strong demand from either teachers or students. Instead these technologies appear to have been introduced in a largely 'top-down' manner. Often these technologies appear to have been introduced in response to what we referred to in Chapter 2 as 'external' imperatives – not least the acknowledgement that the technology was available for use and that its application would bring education in line with the rest of society. Indeed, all four examples could be said to highlight a trend for technology being introduced into education as a 'solution in search of a problem'. Certainly, we have seen throughout this chapter how the separate introductions of film, radio, television and microcomputing into education were accompanied by a considerable degree of salesmanship, hyperbole and exaggeration. Many claims were made about the enhanced nature of technology-based learning, the resulting improvements to individual learners, as well as the establishment of 'fairer' conditions for 'rich' and 'poor' students and schools. We also saw how bodies of 'evidence' were produced quickly to 'prove' the 'effect' of these technologies, especially in terms of learning gains – regardless of the fact that this evidence was, more often than not, inconclusive and 'equivocal'.

It could therefore be concluded that film, radio, television and microcomputing all perpetuated a tendency to use new technology as a 'technical fix'. Of course, education was certainly not the only area of twentieth-century society in thrall to the transformative potential of these different technologies. Any educational enthusiasm for new technology during the twentieth century must be seen as a subset of wider societal enthusiasms – first for the emergence of electrical engineering during the early decades of the 1900s and then for the subsequent post-industrial 'white heat' of new telecommunications and computerized technologies. In general, the twentieth century witnessed an indecent haste among those in public and political circles to imbue all manner of technologies with the 'power' to affect substantial societal change. Alvin Weinberg, a physicist who had worked on the Manhattan Project, wrote a seminal paper in the 1960s criticizing the eagerness of governments to seize upon almost any 'quick technological fix for profound and almost infinitely complicated problems' (1966, p. 69). The flaw in this reasoning, Weinberg argued, was that 'social problems are much more complex than are technological problems' (p. 68) – requiring 'social engineering' rather than technological remedies. Although Weinberg was more concerned with issues of war and poverty than education, his analysis holds true in terms of the burgeoning interest throughout the twentieth century for audio-visual and computerized technologies as potential solutions for the perceived shortcomings of national education systems.

Most of the commentators who have charted the history of educational technology throughout the twentieth century have made sense of these observations in terms of a clear 'cycle' of events that is more or less repeated with each 'wave' of technology in education. This cycle is seen to begin with substantial promises for the transformative potential of the technology backed by research evidence and other instances of scientific credibility. Yet despite initial enthusiasm and expectations, educators then go on to only make inconsistent use of the new technologies for a variety of technical, professional and personal reasons. Perhaps most importantly, few changes appear to occur in the arrangements of educational institutions. A number of rationales are then proposed to explain this 'lack of impact' such as resourcing, funding, educational bureaucracy or a general 'teacher resistance' to the technology. Then, as memories of initial enthusiasms for the technology begin to fade, educators are subsequently 'sold on the next generation of technology, and the lucrative cycle start[s] all over again' (Oppenheimer 1997, p. 47). As far as most historians of educational technology are concerned, this cycle of 'hype', 'hope' and 'disappointment' is perhaps the biggest lesson to be learnt form the twentieth century. As Margaret Cassidy concludes:

> While it is never entirely accurate to claim that history repeats itself, or that patterns and similarities are accurate predictors of future events, it is probably fair to think that some of the obstacles that stood in the way of radio, television and computer assisted instruction are still in place. (1998, p. 181)

As our own chapter has shown, there would certainly appear to be a number of recurring issues arising throughout the history of film, radio, television and microcomputing in twentieth-century education. All these technologies could be said to have been hampered by a number of practical issues such as inadequate resourcing, technological unreliability, increased financial cost of upkeep, teachers' lack of confidence in the technology and inadequate training. Many of the recurring issues throughout the different 'phases' of educational technology highlighted in this chapter also hint at deeper structural issues and 'clashes' – not least issues of congruity and 'goodness of fit' with pre-existing educational structures. As Margaret Cassidy (1998, p. 178) observes, all of these twentieth-century technologies certainly 'posed problems in terms of fitting into the schedule of the school day'. As many of the examples illustrated in this chapter suggest, this lack of 'fit' related to issues of time, content and relevance to the curriculum. There is also a sense that these technologies found it difficult to find a prominent place within the social and cultural contexts of the educational institutions they were meant to be implemented into. Indeed, two of the recurring obstacles to successful implementation identified by Larry Cuban (1986) were the nature of 'the classroom and school as work settings' and the 'situationally constrained choice' that teachers face when working in schools, colleges and universities.

If nothing else, this chapter has illustrated the complex nature of technology implementation in education. We have seen that there are few historical grounds to assume that technology use leads to inevitable and sustained educational improvement. Instead, we have seen plenty of evidence to suggest that the implementation of technology in education is rarely a predictable or even controllable process. As Robert Reiser concludes, 'of the many lessons we can learn by reviewing the history of instructional media, perhaps one of the most important involves a comparison between the anticipated and actual effects of media on instructional practices' (2001, p. 61).

So what lessons can we take from this chapter's 'contextual' account of technology and history? All of the examples in this chapter have certainly shown how educational institutions and the classrooms within them are social spaces that mediate the choices offered by new technologies. Indeed, the main benefit of taking a contextualist approach has been to highlight the socio-technical nature of technology-related 'change' in education. All of the examples in this chapter have illustrated clearly how the use and non-use of technology in educational settings is a social as well as a technical matter. We have also seen how the implementation of technology in educational settings is the result of human actions, decision-making, expectations and institutions – not simply the result of the relentless march of technological progress.

So while film, radio, television and microcomputing can all be associated with some specific changes and adjustments to education over the twentieth century, none of these technologies could be said to have 'caused' or generated any widespread change or systemic improvement. Instead, any changes or adjustments are perhaps better understood in terms of the ways in which a technology is appropriated within the social relations that surround any educational context. This goes some way towards explaining the seemingly slow, unpredictable and often frustrating nature of educational change throughout the twentieth century – a period that was otherwise an era of swift and far-reaching technological advancement. As Brigitte Wessels contends, 'although some aspects of technological change may be fairly rapid, social and cultural change usually occurs more slowly . . . reflect[ing] the complexity and indeterminacy of the social' (2010, p. 28). As we have seen throughout this chapter, this would seem to particularly be the case with the social and cultural aspects of twenty-first-century education.

Conclusions

The remainder of this book will now go on to account for the uses of technology in twenty-first-century education. In doing this we should certainly remain mindful of the likely continuities from earlier forms of educational technology – be they technical, social, cultural or political. As Neil Postman put it, the high-profile 'failures' of educational television, film and radio should mean that there is no excuse for educators to approach the implementation of any new technology 'with their eyes closed' (cited in Oppenheimer 1997, p. 62). However, all the examples in this chapter can also help us think about how contemporary educational technologies may differ from their predecessors. What possible *dis*continuities as well as continuities may be apparent with current and emerging forms of educational technology? We should not automatically assume that educational technology use in the 2010s is necessarily a certain case of 'history repeats'. It may well be that current forms of personalized digital technologies and social media applications encounter many of the issues that have recurred in the past. But there may also be good reason to expect the current phase of digital technologies to be 'the one' that finally overcomes these issues, and goes some way towards achieving the long-anticipated technological transformation of education. Although the weight of history would suggest otherwise, many technologists certainly expect this to be the case.

Indeed, many technologists would contend that the educational technologies of the twenty-first century are now qualitatively and quantitatively different from the technologies of the twentieth century. As we discussed in Chapter 1, contemporary digital technology can now be characterized by a 'convergence' of different media and uses which means that the digital technologies of today are perhaps not directly comparable to the technologies of the twentieth century. A modern 'multifunction' digital artefact such as a tablet computer can function as a film player, radio, television *and* a computer (as well as a telephone, camera, internet device and games machine). These contemporary technology devices are often highly portable, not reliant on fixed sources of power or internet connectivity, and owned and brought into the classroom by the individual teacher or student rather than remaining the property of the educational institution. Contemporary technology is seen to be largely 'interactive' in nature, rather than relying on the 'broadcast' mode of transmission that characterized twentieth-century technology. In all these ways, many people would argue that the multifunction digital technologies of today are more than capable of meeting the promises made on behalf of the less capable technologies of the twentieth century. Many people would argue that the likes of Thomas Edison may not have been wrong when enthusing about the transformative potential of new technologies *per se*, merely that these promises were perhaps being made one hundred years before their time.

It is equally as important to bear in mind the claims currently being made for the apparently distinctive nature of twenty-first-century learning. Indeed, many educationalists would contend that contemporary forms of technology can now support radically different forms of learning than in the twentieth century. Whereas film, radio, television and microcomputing did little more than support the presentation of content and provide resources for the passive receiving and 'doing' of learning tasks by individual learners, contemporary digital technologies are seen to be capable of supporting new active forms of learning which are based around dialogue and collaboration within large communities of learners. Many of the teaching and learning activities associated with the classroom application of film, radio, television and microcomputing many now appear in hindsight as being profoundly 'formal' in nature, with the technology often doing little more than reinforcing the teacher controlled 'broadcast' of information. Yet as was detailed in Chapters 1 and 2, contemporary digital technologies are seen to be far more centred on the needs of the individual. In these terms alone, many educationalists and technologists now expect digital technology to break out of the 'Groundhog Day' cycle of hype, hope and disappointment, and finally realize its potential (see Mayes 1995, 2007). With all these expectations for a brighter future in mind, we can now move on to the next set of key issues and debates as discussed in Chapter 4 – 'does technology improve learning'?

Further questions to consider

- In what areas of education have the use of film, radio and television endured, and could even be said to still play an important role in the 2010s? What reasons can explain this longevity when compared to the relatively low use of these technologies in the formal classroom settings of the school, college and university?
- The contemporary tablet computer could be seen as a telephone, television, computer, radio, photograph and video camera all rolled into one. To what extent do multifunction digital technologies like this represent the 'convergence' of previous technologies? Are any of the issues associated with the historical use of 'separate' technologies still applicable to the converged technology 'platforms' of today, or are these issues now largely overcome?
- How would the history of a recent educational technology be written in 20 years time? For example, consider the educational use of blogging. What examples of 'hype', 'hope' and 'disappointment' can already be associated with blogging? What wider issues and factors already appear to have compromised the educational potential of blogs and blogging?

Further reading

Larry Cuban's book on the history of classroom technologies in the twentieth century expands upon all of the different technologies discussed in this chapter. It is well worth finding a copy if you can:

- Cuban, L. (1986) *Teachers and Machines: The Classroom Use of Technology since 1920*, New York, Teachers College Press

Although not related directly to educational use, this book provides an interesting and entertaining overview of the social history of technology:

- Pursell, C. (2007) *The Machine in America: A Social History of Technology*, [Second Edition] New York, John Hopkins Press

Although not easily found, these older pieces of writing offer some interesting overviews of the history of educational technology throughout the nineteenth and twentieth centuries:

- Saettler, P. (1990) *The Evolution of American Educational Technology*, Englewood CO, Libraries Unlimited
- Cassidy, M. (1998) 'Historical perspectives on teaching with technology in K-12 schools' *New Jersey Journal of Communication*, 6, 2, pp. 170–184

These two pieces of writing from Terry Mayes reflect a shift in his thinking over the 1990s and 2000s. The first article reasons that educational technology is stuck in a frustrating cycle of partially fulfilled promises. The second piece revises this opinion in light of social media and 'web 2.0' technologies – arguing for the potential for change and 'real' transformation of education:

- Mayes, T. (1995) 'Learning technology and Groundhog Day' in Strang, W., Simpson, V. and Slater, D. (eds) *Hypermedia at Work: Practice and Theory in Education*, Canterbury, University of Kent Press
- Mayes, T. (2007) 'Groundhog Day again?' Keynote speech to JISC Conference, Innovating e-Learning 2007: Institutional Transformation and Supporting Lifelong Learning

4 Does Technology Improve Learning?

Chapter outline

Introduction

As we discussed in Chapter 1, learning lies at the heart of most people's understandings of what 'education' is. The majority of technology use in education is therefore concerned with supporting the act of learning in one form or another. In fact many academics working in the area of educational technology would describe themselves as being 'learning technologists' and would characterize their work as part of the 'learning sciences'. As such, we cannot fully understand education and technology unless we consider the key issue of how the use of technology can support, enhance and even improve learning.

The links between digital technology and matters of thinking, intelligence and learning stretch far back into the history of computer development. As outlined in Chapter 3, the development of the computer during the 1950s and 1960s was rooted in the field of artificial intelligence. This led to an early emphasis within computer science on the challenge of teaching a machine to think intelligently, or at least being able to add 'thinking-like' features to technology. A belief that computers are 'machines for thinking' has therefore long persisted in technological and educational circles. As Martin Cohen reasoned at the beginning of the 1990s, 'computers are not just machines that seem to think – they promise to do people's thinking for them and much else besides. It is in this sense that the computer is an "educational tool"' (Cohen 1993, p. 57).

An interest in learning and thinking continues to drive the development of digital technologies into the 2010s. Now it is argued that computer technologies can have a profound influence on how humans think. Over the past ten years, for example, cognitive neuroscientists and others concerned with the study of brain development have begun to document the possible links between technology use and young people's capabilities for learning and processing information. This has prompted excitement among some academics and educational commentators over the technology-induced capacity of young people to 'think and process information fundamentally differently from their predecessors' (Prensky 2001, p. 1). One of the key neurological and cognitive changes is seen to be the increased quantity of learning that can take place. The vast networks of information, resources and people now available through digital technologies such as the internet is seen to be restructuring and extending young people's mental facilities and ability to learn. As Prensky (2009, n.p.) speculates:

> given that the brain is now generally understood to be highly plastic, continually adapting to the input it receives, it is possible that the brains of those who interact with technology frequently will be restructured by that interaction. The brains of wisdom seekers of the future will be fundamentally different, in organisation and in structure, than our brains are today.

These claims about the science of learning lend support to wider 'commonsense' feelings that technology enhances the learning process. Indeed, few educators would contest the idea that technology use often leads to *some* form of learning gain or benefit. Digital technology is now used throughout educational institutions as a means to support learning – either as an information tool (i.e. as a means of accessing information) or as a learning tool in its own right (i.e. as a means of supporting learning activities and tasks) (Tondeur et al. 2007). There is also much enthusiasm for the ability of digital technologies to support people's learning beyond formal education. It is no coincidence, for example, that one of the most popular computer games in recent times has been *Dr Kawashima's Brain Training* – a mental agility game for children and adults that has sold tens of million of copies since its launch in the mid-2000s.

As all these examples suggest, most people in education consider digital technology and learning to be inextricably linked. The key issue now is to consider exactly how, what and why this may be. *How* exactly can technology support learning? *What* types of learning result from technology use? *Why* can technology support learning that would not otherwise take place? We therefore need to examine the ways in which digital technologies are associated with learning – and think a little more carefully about what learning 'gains' and improvements can be said to derive from technology use. In order to do this, we first need to review the key theories of learning that have been developed since the beginning of the twentieth century, and consider what explanations they provide for the role of technology in learning. The chapter now goes on to review four of the key learning theories developed over the past hundred years – that is, behaviourism, cognitivism, constructivism and socio-cultural psychology. Just what contribution have these theories made to the use of technologies for learning?

Behaviourist theories of learning and technology

As we saw in Chapter 3, the history of 'pre-digital' technology use in twentieth-century education was often aligned with 'behaviourist' theories of learning advanced by psychologists such as B. F. Skinner. In particular, behaviourism grew to be a highly influential learning theory during the 1950s and 1960s, and continues to remain relevant to the use of digital technology in contemporary education. Put simply, behaviourist accounts describe what goes on in the mind largely in terms of a closed 'black box'. Behaviourists are far more interested in the effects of learning rather than the processes of learning. Underlying the behaviourist view of learning is the idea of the learner's behaviour being 'conditioned' by a series of reactions and responses to various stimuli in their environment. In other words, the behaviourist approach suggests that when faced with a stimulus then a human will respond (i.e. behave) in a particular way. What then happens subsequently will influence how the human responds (i.e. behaves) when faced with the same stimulus again. If the consequence of this behaviour is reinforced by a reward or suppressed through a punishment, then it is likely to be repeated or curtailed according to the nature of the reinforcement.

For example, in the model of 'classical conditioning' behaviour is explained in terms of a series of stimulus/response interactions based on punishment (perhaps best known through Ivan Pavlov's experiments on the digestive glands in dogs). In this manner, learning can be seen as the formation of a connection between the stimulus and the response. This chain of events was illustrated in John Watson's experiments during the 1920s with human subjects – most notably the purported 'little Albert' experiment. These experiments were based upon Watson's belief that the majority of human behaviours are based on conditioning. Watson set out to test this hypothesis by conducting a series of experiments to make young children (such as 'little Albert') afraid of rats. He achieved this through the association of a loud and unexpected noise whenever a rat was touched. After a series of similar events Watson demonstrated how this fear could then be generalized to other small animals. This fear could also then be 'extinguished' by subsequent exposure to animals without the noise.

While offering a compelling explanation of a number of behaviours, the idea of learning being rooted in reactions to punishment was gradually superseded by the model of learning through 'operant conditioning'. Here learning was seen to be rooted in the occasion of being rewarded after a correct response. B. F. Skinner's experiments on conditioning the behaviour of rats, pigeons and dogs showed how certain kinds of behaviours could be generated easily through a response/stimulus process of feedback and reinforcement. Skinner's work on operant conditioning highlighted the importance of 'behavioural chaining' where a behaviour was learnt in a series of steps, with the learner incrementally mastering each step in sequence until the entire sequence is learned. Skinner demonstrated the concept of behavioural chaining through a series of experiments with animals learning to perform certain tasks. For example, in terms of his experiments to condition pigeons to learn to pull levers in order to gain food, a succession of behaviours were first rewarded, but then later left unrewarded as the sequence of actions were internalized (e.g. touching the lever, moving the lever, moving the lever to the left, and so on).

As these descriptions imply, the behaviourist view of the learner is largely as a passive recipient of the learning experience. In this sense, many people would argue that behaviourism is more accurately described as a teaching theory rather than a learning theory. Indeed, much of Skinner's work was implicitly critical of conventional classroom teaching techniques. Skinner was particularly frustrated by the time-lapse that normally exists between a student's response and the feedback that a classroom teacher is able to provide. Skinner also bemoaned the infrequency of such reinforcement, and the lack of individual attention that could be given to students in large classes. As with many of the learning theories of the twentieth century, behaviourism soon became the driving motivation for proposed reforms to the existing educational system.

As the 1950s progressed, many behaviourists began to advocate a system of teaching and learning that became known as 'programmed instruction'. As Saettler (1990, p. 14) describes, this involves 'a curriculum that is programmed step by step in small units, focused on immediately observable and measurable learning products'. Here the links between technology and behaviourist theories of learning were made explicit. In particular, the programmed instruction movement was built around the development and use of a number of educational technologies and 'mechanical devices'. As Skinner reasoned at the time, the advantages of device-based learning were plentiful:

> If the teacher is to take advantage of recent advances in the study of learning, she must have the help of mechanical devices. The technical problem of providing the necessary instrumental aid is not particularly difficult. There are many ways in which the necessary contingencies may be arranged, either mechanically or electrically . . . The important features on the device are these: Reinforcement for the right answer is immediate. The mere manipulation of the device will probably be reinforcing enough to keep the average student at work for a suitable period each day, provided traces of earlier aversive control can be wiped out. A teacher may supervise an entire class at work on such devices at the same time, yet each child may progress at his own rate, completing as many problems as possible within the class period. If forced to be away from school, he may return where he left off. The gifted child will advance rapidly, but can be kept from getting too far ahead either by being excused from arithmetic for a time or by being given special sets of problems which take him into some of the interesting by-paths of mathematics. The device makes it possible to present carefully designed material in which one problem can depend upon the answer to the preceding and where, therefore the most progress to an eventually complex repertoire can be made. (Skinner 1958, p. 95)

Early instances of programmed instruction techniques included mechanical multiple-choice machines and so-called chemo-sheets where learners were required to check their answers with chemical-dipped swabs. Skinner himself devoted much time to the development of the 'teaching machine'. Based on the principles of operant conditioning these machines required the learner to complete or answer a question and then receive feedback on the correctness of the response. Skinner's approach to the design of teaching machines was to divide the learning process into a large number of very small steps, with positive reinforcement dependent upon the successful accomplishment of each step. By relying on a series of small learning steps, the teaching machines were designed to give frequent positive reinforcement to increase the rate at which the learner correctly learnt each step. The teaching machines also operated on the principle that students should compose their responses themselves rather than select responses from a set of prewritten multiple-choice options – Skinner's reason being that responses should be recalled rather than simply recognized. Unlike conventional classroom-based learning, teaching machines were designed to keep students continuously and actively engaged with the learning task, with immediate feedback provided on every response.

Teaching machines were generally considered at the time to be a success. Soon after developing the first machines for use in schools and universities, Skinner reflected that 'with the help of teaching machines and programmed instruction, students could learn twice as much in the same time and with the same effort as in a standard classroom'. Although the popularity of programmed instruction began to wane in the 1960s its basic structure and behaviourist approach played an important role in the then emerging field of 'computer-assisted instruction'. Early forms of computer-assisted instruction borrowed heavily from behaviourist principles – especially in terms of so-called drill-and-practice computer programs. Drill-and-practice software continues to be used into the 2010s – most commonly designed to reinforce basic skills such as spelling words, development of reading vocabulary or typing programs. There is also a wide variety of drill-and-practice software available for more specific competencies, such as improving letter recognition and developing phonics skills. Many contemporary drill-and-practice programs allow the learner to determine the sequence of instruction or to skip certain topics – although in essence the technology is used to present instruction to the learner whose responses are then reinforced. Behaviourist principles also inform 'tutorial' software packages which present new concepts and provide step-by-step instructions on how to complete certain objectives. In all these cases, behaviourist learning theory continues to underpin the design and development of educational technology, many decades on from the first teaching machines.

Cognitivist theories of learning and technology

Behaviourist theory can be seen as one of the guiding influences on educational technology throughout the twentieth century. However, behaviourist principles are now often criticized as providing a rather bounded 'input/output' understanding of learning. As we have just seen, behaviourist accounts are concerned primarily with the individual's observable behaviour rather than the cognitive processes taking place within their head. This distinction is made clear when one considers behaviourism's close links with methods of animal training. At best, behaviourism relies on observable changes in behaviour as an indication of what is happening inside the learner's mind. As such behaviourism is limited in its ability to explain exactly how learning takes place and how knowledge is constructed within the human mind.

In contrast, the theories of learning that have emerged from the field of cognitive science offer a very different perspective. Here, learning is understood more in terms of the thought processes that lie behind any observable behaviour. Unlike the behaviourist theories just described, learning is seen as an internal process of mental action. In particular, these 'cognitivist' theories of learning seek to describe the mental processes that underpin the act of learning within the human mind. The language of cognitivist theory therefore involves quite complex descriptions of how stored representations are mentally processed. By describing and modelling how the mind should work, methods can be developed to support individuals in matching this 'ideal' performance.

This interest in describing the mental processes of learning provides common ground for the alignment of cognitive psychology and technology-based education. Throughout the latter half of the twentieth century, cognitive psychologists became increasingly interested in developing computational metaphors of the mind – that is, descriptions of how the mind processes and 'computes' information. In particular mental processes began to be conceived in terms of an internal knowledge structure where new information is compared to existing cognitive structures called 'schema'. It was argued that these schema could be combined, extended or altered to accommodate new information as it is acquired and processed by the mind. This computational orientation of cognitive psychology led to the development of computer-like models of the mind, involving three main stages of information processing where 'input' first enters a sensory register, then is processed in the mind's short-term memory, and is then sometimes transferred to long-term memory for storage and retrieval.

In imagining this kind of information processing 'computer', cognitive psychologists see the mind as relying on a number of components that would be familiar to any computer scientist. Indeed, cognitivist theory was soon informing the development and design of technology-based learning from the 1960s onwards – in particular providing the basis for the development of 'intelligent tutoring systems' and 'cognitive tutors'. Here computer technology is used to host a series of teaching exchanges between the learner and an 'intelligent system'. The intelligent system is designed to respond to a model of what the learner should ideally be doing during a task. The learner's performance is then compared with this model and the system is able to 'troubleshoot' where the person's mental actions have deviated from the ideal. On the basis of this comparison, the system is then able to provide 'intelligent feedback' to guide the learner in another attempt at a similar task.

This approach is based around the idea of programming a computer to 'think' like a human mind – a process that lies at the heart of the field of artificial intelligence. Indeed, principles of artificial intelligence have underpinned a range of technologies that have been used in education over the past 50 years, often in the form of computer-based troubleshooting programmes as described above. A range of applications have been developed from the 1960s to the present day to diagnose students' understanding of the skills involved in mathematical and scientific procedures, with the system providing a complete diagnostic model of common learner errors which an individual's performance could then be compared against.

Although applicable to all stages of education, such technology-based learning is especially popular in adult and vocational learning. Many of the 'intelligent learning environments' currently being used in work-based training contexts still follow cognitivist lines. A range of simulation-based intelligent tutoring systems is regularly used in industrial and military settings to train professionals ranging from airline pilots and surgeons, to tank commanders and Naval weapons officers. Such systems often provide 'free-play' simulations that enable students to act in roles in realistically complex work-related simulations. As well as simulating models of complex cause-and-effect relationships these systems are designed to provide comprehensive and useful instructional feedback – allowing students to reflect on the appropriateness and effectiveness of their many actions and decisions. Many of the latest intelligent learning environments are based around graphical manifestations of the system's intelligence in the form of so-called pedagogical agents. These often take the form of 'conversational companions' such as cartoon characters or more realistic 'avatars' who directly talk with the learner on behalf of the intelligent system.

As Gertner and Van Lehn (2000) describe, the fundamental principles underlying the design of many of these intelligent tutoring systems can be best described as computer-based 'coached problem-solving'. Often the computerized-system encourages the learner to construct new knowledge by providing minimal hints that require them to derive most of the solution on their own. In a similar fashion to behaviourist views of learning the technology gives immediate feedback after each action to minimize the amount of time spent on incorrect activity. These systems often offer the student flexibility in the order in which actions are performed – sometimes allowing them to skip steps when appropriate. Many intelligent tutoring systems are based around a 'mastery' model, with students allowed to progress through tasks after mastering a large proportion of a given task. However, in contrast to the programmed learning technologies described before, students using an intelligent tutoring system are seen to be learning by 'doing' rather than learning by being instructed.

Constructivist and constructionist theories of learning and technology

The computational metaphor of information processing that underpins cognitive psychology offers a powerful explanation of learning. As the example of intelligent tutoring systems suggests, cognitivist theory certainly moves the emphasis of technology-based learning beyond issues of behaviour and introduces an enhanced notion of learner control. However, cognitivist theories can be criticized for encouraging a strongly individualistic approach to learning and knowing, and perhaps losing sight of the social nature of human learning. It is not surprising, therefore, that while behaviourist and cognitivist theories of learning have continued to influence the ways in which technologies are used in education, the past 30 years have seen psychological accounts of learning take a distinctly 'social turn'. In particular, so-called constructivist theories of learning came to dominate the field of educational technology during the 1980s and 1990s. Much of this work drew inspiration from well-established learning theories developed by psychologists such as Jean Piaget and Jerome Bruner – although as we shall go on to discuss, a number of distinctive theories of learning can be classed as being constructivist in nature. It therefore makes sense to consider these theories and the implications they have for technology and learning in a little more detail.

Much of the enthusiasm for computer-based learning throughout the 1980s and 1990s was driven by the notion of people learning by constructing their own understanding. Constructivist theories – not least the work of Piaget and his followers – describe learning as taking place best when it is problem-based and built upon the learner's previous experience and knowledge. In this sense, learning is rooted in processes of exploration, inquiry, interpretation and meaning-making. Constructivist theories therefore portray learning as a much more active process than in behaviourist and cognitivist accounts. The constructivist learner is not solely receiving and acting upon information that is transmitted to them from others. Instead learners are seen as constructing their own perspective of the world through individual experiences. One of the central ideals of constructivism is that human knowledge is built through individual exploration, with learners constructing new knowledge upon the foundation of previous learning. Human learning is therefore seen to be highly iterative and exploratory in nature – often deriving from the learner being able to problem-solve in ambiguous situations.

In presenting learning as an iterative process of using current experiences to update one's previous understanding, constructivist accounts place great importance on the individual learner's ability to reflect upon their learning. Piaget described the developing mind as in an ongoing process of maturation – seeking equilibrium between what is already known and what is being currently being experienced. From this perspective the notions of 'assimilation', 'accommodation' and 'adaptation' are seen as crucial elements of learning. Assimilation refers to the ability to alter and modify incoming information to fit with what is already known. Conversely, accommodation is the ability to alter what is known in light of new, incoming information. In ideal circumstances the process of cognitive adaptation involves the learner using both assimilation and accommodation as they explore and make sense of their environment.

As these concepts suggest, constructivist accounts tend to support models of learning that are looser and more activity based than is the case with behaviourism and cognitivism. These learning activities often take the form of problems that can be solved in many different ways according to an individual's approach. How individuals approach a learning experience will depend upon their existing knowledge and how they filter their current experiences through their previous experiences. Attempts to encourage and support constructivist learning therefore seek to provide learners with opportunities to explore and learn through successful and unsuccessful experiences. The role of the teacher is one of orchestrating and supporting the learner's exploration rather than directly providing instruction.

In this sense, technology is seen as a key means of facilitating a learner's exploration and construction of knowledge. The past 30 years have seen a growing belief among educationalists that technology is one of the most suitable means of supporting constructivist principles in a learning environment. As David Jonassen (1994) describes, these principles include:

- providing representations of real-world settings or case-based learning instead of predetermined sequences of instruction;
- emphasizing authentic tasks in meaningful contexts rather than abstract instruction out of context;
- avoiding oversimplification and representing the complexity of the real world;
- providing multiple representations of reality to be explored and made sense of;
- emphasizing knowledge construction instead of knowledge reproduction;
- supporting collaborative construction of knowledge through social negotiation, rather than competition among learners for recognition;
- encouraging thoughtful reflection on experience.

These principles can be found in a range of popular digital educational technologies. For example, during the 1990s Jonassen focused on the learning potential of *HyperCard*. This application was a forerunner of the worldwide web, allowing information (in text, picture, audio or video form) to be stored in a series of 'cards' that were arranged into 'stacks'. Cards could be linked to each other through the use of a built-in programming language that used plain-English commands. Although HyperCard was often used in schools to teach programming concepts it also allowed learners to create interactive learning materials, build databases and generally support the construction and problem-solving processes that constructivist learning entails. More recently, much enthusiasm and attention has been paid towards the use of gaming environments to support constructivist forms of learning through exploration, problem-solving and reflection on experience. In particular, some commentators are arguing that 'realistic' simulations like *The Sims, SimCity* or *Railroad Tycoon* offer a ready means of supporting exploratory spaces for constructivist learning (e.g. Collins and Halverson 2009).

Perhaps the most prominent example of technology-based constructivist learning has come through the work of Seymour Papert – himself one of Piaget's students and collaborators. Papert is perhaps best known in educational technology circles for developing the notion of 'constructionism'. This is an extension of the constructivist approach that is based around the notion of learning best taking place through the exploratory building of objects that are themselves then able to do something. By building an object and then manipulating it to do something, Papert reasoned that learners are able to learn from the process of thinking about how to get something else to think. Constructionists therefore talk of encouraging a learner's conversations with an artefact, positioning the technologies as tools to learn *with*, rather than learn *from*.

In his 1980 book, *Mindstorms: Computers, Children and Powerful Ideas*, Papert reasoned that the use of computers for self-directed learning could result in the construction of what he called 'Microworlds'. These are learning environments that are created as learners build things and naturally encounter problems that require creative solutions. As a result, formerly abstract concepts can take on a real meaning, and tangible rewards can be experienced for exploring and experimenting with these concepts. As Papert put it, a Microworld can be seen simply as 'an object to think about other things with' (1983).

One of the implicit characteristics of the constructionist approach is the use of technology to support the emotional aspects of learning, especially in terms of encouraging a childlike view of learning through building, making things and attributing inanimate objects with their own intelligence. Papert talked of 'animating learning' and 'capturing the imagination' of young and old learners alike. These characteristics are all evident in the learning artefacts that stemmed from Papert's development of the 'Logo' computer programming language that was used in many schools during the 1980s. Here learners used simple English language programming commands to provide movement and drawing instructions to an on-screen cursor (the 'turtle') and its associated 'floor Turtle' robot with retractable pen. Logo allowed learners to program the computer to produce line graphics – from a simple square or triangle, to extremely complex geometric patterns.

Yet Logo was not merely a fancy geometric drawing device. By making the turtle do something Papert saw Logo as a tool to improve the way that children think and solve problems along constructivist lines. The legacy of Logo and Turtle Graphics has been since extended into a number of projects. These include the use of sets of 'Lego' construction bricks (most recently the programmable *Lego Mindstorms* robotics kits) as well as an online manifestation of *Net-Logo* where Logo-like programming commands can be used to explore and manipulate models of emergent phenomena (such as the evolution of a butterfly population or a country's economic performance). By building, testing and refining models of how complex systems develop over time, all of these applications involve learners in the type of self-directed exploratory learning that lies at the heart of the constructivist philosophy.

Sociocultural theories of learning and technology

As the examples of Logo and HyperCard illustrate, much of the appeal of constructivist and constructionist models of learning lies in their emphasis on learner-centred and learner-driven forms of education. That said, these learning theories can be seen to position knowledge as something to be acquired from autonomous and, often, solitary investigation. Indeed, all of the different theories described so far tend to present learning as individually centred. In contrast, growing numbers of psychologists over the past 20 years have turned their attention to understanding the influence of the social and cultural environments that surround an individual's learning and cognitive development. In this sense many psychologists would now share the view that learning is a profoundly social process. While not disagreeing with the general principle of the learner constructing their own knowledge and understanding, more emphasis is now being placed on how these learning processes are located within 'socio-cultural' environments.

Much of this thinking relates to the earlier work of psychologists such as Lev Vygotsky and the development of so-called socio-cultural theories of learning. Vygotsky is associated with a number of concepts relating to the social and cultural nature of learning, not least the idea that learning is mediated through the learner's culture. Vygotsky saw most human action as involving what he called 'cultural tools' and resources. These tools and resources related to all of the significant things that could conceivably exist in a learners' environment – ranging from material artefacts and technologies, to symbol systems and language. In this manner the successful learner can be seen as someone who is able to appropriate and deploy all of these resources in their actions.

Vygotsky's work stressed the integral role of language in learning. In particular Vygotsky saw cognitive development as linked inexorably to speech – be it spoken oral language or silent inner speech. The socio-cultural approach therefore stresses the importance of interaction with other people as a key resource for supporting cognitive activity and learning. In particular, other people are seen to play an important role in first selecting and shaping the learning experiences that are presented to individuals, and then supporting them to progress into the next stages of knowledge and understanding. This view of socially supported cognitive development sees learning as often being based around the less-able learner being able to reach shared meanings with the more-able others in their social environment. In this sense Vygotsky's concept of the 'zone of proximal development' described how tasks that were too difficult for an individual learner to master alone could be learned with the guidance and assistance of more skilled or more knowledgeable others. As the learner becomes more proficient or knowledgeable then this support can be gradually withdrawn until it is no longer required – a process referred to by psychologists such as Peter Woods and Jerome Bruner as 'scaffolding'.

The notion of learning as a collaborative and socially situated process has found particular resonance with many academics working in the area of educational technology (see Luckin 2010). First, many academic psychologists and technologists agree that digital technologies can act as powerful social resources in an individual's learning context. It is argued, for instance, that people often treat technologies as social beings – even interacting with digital devices as if the technology is more able and more knowledgeable than the human (Bracken and Lombard 2004). Digital technology is also seen as a key means of providing learners with enhanced access to sources of knowledge and expertise that exist outside of their immediate environment. There is now considerable academic interest in the field of 'computer supported collaborative learning' where individuals collaborate and learn at a distance via online tools such as wikis, blogs and other online collaborative workspaces. As Leask and Younie (2001) argue, online technologies can support access to knowledgeable others beyond the learner's immediate environment and become an important part of the 'scaffolded' learning process. In this sense learning is now felt to be a technology-supported matter of a collaborative 'we think' or 'we all learn' rather than an individualized concern of what 'I think' or 'I learn' (Leadbeater 2008b, Bonk 2009).

Many people's enthusiasm for these forms of digital learning is rooted in the wider socio-cultural principles of 'situated learning' and the associated notion of 'communities of practice'. These terms describe learning as best taking place in the form of 'real-world' activities and interactions between people and their social environment. Learning is seen to be a highly social activity that takes place in realistic contexts and activities – often centred on the social groups that are involved in these activities and contexts. This concept is made clearer if we consider how a worker learns to do their job. Most occupations will involve groups of people all involved in the same work-based activity or practice. Within these communities of people all involved in the same practice, incoming members will often learn from pre-existing members how to do things. Indeed, Lave and Wenger's (1991) original coining of the phrase 'communities of practice' derived from their anthropological study of how butchers, midwives, tailors and Navy quartermasters learnt their occupations 'on the job'.

Socio-cultural accounts often describe learning that is highly social and often informal in nature. While some learning may take place as formalized training or instruction, the individual learner is often socialized on an informal basis by others into the process of finding, sharing and transferring knowledge 'artefacts'. The act of learning a particular skill or understanding specific cultural and social practices is seen to largely be a tacit process – involving the individual learner imitating what is observed from the actions of others. Often learners will be first shown the 'big picture' by a knowledgeable or expert other, then shown how to deal with it, and then led through the different components of the task. Situated learning therefore relates to learning through active participation and apprenticeship – with the learner involved in the co-construction of knowledge with more-able peers and, importantly, being held to account for the competence with which they perform. Crucially, this learning is ideally situated in the 'real-life' environment where the practice or activity takes place.

The idea that learning involves participation in a full version of what is being learnt has led to a growing interest in the design of educational environments that attempt to approximate the conditions for 'authentic' learner participation. In these terms, many educators see technology-based environments as an ideal means of supporting *in situ* forms of socially 'augmented' learning.

For instance, recent developments in mobile technology, wireless connectivity and global positioning systems have allowed the development of outdoor role-playing games that respond to learners' physical environments as well as their interactions with other learners who are also playing. Using mobile technologies, for example, different features can be imported into the same environment, so that a classroom becomes a surgical operating theatre, or a small wood can become a vast Amazonian rainforest (see Klopfer 2008).

It is argued that these forms of 'mobile gaming' can support learning that is both 'social' (meaning that it can involve 'real' social relationships between learners) and 'authentic' (meaning that it relates to actual people, places and events). In Scott Grabinger's terms, these technologies can support 'rich environments for active learning' (Grabinger and Dunlap 1996). Mobile technologies have also been used to support digitally connected but otherwise remote 'real-life' communities of practice. The nature of these learners can range from dispersed groups of veterinary students learning on rural work-placements to sailors pursuing their continuing professional development while at sea. In all these instances, digital technologies are used to create more direct participatory experiences among remote learners – allowing learners to work together with peers, tutors and other learning materials in a variety of formal and informal ways.

Of course, these activities do not have to be situated in real 'real-life' environments. Much interest has also been shown in the socio-cultural learning potential of participating in 'virtual worlds' and 'massively multiplayer online games' such as *SecondLife* and *World of Warcraft*. Indeed, it is now recognized that a number of learning activities and processes are associated with inhabiting and exploring these online environments. For example, these applications are based on large groups of users encountering, interacting and engaging with other users. These processes often lead to the formation of informal and formal communities where users will work together in groups with hierarchies of expertise and learning. As Carr and Oliver (2010) reason, participating in virtual worlds can involve a range of learning practices – from ongoing processes of developing expertise, to learning socially produced conventions relating to identity, etiquette and trust. Perhaps most significantly, much of what takes place in a virtual world involves collaborative activities between users (such as pursuing collective 'quests') all of which involve creative and collaborative learning practices. Whether one is running a virtual clothes shop or learning to be a warrior-king on an alien planet, virtual worlds and online gaming can support the 'social dynamic' that many people now feel is at the heart of effective learning. As Tom Chatfield concludes:

> We are deeply and fundamentally attracted, in fact, to games: those places where efforts and excellence are rewarded, where the challenges and demands are severe, and where success often resembles nothing so much as a distilled version of the worldly virtues of dedicated learning and rigorously co-ordinated effort. (Chatfield 2010, p. 28)

Alternative accounts of technology, learners, information and knowledge

All of the various learning theories described so far in this chapter have had a substantial influence on people's expectations and assumptions about education and technology. Although academics and other educational technologists differ with regards to their preferred theoretical approach, very few would question the fact that digital technologies can greatly improve learning if used in an appropriate manner. However, while these theories may provide powerful explanations of how technologies *could* be designed and used to support, enhance and even improve learning, they do not always provide realistic accounts of how technologies are actually being used to support learning. It should be remembered that none of the learning theories outlined above were developed specifically with digital technology-based learning in mind. Many of the descriptions provided so far in this chapter rely on the adaptation of well-established learning theories in light of technologies that have been developed many years later.

Some academic commentators would therefore question the 'goodness of fit' between twenty-first-century technologies and twentieth-century theories of how individuals learn. Indeed, some people argue that technology-based learning requires *new* theories of learning that account directly for what takes place when individuals use digital technologies. In particular, an argument is emerging that the influence of digital technology on learning is perhaps not as straightforward as simply improving learning *per se*. Returning to a distinction made at the beginning of this chapter, digital technologies are perhaps more commonly used as an 'information tool' than as a 'learning tool'. It is perhaps more accurate to say that the technologies that are used most in everyday life appear to alter learners' relationships with information and knowledge.

Put in these terms, the main relationship between the learner and technology may not be related to processes of learning *per se*, but is based around their relationship with information.

These emerging ideas are reflected most explicitly in the notion of 'connectivism' – the idea that learning is the ability to access and use distributed information on a 'just-in-time' basis (see Siemans 2004). From this perspective, learning can be seen as an individual's ability to connect to specialized information nodes and sources as and when required. Similarly, being knowledgeable can be seen as the attendant ability to nurture and maintain these connections. Connectivism therefore attempts to account for the changing nature and increasing complexity of learning in a networked world (see Chatti et al. 2010). As George Siemans (2004, n.p.) puts it, learning can therefore be conceived in terms of the 'capacity to know more' via digital technologies such as the internet rather than a reliance on the individual accumulation of prior knowledge in terms of 'what is currently known'.

Of course, these concepts are by no means new. The British writer Samuel Johnson was thinking along similar lines nearly three hundred years earlier when arguing that 'knowledge is of two kinds. We know a subject ourselves, or we know where we can find information upon it' (cited in Boswell's 'Life of Johnson'). Johnson was, of course, referring to the use of book-based information repositories and libraries, yet such arguments have accompanied the development of various information technologies throughout the twentieth century. Vannevar Bush in his seminal 1945 essay 'As we may think' talked of how new technologies such as microfilm viewers would render all previous collected human knowledge more accessible. Bush argued, for example, that 'the *Encyclopaedia Britannica* could be reduced to the volume of a matchbox. A library of a million volumes could be compressed into one end of a desk' (1945, p. 113). Fifteen years later the technologist Ted Nelson extended this reasoning into the notion of *Xanadu* – a world where the entire world's information would be published in a hypertext format and then shared between all people as equals.

Given this pedigree, it is perhaps unsurprising that ideas such as Siemans' notion of 'connectivism' are growing in popularity, especially in light of the rapid development of internet technology over the past 20 years. These approaches therefore reflect a growing sense among some twenty-first-century educators that the primary skill of learning is the ability to successfully identify and retrieve information from online 'knowledge spaces'. As authors such as Pierre Levy (1997) describe them, these are spaces that are non-linear and non-hierarchal, fluid rather than rigid in structure, and where human cognition can be expanded and enhanced to the point where people enjoy a 'new relation to knowledge'. As we saw in Chapter 1, through the use of 'social media' these digital stores are no longer static repositories of information that an individual simply accesses. Instead online stores of information can now be networked, connected and constantly augmented and edited by all users. As such the ability to passively retain information is less important than the skills to access and actively augment information stored elsewhere when required. In this respect, commentators such as Marc Prensky are beginning to talk of 'digital wisdom' instead of intelligence – that is, 'wisdom arising *from* the use of digital technology to access cognitive power beyond our innate capacity and to wisdom *in* the prudent use of technology to enhance our capabilities' (2009, n.p.).

All these perspectives suggest that concepts such as intelligence and learning now need to be described in wider and more expansive ways than before. For example, in the business world much attention has been paid recently to the idea of 'collective intelligence'. This refers to the use of digital technology to support mass communities of information producers and consumers in their (re)creation of collectively produced bodies of content. This is sometimes referred to as a process of 'produsage' – that is, 'where knowledge remains always in the process of development, and where information remains always unfinished, extensible, and evolving' (Bruns 2008, p. 6). In these terms the process of using and learning from these ever-evolving forms of information takes on a quicker and more dynamic and fluid form than before. As Jamais Cascio describes, one of the main learning competencies of this 'fluid intelligence' is the ability to 'find meaning in confusion' and to solve new problems independent of acquired knowledge:

> Fluid intelligence doesn't look much like the capacity to memorise and recite facts, the skills that people have traditionally associated with brainpower. [But] the information sea isn't going to dry up, and relying on cognitive habits evolved and perfected in an era of limited information flow – and limited information access – is futile. Strengthening our fluid intelligence is the only viable approach to navigating the age of constant connectivity. (Cascio 2009, p. 2)

Whereas many technologists see these changes wholly in a beneficial light, others are more cautious. In contrast to the likes of Siemans, Pensky and

Cascio, some educational technology commentators see the apparently increasing fluidity of access to knowledge as having a detrimental effect on thinking, learning and people's general intellectual abilities. Concerns have been raised, for example, over an intellectual 'dumbing-down' associated with using digital technologies to access information and knowledge. Some critics argue that excessive use of online resources is now hampering the ability of many learners to gather information in a discerning manner. As Andrew Keen (2007) puts it, current generations of school children and college students are often doing little more than 'taking search-engine results as gospel'. These concerns are often expressed in terms of differences between old and new generations of learners. In particular current generations of learners are argued to have a declining awareness of issues such as the authorship, authenticity or authority of a piece of information. Keen, for example, bemoans the 'younger generation of intellectual kleptomaniacs, who think their ability to cut and paste a well-phrased thought or opinion makes it their own' (2007, p. 23). Similar issues were raised in Nicolas Carr's well-received polemic that 'Google is making us stupid'. As Carr contended, 'as we come to rely on computers to mediate our understanding of the world, it is our own intelligence that flattens into artificial intelligence' (2008, n.p.).

As Carr, Keen and others are now arguing, one of the unintended consequences of digitally driven learning could be that individuals are now increasingly incapable of learning for themselves. Although rarely based on robust research evidence, such arguments have proved to be remarkably popular. There is even evidence that young learners themselves believe current generations of digital technology users to be less effective at learning. One recent study of Israeli teenagers found over two-thirds to believe that 'this generation is worse at learning than the pre-ICT generation' due to the decreased demands and increased short-cuts and temptations of internet-based learning (Ben-David Kolikant 2011). Growing numbers of commentators are now beginning to concur that many young learners now find themselves in a state of intellectual inertia – what Drew Whitworth (2009) terms 'information obesity'. This leaves the individual increasingly incapable of dealing with the vast quantities of information now available to them. In particular, Whitworth points to the growing quantity of poor quality information accessible through the internet – not least 'counter-knowledge' such as conspiracy theories, creationism, health scares, and so on. Also of concern are the mounting pressures and expectations in contemporary society to consume information before people are able to properly evaluate its worth. As the popular philosophy writer and media commentator Alain de Botton bemoaned:

> *Google*, *Twitter*, *Facebook*, email, the iPhone, the Blackberry and the web have all finally conspired to kill our ability to be alone and unstimulated. Our unaided minds can no longer possibly hope to emulate the thrills available from these devilish technologies. Sales of serious books have plunged 39 percent since this time last year. We are at an epochal moment. Our intelligence has ended up making us stupid; it's a miracle if you are still reading. (de Botton 2009, p. 36)

Evidence for the influence of technology on learning

While sometimes persuasive, many of these visions of the transformation of learning outlined in the previous section are simply reactions to general changes in society associated with technology. Many of the negative perceptions of twenty-first-century learning and learners outlined above should perhaps more accurately be seen as reflections of wider societal fears over digital technology – that is, 'a prognosis of isolated individuals, the breakdown of community and loss of social interaction' (Wessels 2010, p. 5). Moreover, many of these accounts are based on conjecture and supposition rather than credible empirical evidence. Alain de Botton, for example, admits to basing his analysis above on little more than 'a straw poll of friends and a little soul searching'.

Even the more theoretically informed debates and discussions outlined in the first half of the chapter are largely abstracted. While such accounts are very good at telling us why something could or should be happening, they are far less certain of what is actually happening and why. Here most academic commentators would turn to empirical investigations and measures to ascertain precisely what the relationship is between technology use and learning. Yet achieving any degree of confidence or certainty over a discernable 'cause-and-effect' relationship between technology and learning is nigh on impossible. Put simply, it has proved tremendously difficult to design and carry out empirical studies that can show that digital technology of any kind has an 'impact' or 'effect' on learning.

This has certainly been the experience of researchers who have attempted to apply rigorous 'scientific' methods of enquiry to the topic of teaching and learning with technology. Because education and technology are entwined with all manner of other social, cultural, economic and political 'variables', it has proved very difficult to design any kind of experimental study to investigate the influence of technology use in learning settings. Those researchers that do attempt to pinpoint causal effects of using technology on learning produce what can be charitably be termed as 'mixed results'. For every large-scale study or 'meta-study' (a study that analyses the results of many other studies) that concludes that technology use can be associated with improvements in learning performance, there are many others that find no difference, or even a negative relationship.

This situation has persisted from the 1980s into the 2010s. For instance, there is much current interest in the potential of online learning for school-aged learners. Yet as the authors of a recent US government synthesis of research were forced to conclude, very few rigorous empirical studies of online learning for these students have been published (Means et al. 2009). Moreover, the methodological design of such studies 'almost guarantees that the desired outcome will be attained – that indeed [online] learners perform as well as campus-based students' (Lockee et al. 1999, p. 33). Thus despite repeated attempts by policymakers, IT firms, researchers and practitioners to identify 'impacts' and 'effects' of the recent growth of digital technology use in schools, tangible evidence for sustained beneficial change is proving elusive.

The main problem for all these groups is the difficulty being certain of a causal 'effect', or even association, between technology use and learning. This is an incredibly frustrating situation for the educational technologists, policymakers and teachers who feel sure of the learning benefits offered by digital technologies. Yet even when digital technologies are being used in what could be considered appropriate and equitable ways, there are few robust empirical studies to suggest that this is resulting in sustained educational benefit. This apparent lack of change was illustrated throughout 2000s when a number of separate quasi-experiment studies in Israeli, German, Dutch and Columbian high schools all reported non-existent or even negative correlations between levels of computer use and eventual learning outcomes (Angrist and Lavy 2002, Lauven et al. 2003, Fuchs and Woessmann 2004, Barrera-Osorio and Linden 2009). At the very least, these large-scale studies and others like them begin to raise doubts over many of the more strident claims for improved learning.

This lack of evidence is not unique to the area of digital technology and learning. Indeed, there is a long history of educationalists being unable to prove the effectiveness or impact of educational innovation and change. Thomas Russell's (2001) work on the 'no significant difference phenomenon' provides a comprehensive synopsis of over 350 research reports that document no significant differences in learner outcomes between 'conventional' and alternate modes of education delivery. Of course, the inconclusive nature of these studies often stems from the difficulty of objectively measuring 'learning'. This sense of imprecision and ambiguity exists even in the ostensibly 'scientific' area of neurological and cognitive development. For example, an emerging body of evidence from neuroscience suggests that internet use *enhances* the capacity for young people to possess greater working memory and be more adept at perceptual learning (see Small and Vorgon 2008). However, a counter-body of evidence exists that associates internet use with similar *declines* in young people's cognitive skills and mental performance, as well as the unbalancing of their hormone levels (see Sigman 2009). Even in this more 'quantifiable' area of investigation, debates often descend into subjective claims and counter-claims (e.g. Healy 1999, Prensky 2001, Greenfield 2009). At best the 'evidence' over the influence of digital technology on mental and cognitive development and performance is mixed and inconclusive. At worst these debates descend into the realms of what can be termed uninformed conjecture and 'neuro-myth' (see Schultz 2009).

While many researchers remain committed to searching for clear 'proof', others are now reasoning that the lack of evidence for the influence of technology use on learning could simply suggest that the wrong questions are being asked altogether. Although some critical commentators see the finding of 'no significant difference' as proof of technology 'not working', others are beginning to argue that learning gains are not the most appropriate outcome by which technology use should be judged. As Bill Dutton (2008) contends, 'are we looking at the wrong outcomes for judging the impact of technical change? In my opinion, [digital technologies] are transformational in reconfiguring access, changing how we get information, but perhaps less so in terms of also what we know.' In raising this point, Dutton reasons that much empirical research on education and technology is mistakenly following a simple substitution paradigm – that is, that technology-based learning is better than non-technology-based learning. However, as he continues, this is perhaps an incorrect perspective to take:

> it's the wider benefits of learning with [digital technology] that matter – not least the transformational view of technologies reconfiguring access to information,

people, services and technology. Such a perspective would lead us to study developments outside as well as inside the classroom.

Dutton's arguments mirror those made over 20 years before by the media theorist Richard Clark (1983, 2001). Clark argued that few clear reasons exist to assume that learning benefits will result from using technology for instructional purposes. To illustrate his point, Clark used a 'grocery truck' analogy. In this, Clark argued that technologies are 'mere vehicles' for delivering instruction and are therefore no more likely to influence student learning or achievement than 'the truck that delivers our groceries causes changes in our nutrition' (1983, p. 446). On the other hand, Clark acknowledged that there were significant 'economic' benefits to be had from using technology to deliver learning – not least benefits of time, cost, logistics and other institutional concerns. These benefits, he argued, are of more relevance in judging the educational worth of digital technology. Of course, there are many conceptual problems with seeing any technology as neutral and without value – for instance, Clark's analysis is often criticized as being almost the exact opposite of Marshall McLuhan's notion that the 'medium is the message'. Yet although it can be contested for other reasons, Clark's viewpoint is useful in raising the possibility that, in and of themselves, 'media do not cause learning' (1983, p. 446).

Conclusions

As with all of the issues addressed in this book, 'does technology improve learning?' is not a straightforward question with a straightforward answer. Indeed, a mass of conflicting debates and arguments surround this topic – reminding us of the need to think carefully about the relationships between education and technology. On one hand this chapter has highlighted the benefits of using learning theory to think about why technologies are being used in education. All the theories outlined in this chapter offer ways of thinking about the effective use of technology to support learning. Yet these accounts can all be challenged and criticized. In particular, all of the theoretical approaches presented in the first half of the chapter make different assumptions about what it is 'to learn' and what it is to be 'a learner'. As such they all present different sets of beliefs about the processes of learning with technology. These include different beliefs about the psychological basis of learning and cognition; different educational beliefs about pedagogy and the best way to support learning; and different epistemological beliefs about the nature of reality and knowledge. None of these approaches can be objectively reckoned to be 'better' or more 'accurate' than others. Instead these theoretical accounts offer different insights into how technologies can be designed and used to fit different types of learning – be it rote-learning or problem-solving, 'knowing what' or 'knowing how'.

All these theories point to the importance of matching particular types of learning and learner with particular types of technology. There is certainly no 'one-size-fits-all' solution for applying technology to learning. Digital technology will not automatically support and enhance learning processes unless some thought is given to the 'goodness of fit' between the learning task and the learning technology. For example, the social dynamic of technology-based instruction described by socio-cultural perspectives is clearly less suited to some forms of learning than others. Why is it, for instance, that the classroom-based lecture and seminar continue to be popular modes of learning at many levels of education? One possible reason could be that it is often difficult to capture the vital social elements of face-to-face learning in environments that are mediated through technology. As Charles Crook (2002, p. 33) reasons:

> the cultural view of teaching and learning as socially organised [is] vulnerable to unpredicted consequences of re-mediation through new technology . . . While [digital technologies] offer some powerful possibilities for elaborating the socio-cultural perspective in education, some applications of educational technology seem in awkward tension with the social nature of teaching and learning. [These] effects may often re-mediate our relations with others.

It is therefore important to bear in mind that debates over technology and learning are often driven by personal belief and opinion, rather than being empirically reasoned and informed. Indeed, much of the discussion outlined in the second half of this chapter points towards the limitations of attempting to 'prove' relationships, impacts and effects of technology on learning. If nothing else, it should be clear from these debates that the fields of education and technology are too socially complex to lend themselves to simple analyses of cause and effect. As Cigman and Davis (2008, p. 501) conclude:

> such a consensus would have to depend in turn on agreement about what counts as learning, or, to be even more explicit, what counts as worthwhile learning. We reach a point in any review of the potential of digital technologies which mirrors the situation when we scrutinise the enhancement agenda and the offerings of neuroscience. This is the point where empirical research comes to a halt, and

instead we are in the area of normative debate. Evidently we need to be apprised of all the relevant facts when engaging in such a debate, but the issues now relate to what is important for human flourishing, the point of education and the kind of learning that enhances (in some senses to be explained and defended) human existence.

As this quotation implies, digital technologies are a key battleground for current debates, ideas and arguments about teaching and learning. It is therefore important to remain aware of the values and ideological assumptions that often underpin the extravagant claims made about the potential of digital technology to 'transform' learning or knowledge. Indeed, many debates over technology and learning appear to be driven by wider beliefs of what constitutes 'good' or 'desirable' learning. As such, much of the justification for digital technology use is as a form of a pedagogic corrective – that is, a means to get certain forms of learning into formal educational settings that are otherwise seen to be lacking. This could be argued to be as much the case with the socio-constructivist technologies of the 2010s as it was with the behaviourist-inspired teaching machines of the 1950s and 1960s. Some educational technologists refer to this as the 'Trojan Mouse' approach – that is, using digital technology as a means to 'leverage' a wider philosophy of teaching and learning into educational settings. As Eric Klopfer – when arguing for the learning benefits of mobile games – was honest enough to acknowledge:

It isn't all about the technology. Most of the intellectual capabilities previously defined are relevant to understanding most modern issues and problems. They need not necessarily be associated with technology at all. Many of these skills are equally relevant to constructivist learning that has been promoted by education reformers for decades, and could be fostered without technology. Technology, however, is the vehicle for getting these intellectual capabilities into schools discretely. (2008, p. 12)

With all these issues in mind, it is important to recognize the contested nature of any claims made for technology and learning. It is perhaps best to see technology simply as a focal point through which a range of wider debates about learning, information and knowledge are filtered. As Paul Standish (2008, p. 351) reasons, matters of technology and learning 'cannot be broached without consideration of the essentially ethical question of what counts as worthwhile learning, whether for liberal or vocational ends'. As this chapter has illustrated, many current discussions of education and technology are based around assumptions that worthwhile learning should be active, interactive, learner-centred, social, communal, authentic, and so on. Although many readers may well sympathize with these assumptions it is important to acknowledge that such characteristics involve a commitment to a particular set of values. Moreover, it is important to acknowledge that these values are often at odds with the nature of the educational settings and wider social contexts that learning often takes place in. Against this background, the gap between the rhetoric and reality of technology-based learning looks set to continue for some time yet.

Further questions to consider

- How valid it is to use 'old' theories of learning to make sense of technology-based learning? In what ways can knowledge of how 'traditional' learning takes place be transferred over to technology-mediated contexts? In what ways does existing knowledge of 'traditional' learning lack relevance to contemporary digital technology use?
- Why is it so difficult to accurately measure – or even objectively identify – the 'effect' of technology on learning? Is this question even worth asking?
- To what extent are digital technologies used as a vehicle to promote particular ways of learning (e.g. child-centred learning, play-based learning, discovery-based learning)? To what extent are digital technologies a 'blank canvas' that can be used to promote any type of learning one wishes?

Further reading

Skinner's seminal paper on behaviourism and learning technologies can be found easily online. The full reference is as follows:

- Skinner, B. (1958) 'Teaching machines' *Science*, 128, 3330, pp. 969–977

Some of the classic texts on learning theory and technology are now rather dated, but are worth seeking out:

- Duffy, T. and Jonassen, D. (1992) *Constructivism and the Technology of Instruction*, London, Routledge
- Papert, S. (1980) *Mindstorms: Children, Computers and Powerful Ideas*, Brighton, Harvester Press
- Pea, R. and Sheingold, K. (eds) (1987) *Mirrors of the Mind: Patterns of Experience in Educational Computing*, New Jersey, Ablex

The book has interesting chapters written by John Seely-Brown on situated cognition, David Jonassen in constructivism and Richard Clark on the difficulty of measuring the influence of technology on learning:

- Ely, D. and Plomp, T. (2001) *Classic Writings on Instructional Technology – Volume 2*, Westport CT, Libraries Unlimited

These books offer overviews of some of the more recent thinking about education and technology from a socio-cultural perspective:

- Harasim, L. (2010) *Learning Theory and Online Technology: How New Technologies Are Transforming Learning Opportunities*, London, Routledge
- Luckin, R. (2010) *Re-Designing Learning Contexts: Technology-Rich, Learner-Centred Ecologies*, London, Routledge

5 Does Technology Make Education Fairer?

Introduction

While many debates over educational technology concern matters of learning, these issues are often entwined with what was referred to towards the end of Chapter 4 as the wider benefits of digital technology. In particular we considered Bill Dutton's argument that the real educational significance of technology use in education perhaps lies in the transformation of access to information, people, services and technology – what Richard Clark described as the economic and logistical advantages of institutional media. As well as making education more convenient and cost effective, there has also been much recent discussion of the social advantages of technology use in education – in particular the idea that technology can be used to make the processes and practices of education fairer, more equal and more just.

In order to consider these socially transformational benefits in more depth, we first need to be clear what is meant by phrases such as 'fairer', 'more equal' and 'more just'. All of these terms relate to what is often referred to as 'social inequality'. The concept of social inequality relates to the unequal distribution of power, resources and prestige among individuals and social groups. A range of socially created inequalities and differences can be found throughout any society – not least disparities in people's income, health and housing. Alongside these issues, educational inequalities are perhaps one of the most important influences on an individual's 'life chances'. The ability to access and create knowledge, as well as the ability to gain the credentialization and qualifications that are linked with education, are all considered to be key assets in acquiring power, resources and prestige in contemporary society. Education is seen to be an especially important element of what is termed 'social inclusion' – that is, the extent to which individuals and groups are able to participate fully in society and control their own destinies. In short education is at the heart of how more or less 'fair' contemporary social life is for a person. As Lynsday Grant puts it,

> Learning is a process that can dramatically broaden the opportunities and choices available to an individual. At an instrumental level, learning skills and gaining qualifications opens up possibilities for employment, and access to fulfilling and rewarding employment is one key measure of social justice. This is the definition of learning often used in discussions around social justice and social mobility. But learning is also important to social justice in ways that go beyond this instrumental level. Learning is a process that can enable people to make their voices heard in the wider world and thereby exert agency over the future direction of their own lives and communities. Learning can build individuals' self-confidence and a sense of their own efficacy. Learning therefore has an important role to play in . . . tackling the effects of deprivation, disadvantage and limited opportunities. (Grant and Villabos 2008, p. 4)

If anything, education systems in most developed countries appear to have led to the continuation of inequalities and social stratification over the past 50 years or so. This has prompted many academics to conclude that education is a deeply unfair and unequal process. Despite great efforts to engineer change, even the most efficient education systems end up privileging those who are already privileged, and doing little to improve the relative advantage of those people who are less well-off. Against this background the transformational qualities of digital technologies are clearly attractive – promising to somehow overcome many of the inequalities and inefficiencies of existing educational provision. A great deal of hope is being placed, therefore, in the socially benefi-cial capacity of digital technologies to allow disadvantaged individuals to gain the full benefits of education and learning. As Mark Warschauer (2003, p. 9) put it, the combination of education and digital technology 'is critical to social inclusion in today's era'.

Broadly speaking there are two different approaches to understanding technology and educational inequality. On one hand, technology is seen to be a ready means of addressing inequalities of *educational opportunity*. Put simply, the idea of 'equality of opportunity' refers to the choices and chances that indi-viduals have in life. This approach to equality is based on the belief that every individual should have an equal chance to access resources and opportunities. In this sense, technology is seen as an ideal means of providing individuals with a free choice from a diversity of educational opportunities. This emphasis on choice and diversity is linked to the notion of 'meritocracy'. In a merito-cratic society individuals should have an equal right to compete against each other to succeed, regardless of prior circumstance and background – as Sheldon Richmond (1974) put it, to have an 'equal chance to become unequal'.

A more radical approach is the use of technology to address inequalities of *educational outcome*. The idea of 'equality of outcome' refers to the conditions and circumstances that individuals face, with it being seen fundamentally unfair that large differences in circumstances exist between individuals or groups in a society. This approach to equality is linked to what is often referred to as 'social justice' – that is, the concept of creating a society with a greater degree of egalitarianism in terms of what people actually have. In this sense, digital technology is seen as a ready means of supporting progressive inter-ventions that attempt to redistribute resources, power and prestige, and therefore seek to achieve equality of opportunity *and* equality of outcome. This use of technology attempts to move beyond the meritocratic idea of allowing people an equal chance to compete with each other. Instead, techno-logy is used as part of interventions to force changes that are often talked of in terms of affirmative action or positive discrimination.

Technology, freedom and fairness

As we shall soon see, digital technology now plays a key role in both of these approaches to making education fairer. Of course, a widespread faith in the socially transformatative power of technology is not confined to education.

Indeed, the development of information technologies has long been associated with a general sense of freedom, fairness and liberation. For example, much of the development of computing throughout the 1960s, 1970s and 1980s was rooted in a Californian 'hippy' philosophy of freedom and equality. This spirit and ethos persists in the so-called 'hacker ethic' that persists between many computer programmers and developers. This ethos sees information sharing as a positive moral good, with programmers feeling bound ethically to share their work at all times (see Himanen 2001). As Jaron Lanier puts it, many computer programmers and developers continue to pursue a subtle and often unwitting form of 'stealth-socialism' (2010).

Perhaps the most obvious instance of the freedoms associated with digital technologies can be found in the internet and worldwide web. From its inception in 1969, the internet was always envisaged as a technically 'free' environment. Early incarnations of the internet allowed users to send content anywhere across its networks, while also providing a freedom of association based on mutual respect and collective endeavour. Through his development of the worldwide web, Tim Berners-Lee worked to allow a mass of people to use the internet for a common good regardless of state or bureaucratic regimes. Berners-Lee talked in optimistic terms of encouraging an 'architecture of openness' in technical *and* social terms. While ambitious and idealistic, these principles still underpin the popularity of many social media applications. One of the main attractions of social media is the widely held belief that they are somehow able to 'liberate' the user from social structure and hierarchy, boosting individual freedoms and reducing centralized controls over what can and what cannot be done.

As we discussed briefly in Chapters 1 and 2, many people see the openness and freedom of internet connectivity as heralding a potential reconfiguration of all social arrangements and relations. At a macrolevel of analysis, for example, the internet is seen to be a major part of the 'flattening out' of hierarchies and the looser 'networking logic' that many organizations and institutions now appear to be following (e.g. Friedman 2007, Castells 1996). At a microlevel of analysis the ability to be connected to anything at anytime is similarly seen to be enabling individuals to live their lives along more open, democratic and ultimately empowering lines. As Charles Leadbeater concludes:

> the web's extreme openness, its capacity to allow anyone to connect to virtually anyone else, generates untold possibilities for collaboration . . . the more connected we are, the richer we should be, because we should be able to connect

with other people far and wide, to combine their ideas, talents and resources in ways that should expand everyone's property. (2008b, p. 3)

All of these claims convey a sense of a new politics associated with using digital technologies. In particular, many of these accounts associate digital technologies such as the internet with what could be termed 'libertarian' values. As Matthew Allen reasons, many of the benefits of the internet are now 'expressed in traditional democratic terms, emphasizing freedom of choice and the empowerment of individuals through the "architecture of participation"' (2008, n.p.). Key here is a belief that individuals will gain in power as the overarching control of the institutions in their lives diminishes, with digital technologies supporting what Graham Murdock describes as 'the return of control to users and consumers' (2004, p. 21). Much of this belief in the transformative power of digital technologies is therefore based around a new sense of the empowered technology user. This is an individual 'who is more engaged, active and a participant in the key business of the internet: creating, maintaining and expanding the 'content' which is the basis for using the internet in the first place' (Allen 2008, n.p.).

An important concept here is the notion of 'personalization' of technology-based participation – that is, the idea that digital technologies should be based around the needs and interests of the individual user. Of course, this principle has long been at the heart of digital technology design and development. From the development of the early 'personal computer' to the 'personal digital assistant' there has been a growing emphasis on designing technological arte-facts that fit flexibly around the lives and requirements of individual users. As one of the architects of the personal computer put it, much of the past 50 years of digital technology development has been focused on the development of 'personal dynamic computing' through machines 'designed in a way that *any* owner could mould and channel its power to his own needs' (Kay and Goldberg 1977, p. 31).

Technology and making education fairer for individuals

A great deal of ground has already been covered so far in this chapter. First, we have distinguished between the potential of digital technologies to make education 'fairer' both in terms of the ease with which education can be accessed and – some would believe – its eventual outcomes. We have also seen the personalized and individualized freedoms that are associated with contemporary technology use. With these latter assumptions in mind, it perhaps makes sense to now focus on the particular claims concerning digital technology and equality of educational opportunity. Over the past 20 years, digital technologies have been promoted as an effective means of allowing individuals to play active roles in enhancing their educational prospects. Technology has been associated with 'intrinsically equitable, decentralised and democratic' forms of education based around the needs of the individual learner (Graham 2002, p. 35). These promises can be seen as taking 3 distinctive forms.

Increasing the diversity of education

The promise that digital technologies can support a greater diversity of education provision has proved especially popular since the rise of the internet and so-called virtual education. Through the internet, for example, the individual learner is given potential access to learning from a wide variety of providers. An online learner in rural Australia, for example, can access learning from the best of Australian higher education institutions or, indeed, higher education from anywhere else in the world. The internet has greatly expanded the scope of education provision to the point where major universities now host extensive online distance education programmes offering their courses to a global marketplace. Some academics and educationalists talk of 'borderless education' or, perhaps more provocatively, the 'edgeless university' – implying the unlimited provision of education to a mass audience regardless of place, time or space. As Grant and Villabos (2008, p. 9) contend, technologies can therefore be seen as 'diversifying the range of learning experiences available, and thereby engaging with people who have not achieved their full potential with more traditional approaches'.

Besides extending the market-reach of formal educational institutions, digital technologies are seen to offer new opportunities for informal exchange of expertise, knowledge and folk-wisdom between individuals. Indeed, computers have long facilitated the types of 'informal' learning and self-education outlined in Chapter 1 – not least through the retrieval of information from the worldwide web. Now the trend for the informal consumption, creation, communication and sharing of knowledge via digital technologies looks set to increase with learners' growing use of 'read/write' social media tools and applications. Via social media applications such as *Wikipedia*, for example, knowledge is seen to be no longer held by formal gatekeepers but accessible to all – and perhaps most significantly, creatable by all. The collaborative spirit of these social media activities and many others like them has coalesced into a prevailing sense that education will be increasingly based around the networked creation as well as consumption of content. As David Beer and Roger Burrows contend:

> networks are taking shared responsibility for the construction of vast accumulations of knowledge about themselves, each other, and the world. These are dynamic matrices of information through which people observe others, expand the network, make new 'friends', edit and update content, blog, remix, post, respond, share files, exhibit, tag and so on. This has been described as an online 'participatory culture' where users are increasingly involved in *creating* web content as well as *consuming* it. (2007, 2.1)

Decreasing the barriers to education

Many educationalists and technologists would agree that this diversity of provision is matched by the capacity of digital technology to 'free' education from the barriers that may have otherwise prevented individuals from participating. Specific barriers to learning, such as financial cost, the difficulty of physically travelling to places of educational provision, the need to learn at a slower or faster pace, and lack of recent contact with educational institutions are now believed to be resolvable through the use of technology. Digital technologies are seen to deliver educational opportunities to individuals on a convenient and easy basis, facilitating contact with communities of similar learners regardless of proximity, and generally making learning more flexible. This is especially seen to be the case in opening-up access to education across all groups that have historically been found to be underrepresented in forms of education after the compulsory stage of schooling. These groups often include the unemployed, the disabled, mothers, carers, the busy or simply the disinclined. Barriers to education for these groups, whether they are situational (to do with lifestyle), institutional (related to the opportunities available) or dispositional (related to personal knowledge and motivation), are seen as resolvable through the use of digital technology which can offer education to learners on an 'any place, any pace' basis.

All of these factors have fuelled a general sense that digital technologies now enable forms of education that are more flexible and less compromised.

Allied to claims of the general 'death of distance' and increased 'time-space compression' of modern life, technology-based education is seen to be no longer compromised by the 'frictions' of space and place. In terms of location, for example, learning can take place at times that best suit the individual learner. In terms of pacing, digital technologies are seen to offer learners the option of either 'speeding-up' or 'slowing-down' their learning as required. Learners are also felt to be less encumbered by barriers related to their family, household or work commitments. Many of the emancipatory claims surrounding virtual forms of education therefore derive from a presumption that the lack of commitment to be 'present' lends the learning process a purity and efficiency which is otherwise compromised by the physical and temporal demands of educational institutions. As Mark Nunes (2006, p. 135) puts it, digital technologies now allow for 'a "clean" and efficient transmission of information'.

Increasing individuals' control over their education

Allied to these advantages is a perceived increased individual control of learning. Here technology is seen to support and enhance the capacity of individuals to build and maintain connections with various components of the education system on their own terms. This allows individuals to take responsibility for curating and managing their own learning. In this sense, the technology-supported learner is often celebrated as playing an active role in (re)constructing the nature, place, pace and timing of their learning. As Nunes (2006, p. 130) concludes, digital technology allows education to be:

> a performative event in the hands of the student, thereby repositioning the student in relation to institutional networks. To this extent, the [student] is anything but marginal; as both the operator that enacts the class and the target that receives course content, the student occupies a metaphorical and experiential centre for the performance of the course.

This increased control over learning is reflected in a number of changes to the education landscape that require learners to actively make choices and quickly decide upon courses of action. For example, the successful learner is now expected to be reflective and 'reflexive' – displaying a capacity for constant self-evaluation and self-awareness (Beck-Gernsheim 1996). Individuals are expected to build upon past experiences and react to new opportunities and circumstances as they navigate their way through their 'lifelong learning' careers. This style of education is seen to fit well with the demands of modern life – especially in terms of the employment demands of the knowledge economy outlined in Chapter 2. Individuals of all ages are now seen to require the ability to adapt to different demands and circumstances on a 'just-in-time' basis – learning different skills and gaining new knowledge as their situations dictate.

In this sense, digital technologies are seen to be integral elements of these new ways-of-being, playing important roles in underpinning learners' abilities to make decisions about what they need to do next. It has been suggested that digital technologies offer the opportunity to re-engage individuals with learning and education – promoting a 'critical thinking in learners' about their education (Bugeja 2006). As the sociologist Scott Lash observes, digital technology means that modern life is 'no longer about distanciated decision-making [now] there is no distance at all between knowledge and action' (2002, p. 156). In this sense, digital technologies have been heralded by some commentators to offer 'the capacity to radically change the educational system . . . to better motivate students as engaged learners rather than learners who are primarily passive observers of the educational process' (Ziegler 2007, p. 69).

Limitations to the individual freedoms of technology-based education

As all these examples suggest, many commentators now see digital technologies as an important element of an increasingly democratized systems of educational provision. As Solomon and Schrum (2007, p. 8) concluded when talking about the social media applications that emerged throughout the 2000s, 'everyone can participate [in education] thanks to social networking and collaborative tools and the abundance of web 2.0 sites . . . The web is no longer a one-way street where someone controls the content. Anyone can control content in a web 2.0 world.' Claims such as these may seem plausible, but it could be strongly argued that relatively few learners in practice actually experience the perceived 'transformations' outlined above. It makes sense, therefore, to consider some of the limitations to these assumptions and arguments.

First, it seems that in many cases digital technologies have not necessarily led to an increased diversity of education provision. Anyone looking to engage in online learning, for example, will find that popular and profitable areas of study such as business, IT and English language often dominate provision of courses. This is not to say that there are not many more educational providers than before. Indeed, the increased marketization of online learning has seen the provision of education diversify from traditional and established education institutions to a 'long tail' of other actors and settings. The twenty-first-century educational landscape is now one of commercially provided 'e-learning' and home-based 'edutainment', alongside the extended 'virtual learning environments' of schools, colleges and universities (Buckingham and Scanlon 2005).

However, all these instances of digital provision could be characterized as offering 'more of the same' types of education, rather than necessarily supporting a genuine diversity of different opportunities. Opportunities for more esoteric (and often less popular and profitable) forms of learning are more rare, even when one reviews the opportunities available through user-generated or user-supported informal learning. Technology-based education may be supporting a greater volume of learning opportunities, but these are often homogenous and interchangeable with each other. As Rudy Hirschheim (2005, p. 101) describes it, digital technologies such as the internet could be said to be leading simply to 'a more standardised, minimalist product targeted for a mass market, [that] will further 'box in' and 'dumb down' education'.

Doubts have also been raised over the ability of digital technologies to reduce the barriers to accessing learning. In fact some people would argue that technology may actually add additional impediments to the access of learning – not least in terms of the many (often subtle) barriers that lie behind the ability to access and use technology. Indeed, despite assumptions of 'universal access' and 'ubiquitous technology' an individual's ability to engage with digital technologies remains contingent on a number of different aspects of resourcing. As Jan van Dijk (2005) reasons, using digital technology remains dependent on a number of factors, such as:

- temporal resources (e.g. time to spend on different activities in life);
- material resources above and beyond digital technology devices and services (e.g. income and all kinds of property);

- mental resources (e.g. knowledge, general social and technical skills above and beyond specific IT skills);
- social resources (e.g. social network positions and relationships, such as those in the workplace, home or community);
- cultural resources (e.g. cultural assets, such as status and forms of qualifications).

Put in these terms, there would seem to be a number of enduring 'digital divides' which continue to underpin the ability of many individuals to use technology in order to access and engage with learning. Any claims for increased levels of access to education are therefore compromised by what appears to be a complex and divided patterning of digital technology (non-) use within society. Such is the recurring importance of social and economic factors, that one major US study was led to observe simply that 'demography is destiny when it comes to predicting who will go online' (Pew 2003, p. 41). This conclusion has been reinforced year on year by a number of empirical studies that all suggest that people's use of digital technologies remains differentiated along lines of socio-economic status and social class, as well as race, gender, geography, age and educational background (Dutton and Helsper 2009, Jones and Fox 2009, Jones et al. 2009).

It would also seem that pre-existing barriers and impediments to learning – such as barriers of time, space, place, material resourcing and other life circumstances – remain significant for many people despite the affordances of technology. In particular, digital technologies often do little to alter the fact that the chief obstacles to getting involved with education are not necessarily the physical barriers of time and place, but rather people's lack of interest and motivation. Positively influencing people's decisions to learn is not simply a case of making educational opportunities more convenient via digital technology. If people have not previously engaged in learning and education due to issues of motivation and/or disposition then there is little reason to assume that digital technology will alter this. Although technology can be used to overcome physical and cognitive barriers such as disability or literacy, digital technologies on their own can often do little to alter the social complexities of people's lives and the 'fit' of education in these lives. It would seem that many non-technological issues underpin people's non-engagement in education. These are often hugely complex issues such as poverty, housing, quality of employment and – above all – the reproduction of these inequalities from generation to generation.

Technology and social justice in education

At best, then, we should perhaps remain cautious of claims that digital technologies are capable of engineering the transformation of educational opportunities. Despite the growing provision of education via digital technologies it appears that many of the same inequalities and divides remain intact. From this perspective, we should turn our attention to more radical efforts to use digital technology as a means to intervene in educational outcomes. Rather than assuming that increased equalities will accrue automatically from technology use, these examples relate to the design and implementation of technology to promote social justice in education.

While a number of these projects exist in developed countries such as the United Kingdom, United States and Canada, the most sustained efforts along these lines can be found in developing countries. Indeed, educational projects form a large part of what has come to be known as the 'ICTs for Development' (ICT4D) movement where digital technologies are used as potential solutions to the challenges of community development (see Colle and Roman 2003). Many of the challenges that ICT4D seeks to address are relatively basic. For instance, with only 15 per cent of rural households in sub-Saharan Africa having access to electricity, issues of power are of paramount importance. Another major issue is the provision of low-cost and robust technological devices that are capable of working in poor and under-resourced communities where fundamental necessities such as teachers, books, shelter, water and food are still sparse. Yet despite all these issues, technology is still seen as a major means of overcoming entrenched educational inequalities across the developing world. In particular, digital technology is being heralded as a key part of achieving some of the basic goals of providing access to free universal primary education of good quality, and the development of life-skills and vocational-skills in later life. As Michelle Sellinger reasons:

> ICTs can indeed hold the key to a step change towards improvement in the world's education systems. ICT is certainly not a panacea for education, but it is a powerful tool that when implemented appropriately can catalyse and accelerate education reform and development. (Sellinger 2009, p. 206)

Using technology access as a means to access education

Initiatives of this kind take a variety of guises – not least the subsidized provision of access to computers for those without. For instance, a range of non-governmental organizations such as the Scandinavian Fair Allocation of InfoTech Resources project and the UK Computer Aid International charity all work to supply developing countries with refurbished and recycled computers that have been donated from firms and individuals in developed nations. Many of these initiatives follow what is known as a 'telecottage' or 'telecentre' model, where community-based rooms or buildings are equipped with one or more internet-connected computer. These efforts mirror programmes in North America and Europe throughout the 1990s and 2000s where governments and charities sponsored the public provision of computer and internet access across networks of 'ICT Centres' focused on disadvantaged communities and located in a variety of distributed sites such as libraries, museums and colleges. The aim of these centres was primarily to provide flexible access to new technologies for those without facilities at home or at work.

In developing countries the nature of such interventions has often been necessarily basic. One celebrated example during the 1990s and 2000s was the Hole in the Wall project, which originated in a slum area of New Delhi but has since extended to over 500 sites across India and Africa. As its name suggests, the premise of the project is simple. The monitor of an internet-connected computer is made visible in a hole in a wall with no keyboard, but specially designed joysticks and buttons to act as a mouse. Although a volunteer is usually responsible for the maintenance of the computer, there are no teachers or technical support on hand. Instead, an ethos of 'minimally invasive education' is followed, where local people can access the computer 24 hours a day, and teach themselves how to use the computer on an individually paced basis.

The project was soon hailed a great success, prompting claims that the majority of children visiting the Hole in the Wall computers were soon able to teach themselves basic operational skills of word-processing, drawing and web-searching applications – what the providers termed as 'self activated learning'. The success of the Hole in the Wall programme soon led to extravagant claims about the significance of the project for more conventional educational provision. As James Tooley argued, 'even illiterate slum children had been found to teach themselves easily how to access the internet, and to teach others how to do so . . . schools [will] soon realise that this self-teaching method [is] far superior to any that had tried' (2006, p. 28).

While 'Hole in the Wall' and 'telecentre' projects continue to run, more recent initiatives have responded to the increased portability and personalization of computer hardware as well as the rise of wireless connectivity. These developments have shifted the focus of those seeking to provide technology to poor groups. Now an emphasis tends to be put on providing internet connections and portable computerized devices to otherwise disconnected individuals in order to develop technology skills and, more importantly, support their learning. These interventions have grown in prevalence across developed and developing countries. In the United Kingdom, for example, the Home Access Taskforce initiative promised to dedicate over £300 million on providing computers and broadband internet access to deprived families so that children and parents could enhance their learning at home. Similarly, in Portugal the government's Magellan Initiative sought to provide 500,000 children between the ages of 6 and 10 in basic education with an internet-enabled laptop computer.

Perhaps the most high profile of these initiatives has been the One Laptop Per Child initiative – where developing nations are encouraged to invest in US-produced laptop computers. In ICT4D terms this can be described as a 'pro-poor solution' where technologies from developed countries are brought into developing regions. Yet the One Laptop Per Child initiative does not simply use 'off the shelf' computers. Instead the initiative was intended to 'create educational opportunities for the world's poorest children' by providing each child with a specially designed and produced computer – described as a 'rugged, low-cost, low-power, connected laptop with content and software designed for collaborative, joyful, self-empowered learning' (OLPC 2010, n.p.). The initial 'One Laptop Per Child' scheme (or OLPC for short) was originally labelled the '$100 laptop' programme, and was set up by a team from the Massachusetts Institute of Technology which included the educational technologist Seymour Papert (whose work on constructionism was discussed in the previous chapter). The OLPC model soon prompted other computer companies such as Dell and Intel to follow suit in producing low-specification and low-cost laptop and netbook computers for the developing world.

The OLPC initiative marked an ambitious attempt to bring networked computing – and networked learning – to populations of children and young people who were otherwise living in disadvantaged conditions. Described as 'a striking little green machine with a crank handle' (Naughton 2005, p. 6), the first OLPC 'XO' computer was a low-spec, low-cost, robust notebook computer that was designed to work in large numbers of poor communities. Relying on bulk orders of the computers by governments, the OLPC scheme was accepted most enthusiastically in South and Central American countries – not least Peru, Uruguay and Mexico, with some countries in sub-Saharan Africa also participating. As with the Hole in the Wall initiatives, these interventions were soon accompanied by some impressive claims relating to 'the idea that universal laptop computer use will revolutionise the world for the better' (Luyt 2008, n.p.). As one of the guiding lights behind the OLPC scheme reasoned at the beginning of the programme:

> Laptops, as we know them, are a luxury. Education is not. At $100, this is about learning and exploration, not giving kids costly tools and toys. Almost anything, from healthcare to food to birth control, can be addressed well, if not best, through education. The deeper divides are unequivocally proportional to education. Peace will never happen as long as there is poverty. Poverty can only be eliminated through education. (Nicolas Negroponte, cited in Witchalls 2005, p. 23)

Open source solutions to education and technology

Technology access programmes such as the Hole in the Wall and OLPC are based on the logic of first providing people with ready access to a computer and network connectivity, which they can then use to learn with. An alternative strategy has been to encourage and support communities of people who are already computer users to make the most of so-called open source products and processes to access and build their own learning tools. In a basic sense, Open Source can be defined as computer software or hardware that is left in an ongoing 'open' state of refinement and redevelopment by any user who wishes to improve it. Development of Open Source products therefore relies on an organic 'gift economy' basis rather than any for-profit motive. Yet for many educationalists and technologists the appeal of Open Source reaches beyond the products that are developed. Indeed, due to the perceived collective efficiency of communal content creation and redistribution, Open Source has gained credence both as a technical process *and* as a guiding wider philosophy of empowerment and public good (see von Hippel 2005, Weber and Bussell 2005).

Open Source software products now command a prominent place within contemporary computing culture. Most genres of commercial software application are mirrored by high-quality open source alternatives that have been developed and adopted by Open Source communities. Well-known examples include the much celebrated *Linux* operating system, the *Mozilla* web browser and the *OpenOffice* suite of 'Office' applications. From an educational perspective the *Moodle* online content management package has been developed as an alternative to commercial 'virtual learning environments' such as BlackBoard. Tellingly, the 'One Laptop Per Child' project is organized on open source principles. As Luyt (2008, n.p.) enthused, 'one of the main features of the [OLPC] computer, for example, is that users can drill down into the interface to look at the source code directly, and content development for the machine is strictly in the public domain'.

In one sense, these Open Source software tools and applications simply represent software that is financially free of cost – an obvious benefit to users in developing countries. The widespread use of Open Source software in schools is therefore celebrated as a powerful means of circumventing the constraining 'proprietary lock-in' and dependency on major IT suppliers that many educational institutions otherwise experience (Carmichael and Honour 2002). Countries such as Brazil, for example, are aiming to use free Open Source software to bring computer access to the 80 per cent of its population who are currently without. As the co-ordinator of the Brazilian Free Software Project argued, 'every license for Office plus Windows in Brazil – a country in which 22 million people are starving – means we have to export sixty sacks of soya beans' (Marcelo Branco, cited in Anderson 2009, p. 105). Similarly, the Georgian Deer Leap school computerization program during the 2000s introduced the mandatory use of the Linux operating system throughout the national school system. As Chris Anderson (2009, p. 105) concludes, 'from this perspective, free software is not just good for consumers, it is good for the nation'.

Yet for many proponents the educational potential of Open Source software reaches far beyond the idea of teachers and students using non-proprietary software packages in a passive manner. In particular the idea of Open Source has prompted a growing belief among some educational technologists that teachers and students are themselves capable of reshaping computer-based information and content around their own needs and demands. Much attention is now being paid, for example, to the potential of local, 'bespoke' Open Source production of learning content – thereby providing opportunities for 'customising to fulfil specific educational needs and for the development of collaborative on-line learning communities' (Carmichael and Honour 2002, p. 47).

One prominent instance of this is the 'Open Courseware' and 'Open Educational Resource' movements in higher education, which are concerned with making universities' educational materials available online for no cost. It is reckoned that content from almost 80 per cent of courses at the Massachusetts Institute of Technology are available in this free-to-use manner. Similar commitments can be found in institutions ranging from world-class universities such as Oxford and Yale to local community colleges. In all these cases, course materials such as seminar notes, podcasts and videos of lectures are shared online with a general population of learners who could otherwise not attend.

Often the emphasis of Open Educational Resources is not simply on allowing teachers and learners to use materials as provided, but encouraging users to alter and add to these resources as required. The UK Open University's *OpenLearn* project provides free access to all of the institution's curriculum materials with an invitation for teachers *and* learners to adapt these resources as they see fit. Other ventures rely on educational content that is created by individuals as well as institutions. For example, the 'YouTube.Edu' service concentrates on providing educational videos produced by individuals and institutions alike. As Swain (2009, p. 7) enthuses, 'thousands of hours of material are online for potential students, or educators looking for inspiration'. On a more commercial basis, Apple Computers' collection of educational media – the so-called *iTunes-U* – is seen to allow learners to circumvent traditional educational lectures and classes in favour of on-demand free mobile learning (McKinney et al. 2009). Describing itself as 'possibly the world's greatest collection of free educational media available to students, teachers, and lifelong learners', *iTunes-U* offers free access to over 200,000 educational audio and video podcast files to learners and teachers.

Some instances of this open, communal approach involve communities of educators and technologists in developed countries adopting Open Source methods to provide education to more disadvantaged learners. The International University of the People is one such example – a not-for-profit volunteer university offering courses provided entirely online and largely free of charge. The University is designed around altruistic social networking principles. Groups of students participate in weekly discussion forums where they can access lecture transcripts and associated reading material prepared by volunteer professors (often moonlighting from their 'official' paid university positions elsewhere). Students are also provided with assignments and discussion questions, which then direct their study for the week. Students are expected to contribute to discussions and comment on their peers' ideas. For broader discussions and learning, a university-wide forum of all the university's teaching faculty and students operates to aid the discussion and clarification of points not covered in the weekly 'classes'. As well as seeking to expand higher education access to social groups who would otherwise be excluded, the International University of the People also offers some fundamental conceptual challenges to traditional forms of university education.

Whereas the International University of the People could be characterized as a 'pro-poor' solution, other Open Source collaborative programmes in developing countries have framed disadvantaged users as 'active producers and innovators' (Heeks 2008). One such project was the Open Knowledge Network that ran during the 2000s in countries such as Kenya, Tanzania, Mali, Uganda, Senegal, Zimbabwe and Mozambique. The Open Knowledge Network was promoted to be 'a human network, which collects, shares and disseminates local knowledge and is supported by flexible technical solutions'. As Richard Heeks (2008, p. 28) described, the Open Knowledge Network sought to collect, share and disseminate 'relevant local data content focused on livelihood-appropriate issues such as health, education, agriculture, and rights'. These projects were usually community-based, with individuals often developing content and information offline, and then using the internet, mobile phones and other communication technologies to share with other users. One of the obvious advantages of this user-created content was its relevance and usefulness – not least because content could be produced in a variety of national and local languages.

Limitations to technology-based social justice

These products and programmes – and many others like them – can certainly be seen as innovative and relatively successful examples of how technology can be used to pursue principles of social justice and equality of outcome. Yet although widely celebrated, all these initiatives could be said to ultimately have been relatively ineffective. In most countries educational participation continues to be one of the most unequal areas of society despite 20 years of such initiatives. These entrenched general patterns of inequality suggest that a number of limitations should be borne in mind when considering the relative localized success of such projects.

First, many of these interventions can be seen as presenting 'official' interventions and solutions on the part of governments, organizations like the World Bank and other development bodies. Whereas these organizations have the required economic power to develop such expensive schemes they also have an influence on the nature of how the technology is used, and the nature of what it is being used for. This raises questions about the value and nature of the 'empowerment' that people are being offered through digital technology use. As Masschelein and Quaghebeur (2005) remind us, the forms of 'participation' and 'inclusion' that are promised through any social policy intervention are often based on official 'supply-side' needs and assumptions. For example, many of the initiatives just outlined in this chapter operate ostensibly to promote the increased and active involvement of people in activities and decisions that concern their lives. Yet often these official notions of 'participation' and 'involvement' can be seen as conforming to official expectations of what it is to learn or to gain employment related skills. In other words, the individual 'participant' is not actively self-determining (and self-empowering) but submitting themselves to conform to official agendas. In particular, it could be argued that the concept of 'social inclusion' that underpins the digital inclusion model implicit in many of these programmes could be more accurately described as one of economic inclusion. While understandable from an official point of view, it could well be that many of these 'socially inclusive' benefits are not especially desirable – or even that advantageous – for the individuals concerned.

The role of the private, commercial sector in all of these projects must also not be overlooked. As Richard Heeks (2008, p. 26) acknowledges, the area of ICT4D certainly 'presents opportunities for informatics professionals and offers new markets for ICT vendors'. Of course, many people would concur with Heeks' argument that IT professionals and corporations have a moral obligation to shift their attention from solely 'serving the needs of the world's wealthier corporations and individuals' and instead concentrate on 'applying new technology to our planet's mega problems' (2008, p. 26). Yet this is clearly not a realistic or appealing expectation for most commercial organizations. Instead, it is perhaps more realistic to accept that the intentions of most private sector actors involved in such initiatives are multifaceted but ultimately driven by commercial sensibilities. For example, the provision of a low-cost, low-specification laptop to developing countries certainly has the potential to be 'hyper expansive to the existing market' as Intel chief executive Paul Otellini termed it (cited in BBC News 2008). It is probably not coincidental that towards the end of the 2000s Microsoft engaged in a number of 'pro-poor pricing models' for educational consumers in developing countries – including a $3 'Student Innovation Suite' package of 'slimmed down' versions of their software packages. While some commentators may wish to imagine a degree of 'corporate social responsibility . . . in the new media world' (Withers 2008, p. 7), the realities of commercial gain and increased market share are often quite different.

Of course, many technologists would argue that 'bottom-up', user-created initiatives such as the Open Knowledge Network negate many of these problems (Light and Luckin 2008). However, even these interventions face some specific limitations in terms of using digital technologies to allow people to construct their own technology-based learning and to effectively teach themselves. First, despite claims of 'flattened hierarchies' and democratic participation, clear inequalities and hierarchies remain in such interventions. Most obviously, the inclusiveness of 'open' and collaborative projects is obviously compromised by the programming and coding skills required to participate. Although it is often claimed that 'user/developers come from all walks of life' (Weber 2000, p. 15), meaningful participation is limited to relatively technically skilled individuals. In this sense it would seem optimistic to imagine Open Source software production taking place within heterogeneous communities of experts and non-experts sharing common interests and goals.

It is also fanciful to imagine the unproblematic creation of wide range of content and information by communities of educational computer users. Internet usage statistics suggest that most online applications rely on content (re)creation by around 0.5 per cent of users (Arthur 2006). Even an application as apparently 'open' as *Wikipedia* depends heavily on a 'small core' of a few thousand 'highly active participants' who write and edit entries that are then consumed by an audience of millions of users (Leadbeater 2008b, p. 15). Most social media applications reflect the continued relevance of the so-called 90-9-1 rule of participation. This is a rule-of-thumb among technologists regarding user-generated content in online communities. It is reckoned that only 1 per cent of users are generally willing to create original content on a regular and sustained basis, and only 9 per cent willing to comment and perhaps contribute original content on an intermittent basis. In contrast, the remaining 90 per cent of users are happy to just passively consume other people's work (see Nielsen 2006). In this respect it is not surprising that initiatives such as the 'Open Knowledge Network' and 'University of the People' projects tend to suffer from a lack of diverse content.

Perhaps the most serious limitation of all these interventions highlighted so far is that they do not necessarily 'fit' with the social and cultural contexts in which they operate. This is especially seen to be the case with so-called pro-poor interventions. As Richard Heeks argues:

> pro-poor innovation occurs outside poor communities, but on their behalf. Tele-centres began as pro-poor efforts and the OLPC was largely designed this way. This can be an effective approach for engaging resources from the global North in developing-country problems. However, it runs into the danger of design versus reality gaps: a mismatch between the assumptions and requirements built into the design and the on-the-ground realities of poor communities. (2008, p. 29)

As Heeks implies, such problems were faced by the One Laptop Per Child project which encountered an unexpected reluctance throughout the 2000s of governments to commit to the required mass orders of machines. As one commentator observed four years after the high-profile launch of the initiative, 'after years of deal-making and political machinations, it is still only making relatively slow progress' (Johnson 2009, p. 5). While the reasons for this inertia are varied, it could be argued that the architects of the OLPC initiative held an exaggerated expectation of the vitality of laptop computing outside of the developed world. For instance, as Larry Cuban observed, many of the guiding philosophies behind the 'One Laptop Per Child' initiative could be considered to be 'naïve and innocent about the reality of formal schooling' in developing countries (cited in Markoff 2006). Other commentators have been less reserved in their criticism. As John Naughton argued, the One Laptop Per Child project raises significant questions, not least

> whether the folks who wrote it have any understanding of what it's like to live in a society where the average income is less than $2 a day and the notion of children's rights is as theoretical as time travel . . . It is an article of faith that giving kids computers is a way of aiding their learning . . . [The OLPC initiative] is thus rather grandly contemptuous of mundane questions such as whether there is any evidence that giving kids computers is educationally better than giving them books, hiring more teachers or building more schools – or even paying families to send their kids to school. For Papert – and his MIT colleagues – technology seems to be the answer, no matter what the question. (2005, p. 6)

Conclusions

All of the examples in this chapter contrast the potential for the democratic use of technology in educational settings with a number of practical problems and limitations. One of the key issues underpinning all these examples is the question of whether technology can somehow prompt people to develop *new* patterns of behaviour and types of activity. Indeed, this is an issue that lies at the centre of the concept of digital inclusion. For instance, claims are often made in developed countries that being able to learn through digital technologies rather than within the confines of an educational institution will encourage those people who have ceased to participate in education to re-engage on their own terms. Similar claims are made in terms of technology being able to widen and enhance people's engagement with politics, health services and finding new employment. Yet in all cases, it seems as if technology-based services and interventions help some people more than others. Despite substantial efforts to overcome 'digital divides' it appears that there are still some people who are 'superserved' and many others who are 'underserved' by the technological environment.

In many of the examples featured in this chapter, it would seem that digital technologies often seem to fit around (and be shaped by) the existing patterns of people's lives. In this way, the acquisition of a laptop computer is likely to reinforce – rather than alter – what people do in their lives. This tendency to augment what has gone before suggests that digital technologies in themselves will often do little to disrupt or radically alter pre-existing inequalities. From this perspective, it is perhaps not surprising that researchers often find that access to digital technology 'fails' to make people any more likely to participate in education and (re-)engage with learning. It could be concluded that digital technology, at best, increases educational activity among those who were already learners rather than widening participation to those who had previously not taken part in formal or informal learning.

While increasing educational activity can be seen as a perfectly laudable use of the technology, it remains the case that the technology-based education that is taking place is primarily of benefit to the 'usual suspects', that is, those who have taken part in education before as opposed to the 'previously uninvolved'. Such changes could even be seen to actually exacerbate existing inequalities. In fact this 'usual suspects' conclusion is a phenomenon applicable to most aspects of society. The observation that 'them-who-has-gets' (Sawchuk 2003) is a perennial criticism of attempts to engineer full participation in most 'beneficial' societal activities – from encouraging people to vote, through to maintaining a healthy lifestyle. This is referred to by some sociologists as the 'Matthew effect' – invoking the Gospel saying 'to him that hath shall be given'. As Daniel Rigney (2010) details, the 'Matthew effect' of advantage leading to advantage is prevalent in most areas of societal intervention – from economic well-being, politics, criminal law as well as technology and education. In this way, it would seem that there is little that is 'new' about technology-based education – not even in the nature of its inequalities.

As in previous chapters, it would seem that the idea of technology 'making learning fairer' clearly relates back to wider issues of values and ideology. All of the examples and interventions outlined in this chapter reflect wider ideological beliefs of what education is for, and how education should be arranged. Projects such as the One Laptop Per Child and Hole in the Wall are clearly based around what Brendan Luyt identifies as 'a deep felt need to see the technologies of which [western technologists are] so passionate adopted by people in the developing world' (2008, n.p.). How these technologies are actually used depends very much upon how one sees matters of 'fairness', equality and justice. Certainly the promise of digital technology chimes with recent shifts in many countries' ideology of what 'welfare' is. In particular digital technologies appear to fit well with what Bridgette Wessels terms 'the move from a collectivist approach of universal provision to a consumerist welfare based on choice and conditionality' (2010, p. 6).

However, it could be argued that whatever ideological approach is taken to making education 'fairer', it is clear that technology *on its own* cannot make education 'fairer' or necessarily increase equalities of opportunity or outcome. If we think back to some of the conclusions reached in Chapter 2, social problems often require social solutions rather than 'technical fixes'. From this perspective, the use of technology in the 'improvement' of education should be seen as a deeply social and deeply political matter. Underlying all of the issues raised in this chapter are questions of what sort of society one believes in. Are we really concerned with egalitarian issues of improving the situation of the most disadvantaged? Or are we actually concerned with a meritocratic system of differential rewards and are therefore resigned to the necessity of inequality of outcome? As such, the use of technology to make education 'fairer' is a deeply complex and loaded matter that goes well beyond technical issues of how to 'free-up' access to education. Of all the key issues and debates addressed in this book, the question of equality and fairness is perhaps the least straightforward to answer.

Further questions to consider

- Should technology-based education be left to the market, or is there a role for state intervention? What are the advantages – and disadvantages – of making individuals responsible for their own education? What responsibility do commercial interests have in the provision of technology-based education?

- How useful is the notion of the 'digital divide' in the 2010s? What digital inequalities can be said to exist beyond having adequate access to technology devices? What are the dynamics of these digital divisions – for example, are they largely static or can they be easily changed?
- Can 'Open Source' principles ever work in education or are they simply too idealistic? How 'free' are open educational resources (both in financial and in educational terms)? What restrictions accompany the use of Open Education Resources?

Further reading

There are many good books on the topic of the digital divide and digital inequality. One of the best examples is:

- van Dijk, J. (2005) *The Deepening Divide: Inequality in the Information Society*, London, Sage

Mark Warschauer has spent much of his career investigating various attempts to use technology to overcome social inequalities around the world. Some interesting case-studies are collected in the following book:

- Warschauer, M. (2003) *Technology and Social Inclusion*, Cambridge MA, MIT Press

A good introduction to the use of digital technology in developing countries is provided in this edited collection, which includes a specific chapter on 'ICT in Education':

- Unwin, T. (2009) *ICT4D: Information and Communication Technology for Development*, Cambridge, Cambridge University Press

Here are two publications on the topic of open source approaches in education. The second book contains some very interesting chapters on Open Education and Open Courseware:

- Dillon, T. and Bacon, S. (2006) *The Potential of Open Source Approaches for Education*, Bristol, Futurelab
- Iiyoshi, T. and Kumar, V. (2008) *Opening Up Education*, Cambridge MA, MIT Press

6 Will Technology Displace the Teacher?

Chapter outline

Introduction

The relationship between teacher and learner has been a central component of education and learning throughout history. Whether in the formal guise of a professor, lecturer, trainer or in less formal roles of mentor and guide, the notion of 'the teacher' is an integral element of our understanding of what education is, and how education takes place. In a basic sense, then, a teacher can be defined as a person who educates others – supporting the learning process usually within an organized institutional setting. While teachers will often be responsible for groups and classes of learners, others will work with individual students in a tutoring role. Within adult education – especially the workplace – teachers can take the role of trainers, instructors and coaches. In all these forms, the fundamental process remains one of leading others in their learning. Most formal modes of education frame 'the teacher' as being a prestigious and professional role – that is, as a high status vocation grounded in a period of specialist training and professional socialization.

While these definitions of what a 'teacher' is are fairly straightforward, the nature of 'teaching' is far more contested. Academic commentators continue to disagree as to whether teaching should be approached as a 'science' or as an 'art'. For instance, it could be argued that many of the visible aspects of teaching are best classed as a science – especially in terms of the systematic and procedural ways that a teacher conveys information and communicates with learners. Conversely, other aspects of teaching can be seen as more artistic in nature – involving great amounts of intuition, improvisation and expressiveness. It is often argued that effective teaching depends on high levels of creativity, sound judgement and insight. Some people contend that the artistic aspects of teaching can be compared to those involved in the role of a symphony conductor – with the teacher having to draw creatively upon a repertoire of skills in an attempt to orchestrate what is a highly complex process (Eisner 2005). It is perhaps best to say, then, that teaching involves artistic judgements that also depend on science. As Nicholas Gage (1978) notes, there is certainly a 'scientific basis for the art of teaching'.

Against this background, it is not surprising that the bearing of technology on the role of the teacher has been one of the most contested areas of educational technology discussion and debate over the past 50 years or so. On one hand, some academic commentators hold a strongly held belief that technology will displace the teacher (or as a few people will have it, has *already* replaced the need for a teacher altogether). Conversely, many people would also consider technology as a great support to the human processes of teaching. Of course, as we have begun to see in previous chapters, such debates are rarely cut-and-dried. This chapter, therefore, aims to make sense of the contested relationship between digital technology and teachers. To what extent is digital technology compatible or contradictory with teachers and teaching?

The assumed impacts of technology on teachers

Perhaps the best way to approach this question is to compare and contrast people's expectations and assumptions of change with the realities of how teachers actually make use of technology. This is often referred to by social scientists as comparing 'rhetoric' with 'reality'. As we shall go on to discuss, there are often considerable gaps between popular assumptions about the relationship between teaching and technology and what actually takes place. As is often the case with discussions and debates over educational technology, many people's expectations for digital technology and teaching are based upon expectations of radical change or even complete transformation of what it is to teach and what it is to be taught.

Expectations of enhanced teaching and pedagogy

The first set of expectations focus on technology in an augmentative sense. Many academics and educational experts share an expectation that digital technology can bring a number of enhancements to the science and the art of teaching – that is, what is often referred to as the pedagogical role of the teacher. It is also believed that digital technology can provide valuable support to the professional role of the teacher. For instance, in this latter sense digital technologies have long been seen to assist teachers in the more procedural elements of their job, as well as allowing them to help support students' learning. Indeed, over the recent history of educational technology a succession of various digital technologies have been framed as 'the teacher's friend' (Haigh 2007). These accounts have often focused on technology's ability to support the bureaucratic and administrative aspects of teaching. For example, computer technology can play an important role in reducing teacher workloads and supporting the tracking and monitoring of learner progress, the management of learning materials, and the provision of formative and summative assessment of learners. All of these administrative and procedural 'scaffoldings' are seen to culminate in the substantive improvement and 'freeing-up' of teachers' ability to teach (see Selwood 2005).

Besides providing administrative and procedural support, digital technologies are also seen to offer a number of pedagogical advantages to teachers. It is argued, for example, that digital technologies can provide invaluable support to teachers in planning and preparing their teaching in more diverse and informed ways. Digital technologies are also seen as a means for teachers to enhance their own learning about their subject areas and their professional knowledge about the process and practice of teaching (Somekh 2007). Crucially digital technologies such as the internet are seen to provide teachers with global access to teaching resources and collegial support. In this sense, social media applications such as social networking and blogs as well as other forms of computer-mediated communication have all been welcomed as ideal means for 'a large and diverse community of education professionals' to share their knowledge, experience and good practice with others around the world (Farooq et al. 2007, p. 399).

Digital technologies are also seen to provide a range of pedagogical support inside the classroom. For instance, classroom-based technologies such as the interactive whiteboard are now widely felt to provide teachers with opportunities to alter their styles of teaching and modes of delivery. It is argued, for example, that digital technologies allow a teacher to switch between individualized, communal and communicative forms of pedagogy. This allows the teacher to move from being an organizer of learning activities to being a shaper of quality learning experiences. In this sense, most educational technologists are careful to emphasize the continuation of the role of the teacher at the centre of the digitally enhanced pedagogical process. As David Guile argues, most technology-enhanced gains in learning and achievement 'occur primarily because teachers have designed new contexts as well as new learning processes to support learning with [digital technology]' (cited in Reynolds et al. 2003, p. 152). In this sense, the teacher is seen to be assisted and empowered by digital technologies.

Expectations of the disappearance of the teacher

In contrast to these portrayals of technology-empowered teachers, other commentators argue that digital technology poses a fundamental threat to the role of the teacher. As we have already seen in Chapters 2 and 5, some visions of education and technology are based around the total displacement of the teacher altogether. For example, the notion of depeopled 'virtual campus' and the idea of schools and universities that are hosted entirely online have obvious consequences for the role of the teacher. Indeed, while not foreseeing the complete replacement of the teacher, a number of major current debates about education and technology imply a substantial reduction in the numbers of teachers required to continue the process of education. For example, in the field of international development, there is much interest in using digital technologies to provide a high-quality mass education throughout the developing world via the creation of so-called Mega-Schools and Mega-Universities. Here teaching is provided through a combination of technology-based distance learning and community-based support (Daniel 2010). All of these proposals for learner-centred and learner-managed educational provision pose serious challenges to the need for the physical presence of the teacher. As McWilliam and Taylor (1998, p. 29) concluded, one clear question that has long accompanied the rise of digital technology in education is a simple but significant one – 'are teachers becoming the nobodies of pedagogical work?'

Fears for the technology-assisted 'disappearance' of the teacher are not without theoretical precedence. If we think back to Chapter 4, then many of the learning theories associated with the use of technology in education could be said to imply significant alterations to the nature and role of the teacher. For instance, the behaviourist approaches to technology-based learning outlined in Chapter 4 could be perhaps best described as theories of teaching rather than theories of learning. In one sense, Skinner's notion of the teaching machine and programmed learning imply the technological displacement of the teacher. As the reinforcement theorist Fred Keller (1968) put it in a provocative article titled 'Goodbye Teacher . . .', the behaviourist-inspired model of programmed learning leaves little room for the teacher to continue in her role of provider of instruction. According to Keller, at best the teacher was expected to take the role of 'proctor' or 'assistant' – accompanying the use of tape recorders, computers and textbooks as small segments of instruction were given to learners at their own pace and with frequent feedback. As Keller contended:

> the work of a teacher is at variance with that which has predominated in our time. His public appearances as classroom entertainer, expositor, critic, and debater no longer seem important. His principal job is truly 'the facilitation of learning in others'. He becomes an educational engineer, a contingency manager . . . A new kind of teacher is in the making. To the old kind, I, for one, will be glad to say, 'Good-bye!' (1968, pp. 88–89)

While Keller was justified in identifying a degree of teacher redundancy implied in the behaviourist model of technology-based learning, it could be argued that the behaviourist-inspired development of teaching machines was actually intended to simply relieve the teacher of the burdens of mass instruction. Some behaviourists were keen to argue that the teaching machine was intended to relieve rather than replace the teacher – freeing teachers up to engage in more specialist and individualized aspects of pedagogy. As Skinner himself argued:

> Will machines replace teachers? On the contrary, they are capital equipment to be used by teachers to save time and labour. In assigning certain mechanisable functions to machines, the teacher emerges in his proper role as an indispensable

human being. He may teach more students than heretofore – this is probably inevitable if the world-wide demand for education is to be satisfied – but he will do so in fewer hours and with fewer burdensome chores. In return for his greater productivity he can ask society to improve *his* economic condition. (1958, p. 8)

Despite these underlying intentions to reinstate the teacher to the 'proper role of an indispensible human being' many people have subsequently taken behaviourist and cognitivist theories to advocate the usurping of the teacher. This viewpoint can be seen, for instance, in the arguments of the technologist Patrick Suppes, whose early enthusiasm for computer-assisted instruction was discussed briefly in Chapter 3's discussion of the history of educational technology. Suppes gained prominence in the 1960s when arguing for the introduction of the 'computer tutor' as a means of compensating for the short-comings of the human teacher workforce. Suppes' arguments were eloquent if not a little exaggerated. He was prone to reason, for example, that computer technology had the potential to provide all students with a quality of learning comparable to that envisaged by the ancient Greek philosophers:

We should have by the year 2020, or shortly thereafter, computer-assisted instruc-tion courses that have the features that Socrates thought desirable so long ago. What is said in Plato's dialogue *Phaedrus* about teaching should be true in the twenty-first century, but now the intimate dialogue between student and tutor will be conducted with a sophisticated computer tutor. (1984, p. 306)

Suppes' enthusiasm was shared widely throughout the 1960s, 1970s and 1980s. Indeed, people have anticipated the displacement and disappearance of the teacher for as long as computer-assisted instruction has been considered viable. From a cognitivist perspective, for example, much of the enthusiasm for 'intelligent tutoring systems' during the 1980s centred on the possibilities for computer-driven expert systems and technology-supported tutoring. At best it was argued that human interaction might serve as a 'congenial and effective backup' to technological methods (Sleeman and Brown 1982). In a similar manner, the constructivist, constructionist and socio-cultural theories of learning outlined in Chapter 4 have all been used by some educationalists and technologists to deliberately place the learner at the centre of the educa-tional process at the expense of the teacher. As far as much contemporary thinking about learning is concerned, the teacher is reduced to a peripheral element of the learning process.

Expectations of the diminished teacher

It is important to recognize that not every learning theorist and educational technologist of the past 60 years has envisaged the complete displacement of the teacher. Even the most 'anti-school' of technologists would sometimes recognize the continued value of the teacher's role in the learning process. As Seymour Papert reflected, it is perhaps more accurate to expect the role of the conventional 'classroom teacher' to be recast along different lines through the use of technology in education. As Papert argued when responding to the question of whether 'teacher' would still be a word that people would use in the future:

> Yes. Will they have adult professionals to facilitate the learning process? Yes. Will these teachers be people who are in a privileged position as the ones who know and the source of knowledge? I do not think so. Not at all. They will have a very different role. Sensitive, well-informed adults who understand deeply about learning processes and social interactions will be able to give advice. They will be able to spot that this kid has a problem, or this kid needs more interesting challenges, or put pressure on them and make suggestions. (Papert, interviewed in 1996)

As Papert intimates, the popular notion of learning as a process of the 'co-construction' of knowledge sees the individual learner encountering and engaging with many different resources. The use of digital technology in supporting this type of learning can therefore be seen to herald the diminishment – but not total displacement – of the conventional teacher role. The currently popular notions of socially situated learning, for example, certainly leave room for the teacher as act as a 'more able' and more expert 'other' who the learner can turn towards for support. From this perspective, growing numbers of academic commentators are now describing the role of the teacher recast into one of facilitator and supporter – the 'guide on the side' rather than the 'sage on the stage' according to one often used aphorism. For example, educational commentators such as Marc Prensky (2008, p. 1) argue for a 'new pedagogy of kids teaching themselves with the teacher's guidance'. This sense of allowing young people the opportunity to determine the direction of their own learning is reflected in Don Tapscott's (1999, p. 11) advice to 'give students the tools, and they will be the single most important source of guidance on how to make their schools relevant and effective places to learn'.

From this perspective, a key point of contention is what role the teacher is expected to play if they are no longer the leading component in the teaching and learning process. Indeed, many social-constructivist led accounts of education would see the human teacher as being an often secondary source of learning when compared to the learning that can take place among peers, community members and (of course) the use of technology to access distributed sources of knowledge. This is particularly the case with the forms of collaborative, creative and inquiry-based learning that are associated with social media technologies. All of these forms of technology-enhanced learning are seen to present a fundamental challenge to traditional notions of teacher-led instruction. As David Gauntlett (2008) reasons, one of the major 'problems' with contemporary education is that social media now demand a shift from a 'sit down and be told' culture to a more creative 'making and doing' culture. Many recent descriptions of learning along connectivist lines similarly challenge the need for expert mediation or assistance with the act of retrieving information. If we accept these arguments, then a key question that arises is how much of a 'guide on the side' can teacher expect to be within the learning process?

Amidst all of these debates and arguments, many academic commentators expect recent technological developments to alter the role of the teacher considerably over the course of the twenty-first century. As Papert's earlier response implies, this role of guide or facilitator is markedly different from the traditional notion of the didactic teacher or lecturer. For example, the notion of the teacher-as-facilitator implies teaching and learning as a more collective endeavour, with teachers and students addressing and solving problems and engaging in open-ended enquiry together. At best, the teacher is required to take an 'active facilitation' approach characterized by a high degree of participation and involvement in assisting groups of learners. While some may welcome these changes, teachers certainly face a change in terms of what they do, and the status of what it is they are doing.

While this role of facilitator still involves an aspect of leadership and guidance, some commentators contend that technology actually implies the reduction of teaching to 'scientific' and 'technical' concerns of the design and delivery of instruction. In other words the argument is sometimes made that the embodied 'art' of teaching is 'no longer considered indispensable to learning' (McWilliam and Taylor 1998, p. 29). In this sense, digital technology is seen to be hastening wider trends over the past 20 years for education to become increasingly learner-centred and learner-driven, with predesignated education content replaced by the development of broader competencies (Jensen 2001). According to this line of thinking, digital technology in education is now a key part of efforts to shift the role of the teacher away from matters of 'teaching' to matters of co-ordinating and designing processes of 'delivery'. As such, the role of the teacher is more accurately described as that of 'instructional designer'. As Erica McWilliam observes, 'the stress here is on constructing a more efficient loop from academic manager to instructional designer to "deliverer" to learner and (feed)back to academic manager. The embodied teacher is unnecessary to this process' (McWilliam and Taylor 1998, p. 30).

Considering the actual impacts of technology on teachers

All of these expectations describe significant alterations – for better or worse – to the role of teachers and teaching. As with many of the expectations and assumptions that surround education and technology, it is sensible to approach all of these descriptions and claims with a degree of caution. In particular it is worth thinking carefully about the logic of the arguments being advanced here – especially the prevailing belief that technology and technology-based learning will reshape the nature of teaching. There are at least two conceptual difficulties with this viewpoint. Perhaps most obviously, very few of these anticipated changes have actually come to fruition. In contrast to most of the arguments covered so far in this chapter, the number of people working as teachers continues to remain stable (or even be rising) across most sectors of education. The teaching workforces of most compulsory school systems continue to attract new recruits and expand, with more and more people training to be teachers and entering the profession. Similarly, the adult education sector has seen a proliferation of tutors, trainers, coaches and mentors over the past 30 years. All told, teaching would appear to be a thriving rather than disappearing sector of employment.

Perhaps more significantly, these hopes for the technology-driven reconfiguration of the nature of teachers and teaching can be criticized as lapsing into a reductionist way of thinking about education and technology. While technology-based education may well be linked to changes and shifts in the role of the teacher, it would be unwise to take a determinist view of digital technologies directly 'altering' the teacher's role. If we think back to the 'social shaping' approach outlined in Chapter 2, then it makes sense to also think about how teachers influence the nature of technology use in education. It could be argued, that the main significance of technology for teachers and teaching is not one of complete replacement or transformation, but its relationship to the wider 'job' of being a teacher. In this sense, it is sensible to consider education as being a site of *labour* as well as a site of *learning*. In terms of understanding fully the relationship between technology and teaching we need to consider how digital technology interacts with the labour processes and work of being a teacher. We therefore need to consider how technology interacts with the 'job' of being a teacher – especially in a formal educational setting like a school, college or university.

Approaching teachers and technology from this perspective should prompt us to question many of the issues and debates discussed in this chapter so far. Although some teachers make extensive and imaginative use of digital technology in their day-to-day practice, the majority of teachers experience a largely bounded and restricted engagement with technology. Many teachers' engagements with digital technology in a school or university setting, for instance, continue to be focused on the passive delivery of information through interactive whiteboards and the bounded use of virtual learning environments and 'managed learning systems'. Significantly, many of the key administrative and managerial processes in the day-to-day business of educational institutions appear to remain relatively unchanged by digital practices. These processes include formative and summative assessment, reporting and monitoring, maintaining student discipline, and facilitating communication between staff, students and (where appropriate) parents. Although digital technologies are used in all of these processes, the nature of these processes remains essentially the same. In this sense, digital technology use within the context of the educational institution continues to be largely formalized and bounded in nature.

As is often the case with debates over the 'failures' of education systems, 'blame' for the restricted use of technology in schools, colleges and universities has tended to be attributed most readily to the perceived shortcomings of teachers. In fact, a large number of teacher-based reasons have been suggested over the past 50 years or so for the poor showing of digital technology in formal education. For example, teachers have been deemed to be too old, disinterested or incompetent to integrate digital technology into their teaching. Some educational commentators dismiss teachers as digitally disadvantaged in comparison to their 'digital native' students. Marc Prensky (2001) labelled teachers born before 1980 as 'digital immigrants' forced to adapt to a world of digital media after (many) years of leading 'pre-digital' lifestyles. In this sense, most 'digital immigrant' teachers are seen to be largely 'out of the loop' of technological change, leaving little opportunity for these adults to alter their practices or modes of provision to fit with their students' digital native way-of-being. As Prensky (2005, p. 8) summarizes:

> I refer to those of us who were not born into the digital world as 'digital immigrants'. We have adopted many aspects of the technology, but just like those who learn another language later in life, we retain an 'accent' because we still have one foot in the past. We will read a manual, for example, to understand a program before we think to let the program teach itself. Our accent from the pre-digital world often makes it difficult for us to effectively communicate with our students.

Digital technology use in the classroom is also seen to often come up against issues of self-interest, such as teachers' reluctance to challenge or resist dominant structures of traditional educational provision. It is suggested, for instance, that many teachers have a vested interest in maintaining arrangements and structures that ensure their employment and financial security. In particular, teachers are said to be reluctant to alter arrangements that may destabilize or subvert their authority, status and control in the classroom. Some observers argue that teachers often display what Andrew Feenberg termed a 'humanistic opposition' to educational technology – that is, choosing to not use digital technology in their teaching because of emotional or moral responses to the welfare of their students and the integrity of their learning (see Feenberg 2003).

While all these criticisms may appear harsh, it would seem that teachers vary considerably in their apparent ability to incorporate digital technology in their work practices. Although a minority of teachers are clearly able to effortlessly 'assimilate' and incorporate digital technologies into their teaching, others are seen to reach a pragmatic 'accommodation' of technology into their existing modes of working. At worst, some teachers could be said to display a reluctant use of technology (John and La Velle 2004, p. 323). These responses to technology are said to usually involve various subtle reactions to the 'challenge' presented by digital technologies. That said, some teachers could be said to display outright negative reactions to the perceived threats of technology in their classrooms. As Peter Williams describes:

> the conservative profession of teaching has mediated the introduction of new technologies to render them 'safe' . . . This may be partly a distrust of novelty and partly a lack of basic familiarity with the ways of new technology, but a major reason could be the threats the technology poses to teachers' existing practices and to the perceived maintenance of control. (2008, p. 220)

All of these descriptions and analyses position teachers in rather oppositional relationships with technology. Of course, criticisms of reluctance and recalcitrance are not unique to the technological aspects of teaching – teachers have long been described as conservative and generally resistant to many aspects of change in their work (see Lortie 1975). Yet many of the accounts just described convey a sense that digital technologies certainly exacerbate these general tendencies within the teaching profession. At best, then, a great number of teachers are still felt to be 'cautious onlookers' when it comes to digital technology as opposed to being 'enthusiastic innovators' (Crook 2008, p. 34).

Of course, 'blaming' teachers for not making best use of technology only tells us part of the story. It is all too easy for enthusiastic academic commentators to indulge in 'teacher bashing' and portray teachers as outmoded, obstructive or ignorant. Such arguments could be said to transfer a set of 'dangerous moral imperatives' onto teachers and schools to change their practices and processes in line with the assumed 'affordances' of digital technology (Convery 2009, p. 30). At worst such thinking can lead to an unhelpful set of rejectionist conclusions where traditional forms of teaching and teachers are branded irrelevant to contemporary digital society. With these limitations in mind, we need to develop a more rounded picture of the relationship(s) between teachers and technologies. We should therefore think more carefully about how digital technologies find a place within teachers' experiences of education – not least how digital technologies 'fit' with the demands of the 'job' of being a teacher.

Digital technology and the 'job' of teaching

In order to think of teaching as an occupation, we need to acknowledge all of the negotiations and tensions that a teacher's labour and work can entail. From this perspective, the use of digital technologies in educational institutions should be understood (at least in part) in terms of teachers' ongoing negotiations during the course of their day-to-day work. In other words, we should understand teachers as having to engage in an ongoing process of making sense of the various technologies that they encounter during their working-day and then fitting these technologies with the 'job' of being a teacher and, conversely, fitting the 'job' of being a teacher with the demands of digital technology. If we think back to our discussions of social shaping of technology in Chapter 2, then we would not expect these negotiations to be necessarily straightforward. For example, teachers will be often constrained by the complex social contexts of educational institutions that are sometimes based around concerns that have little or nothing to do with helping learners learn *per se*. This is clear if we consider the expected roles of the teacher within the organizational culture of an educational institution such as the school. Of course, these roles include the teacher acting as an authoritative source of information and supporter of learning. Yet the teacher is also put in a role of disciplinary agent – enforcing hierarchies of knowledge and expertise, regimes of assessment and ranking, and routines of physical and temporal confinement. All told, there is a mass of factors underlying how digital technology interacts with the 'job' of being a teacher. Conversely, there are a number of different reasons why teachers may – or may not – make use of digital technology.

Digital technology and teachers' strategic concerns

First, a teacher's use of digital technology during their work is partly a strategic concern. In this sense, a teacher's use of digital technology is often based on a combination of tactical and habitual decisions that allow teachers, in David Tyack's words, to 'discharge their duties in a predictable fashion and to cope with the everyday tasks that school boards, principals and parents expected them to perform' (Tyack and Tobin 1995, p. 476). In contrast to the criticisms of reluctance and conservativeness outlined above, teachers could be argued to often be pragmatic, strategic users of digital technologies – only utilizing technologies in ways that 'fit' with the wider 'job' of being a teacher and appearing to 'resist' technology use only when it is of little direct benefit to their job. In these terms, the (non-)use of digital technologies could be seen in light of teachers' concerns of ensuring that students achieve 'good' grades in external and internal assessments of learning, or that classroom activities follow the prescribed curriculum and meet the varied expectations of managers, administrators, parents, future employers and other educational 'stakeholders'.

A number of academic authors and researchers have discussed the idea that digital technologies tend to be used where there is a perceived 'complementarity' and 'workability' with the concerns of the teacher and the job of teaching (Lankshear and Bigum 1999). For example, it has been observed that digital technologies tend to be used less where there is a perceived lack of 'good fit' with the immediate working concerns of the teacher. The ways in which internet applications tend to be used in schools, colleges and even some university settings, for example, mirror potential teacher concerns over the need to maintain authority relationships between themselves and students. It has been argued that teachers are keen whenever possible to avoid the 'de-centring of the teacher as a voice of authority' (Muffoletto 2001, p. 3). This is not to deny that digital technologies influence and shape the nature of teaching. Other studies have described, for example, how technology use may contribute to a tendency for teachers to alter their approaches to teaching and, for example, 'become more constructivist in their pedagogical orientation over time' (Windschitl and Sahl 2002, p. 166). Conversely, technologies such as interactive whiteboards and slideshow software such as *PowerPoint* have been reported to contribute to a growing sense of teaching being largely presentational in nature (Reedy 2008).

Digital technology and teacher performativity

While these latter points illustrate the reciprocal 'strategic' shaping relationships between teaching and technology, there are many other significant influences on the ways in which teachers in schools, colleges and universities use digital technologies. These influences often lie above and beyond the explicit 'official' roles, requirements and demands of teaching – not least issues of time, discipline, authority and what can be termed 'performativity'.

One prominent example of this is the pressures of time that many teachers face. The issue of time is often highlighted as an overriding concern in studies of teachers' work. As Dan Lortie was led to conclude from his exhaustive study of teaching as a labour process, 'time is the most scare resource' in educational institutions (2002, p. xii). Although teacher time is laden with concerns of being 'productive' and 'effective' it is important to recognize that technology use sometimes intensifies rather than reduces the pressures of time. At best, digital technologies are often used to simply cope with the increasing time-related pressures of teaching – as Michael Apple put it, 'getting done is substituted for work well done' (Apple and Jungck 1990, p. 235). Similarly, teachers' concerns with issues of authority and discipline also appear to contribute to modes of technology use that mirror a concern with maintaining control. Indeed, discipline-related uses of digital technology in the classroom are often seen in terms of using 'technology-as-reward'. This form of technology use is especially prevalent with younger students, where teachers permit technology use as remuneration for finishing their 'proper' work or for good behaviour.

These issues of time, intensification of work and the need to maintain discipline can all be seen to relate to the wider issue of what can be called 'performativity'. As with a great number of contemporary professions, teachers in many countries are now party to growing numbers of targets, indicators and evaluations during the course of their work. While it would be misjudged to conclude that digital technology use in educational institutions is driven entirely by issues of assessment and test scores, concerns over accountability and assessment certainly have a significant bearing on the ways in which digital technologies are used. As Mark Garrison and Hank Bromley concluded from their study of technology use in US high schools:

> At all levels, whether it is teachers requiring evidence of student productivity, schools requiring evidence of teacher effectiveness, or state requirements for higher test scores, efforts to cope with demands for accountability end up interfering with the actual accomplishment of what is putatively being demanded. (2004, p. 607)

Digital technology and teacher resistance

While some teachers will strive to fulfil these demands and pressures, others may be left with feelings of resistance to using digital technology in this manner. In particular, much has been written about the role of technology in contributing to the 'deprofessionalization' and even 'alienation' of teachers as a profession. Long before the mainstream use of the internet, educational computing was being described by some critics as supporting a fragmented and atomized educational 'assembly line' (Sarason 1990, p. 123). In this sense digital technologies have long been argued to contribute to the ongoing degradation of teaching as a profession – something that some teachers will understandably resist and even reject.

For example, some academic commentators on the relationship between computers and university teaching have pointed to a number of characteristics of the digital 'automation' of higher education. The online delivery of courses, for example, may well make good 'business-sense' for a university in terms of reaching a wider market of students. However, delivering courses online has a number of destabilizing implications for the traditional role of the higher education teacher. Once a course has been delivered online a teacher has little or no intellectual property rights over the future use of that material. A teacher's work online is made more visible – and therefore – more easily monitored and 'assessed' by their employers. Overall it could be argued that digital technologies contribute to an 'erosion of academic freedom' (Petrina 2005), and hasten the transformation of university education into what David Noble (2002) has termed a 'digital diploma mill'.

Many of these concerns centre on the role of digital technology in rationalizing and standardizing the job of being a teacher, and therefore contributing to the separation of the 'conception' of teaching from the 'execution' of teaching. While this fragmentation of the teaching process may make technical sense, it can have significant consequences for the teacher. As the sociologist Michael Apple has observed:

> When complicated jobs are broken down into atomistic elements, the person doing the job loses sight of the whole process and loses control over her or his own labour because someone outside the immediate situation now has greater control over both the planning and what is actually to go on. (Apple and Jungck 1990, p. 230)

Although over 20 years old, much of this 'deskilling' analysis holds true in the current context of virtual learning environments, digital portfolios and shared learning resources. Of course, these criticisms of technology-based education are rooted in established criticism of the increased automation of factories and production lines during the twentieth century. In his analysis of the deskilling of factory workers, Harry Braverman (1974) noted how seemingly 'helpful' technologies were used in a variety of ways to enhance ways of controlling the workforce. For example, technology has long been used in the workplace to eliminate the need for direct supervision of workers, with management controlling workers by either automating work, or breaking down jobs into fragmented work processes that require little conceptual ability. So too in education, digital technologies such as the virtual learning environment can be argued to depend on the deskilling of teachers and their students, engendering a 'tool' mentality towards the mechanisms of teaching and learning (Monahan 2005).

Technology and the continuation of 'the teacher'?

All of these discussions and debates illustrate how technology forces us to think carefully about the role of the teacher and the nature of teaching. Despite the convictions of some commentators, digital technology does not look likely to soon 'displace' the teacher except in a few specific instances. At best, digital technology can be said to perhaps reconfigure or remediate the nature of teaching and what it is to be a teacher – sometimes changing but often reinforcing the core aspects of the job of teaching. This chapter has suggested that while most teachers cannot simply ignore technology, they are sometimes able to have an influence on how it is used in educational settings – shaping the use of digital technologies in ways that better fit their immediate context and concerns. However, as the more pessimistic portrayals of deskilling and deprofessionalization suggest, this is not always the case.

There are many issues to consider here. Above all there is a need to more clearly define and defend the role of the teacher in technology-based learning. What reasons are there for the teacher to have an enhanced rather than diminished role in the learning process? For most people this question will invoke an almost instinctive response. Many educators, parents and learners would argue that it simply 'feels right' and 'natural' that learning is a face-to-face process that involves a teacher. It is argued that learning at all levels of education is fundamentally a 'human process enhanced by human beings' (Volungeviciene and Leduc 2006, p. 26), with a teacher playing a large part in this arrangement. This point of view has long underpinned criticism of the 'disembodied' nature of technology-based learning. Nearly 50 years ago, for example, Lewis Mumford (1964) complained that there appeared to be little or no room for 'the human personality' within the 'complex mechanism' of what he described as the technology-driven 'automation of knowledge'. Mumford bemoaned the lack of human presence within 'humanless' courses with 'their cybernetic apparatus, their computers, their TV sets and tape recorders and learning machines, their machine-marked yes or no examination papers' (1964, p. 15). Fifty years later, much of this critique remains relevant.

While such commonsensical notions may 'feel' intuitively to be correct they do not form the basis for a robust defence of the continued place of the teacher in the educational process. We therefore need to move beyond simply relying on romantic notions of teaching being a 'human process' and, instead, consider the specific reasons why teachers should be an integral element of any technology-based learning arrangement. As Erica McWilliam argues:

> it is time to consider carefully what difference a teacher's material body can make. This means pushing beyond simplistic notions of the human need for social interaction on a 'real' campus by coming to grips with some fundamental

epistemological concerns about corporeality, knowing, and pedagogy. (McWilliam
and Taylor 1998, p. 30)

In 'coming to grips' with why technology-based education needs the teacher, at
least three areas of debate require further thought. First is the argument that
many aspects of education are social and embodied in nature, and that these
qualities are not easily mediated through technology. The philosopher Herbert
Dreyfus (2001) touches upon this point when arguing against the dominance
of online learning. Here Dreyfus reasoned that many forms of learning and
expertise are dependent on being in the *physical* presence of a more knowledgeable other. As Dreyfus concludes, technology-based teaching without the
accompaniment of a teacher 'will produce only competence, while expertise
and practical wisdom will be out of reach' (2001, p. 49). This viewpoint is
also echoed by McWilliam and Taylor's (1998) argument that the 'corporeal'
presence of a teacher facilitates learning through the teacher's 'embodiment
of the curriculum' and the 'nature of their utterance'. Although these reasons
may appear somewhat abstract they provide a convincing explanation for the
enduring appeal of the lecture, the group tutorial and the one-to-one meeting.
Issues of presence and embodiment are subtleties that are perhaps lost in some
technology-mediated environments.

Secondly, the idea that all learning should take place in immersive 'situations' of authentic learning can also be challenged. As Charles Crook (2008,
p. 33) argues:

> Surely the extraordinary achievement of human beings is the ability for
> *un*-situated learning. We can learn by being *told* things – way outside of the times
> and places (the 'situations') where those things are experienced. The challenge is
> a matter of integrating that teaching which is dismissively termed 'delivery' with
> authentic involvement in the situations being articulated in such delivery.

In this sense, the 'inauthentic' situation of the classroom could be said to have
considerable educational merit. This view is reinforced by a range of psychological research that suggests that 'unguided' learning is often far less effective
in developing deep understanding in learners than learning that is linked to
direct instruction. If this is the case then there is certainly room for teacher-led
learning in twenty-first-century education. In particular, we should not discount the value of what Schwartz and Bransford (1998) describe as 'a time for
telling' – where teachers take responsibility for outlining the major concepts

that any learner experiences, as well as providing illustrative examples, explanations and opportunities for clarification. In this sense, there continues to be 'a place for lectures and readings in the classroom if students have sufficiently differentiated domain knowledge to use the expository materials in a generative manner' (Schwartz and Bransford 1998, p. 475). It could well be, then, that any discussion of technology replacing the teacher is better advised to focus on the 'blending' of learner-centred and learner-led modes of technology use with teacher-led, face-to-face instruction. Even with well-educated adult learners, growing numbers of educators are now reaching the conclusion that technology is best used only as part of 'the thoughtful integration of classroom face-to-face learning experiences with online learning experiences' (Garrison and Kanuka 2005, p. 96).

As well as benefitting from the experience of being taught by a teacher, it could also be argued that learners benefit greatly from the teacher orchestration and co-ordination of technology-based education. As Charles Crook observes, the increasing complexity and sophistication of emerging digital technologies introduces 'significant distractions and obstructions' that learners must confront. In this sense, teachers play an important role in supporting learners' supposedly self-directed activities. In particular, teachers are often the most suitable people to provide an initial impetus for the collaborative activities that underpin much contemporary technology-based learning. As Crook puts it, teachers can play a key role in 'arranging the furniture' of technology-based learning. Without the 'good core' and 'initial governance and impetus' of teacher guidance and support, uses of digital technology such as social media can often result in little more than 'an intermittent but relentless low bandwidth exchange that is more "coordination" than "collaboration"' (Crook 2008, p. 33).

Some more critically minded commentators are beginning to argue that one of the most pertinent areas of education where teachers can play a role in supporting, guiding and leading students is in terms of technology use itself. In particular it is beginning to be argued by some media educators that teachers need to play a heightened role in supporting young people's use of digital technology, not least in ensuring that the social contexts surrounding digital technology allow young people to develop a critical awareness of their choices. Ensuring that children and young people are informed about their choices and actions when using digital technologies has recently come to be referred to as the development of 'critical digital literacies' or 'new media literacies'. 'Critical digital literacy' can be seen as involving a lot more than just keyboard skills and awareness of internet safety. Instead, it involves helping children and young people develop a full range of creative abilities to make use of digital technology, alongside the critical understandings required to make best use of digital technology. Thus rather than concentrate solely on the technical training, it is beginning to be argued that efforts need to be made at all levels of education to support the development of individuals' critical digital literacies. As David Buckingham argues, within schools, universities and other civic institutions there is a growing need to 'place a central emphasis on developing children's critical and creative abilities with regards to new media', therefore promoting 'a form of "digital media literacy" as a basic educational entitlement' (2007, p. 144).

In terms of these creative abilities, the shift from print to digital technologies is seen to have introduced the need for the development of 'multimodal' forms of literacy as meanings are made in a variety of ways other than print text and its linguistic elements. As Carey Jewitt argues, 'what it means to be literate in the digital era of the twenty-first century is different than what was needed previously' (2005, p. 330). A number of commentators have outlined the ways in which teachers can play an important role in improving the media literacy of children and young people along these multimodal and multimedia lines. Henry Jenkins (2005), for example, proposes a list of 'new literacy skills' to consider in thinking about how teachers can support their students in approaching digital technology:

- *play* – the capacity to experiment with one's surroundings as a form of problem-solving;
- *performance* – the ability to adopt alternative identities for the purpose of improvisation and discovery;
- *appropriation* – the ability to meaningfully 'sample' and 'remix' online content;
- *collective intelligence* – the ability to pool knowledge and compare notes with others towards a common goal;
- *transmedia navigation* – the ability to follow the flow of stories and information across different forms of digital technology;
- *networking* – the ability to search for, synthesize and disseminate information.

Besides these creative skills, perhaps the most important capacity that children and young people should be encouraged to develop is the ability to think critically about digital technology itself. The area of creative thinking is a growing part of school curricula, and it could be argued that the development of better critical understandings of digital technology underpins the success of all forms of technology-based education. As Kay Withers notes, 'the success of self- and co-regulation relies on users themselves being able to make informed decisions: being "media literate" in the way they access and use content and information' (Withers 2008, p. 51). In this sense, it is now being argued that teachers can help children and young people question and challenge the place of digital technology in their everyday lives. A critical thinking approach would be an ideal means, for example, of helping children and young people to get to grips with the many non-technical challenges and issues associated with using digital technologies – not least issues such as discerning the authenticity and academic authority of online information and 'facts', as well as issues of 'privacy' and 'trust' when using the internet. These additional complex aspects can all be addressed by having a critical conception of what it means to be literate and skilled in the twenty-first century.

Conclusions

This chapter has certainly covered a great deal of ground, and there are many issues that require further thought. Yet many of the examples given in this chapter point towards the valuable authoritative role that teachers can continue to play in educating, informing, managing and directing the technological activities of learners. As such, it would seem unlikely that digital technology will lead to the complete disappearance of the teacher. It is also unlikely that digital technology will lead to the displacement of the teacher. Instead, it is perhaps more likely that teachers will continue to play an integral role in education and learning, whether technology-based or not. We shall return to consider the part that teachers can play in the future shaping of educational technology in Chapter 8. For the time being it is perhaps worth keeping the issue of 'blended learning' in mind as we move onto our next set of issues and debates. Here we will consider the role of the educational institution in light of digital technology. Does digital technology imply the partial reconfiguration of educational institutions as implied in this 'blended' analogy? Or does digital technology imply the displacement of the educational institution altogether? While we may be able to construct a case for the continued relevance of the teacher, what can be said of our schools, colleges and universities? Is there a need for educational institutions in the twenty-first century?

Further questions to consider

- What can digital technology do that a teacher cannot? Conversely, what can teachers do that digital technology cannot? How easy is it to use technology to replicate the qualities of face-to-face, personal interaction with a teacher? What is lost and what is gained through the 'mediation' of technology-based teaching?
- To what extent does digital technology contribute to the 'deskilling' of teaching as a profession? Is the comparison of the deskilling of classroom-based teachers and machine-using factory workers a valid one to make? What subtle strategies of resistance do teachers display to technology-based teaching?
- How useful is the notion of 'blended' teaching in understanding the relationship between teachers and technology? What aspects of education need to be blended – that is, different technologies, different pedagogical approaches, or different types of task? Is the notion of 'blended' technology more applicable to particular stages or types of education?

Further reading

There are many good articles on the changing role of the teacher in the twenty-first century. One readable example is from Stone Wiske. A number of online versions of the paper should be available if you search for them:

- Wiske, S. (2001) 'A new culture of teaching in the twenty-first century' in Gordon, D. (ed.) *The Digital Classroom*, Cambridge MA, Harvard Education Letter, pp. 69–77

Chapter 4 of Seymour Papert's book contains a good overview of how the teacher's role is believed to be changing in the face of constructivist and socio-cultural technology-based learning. Although sometimes polemic, Papert's writing typifies how many educational technologists think about teachers and teaching:

- Papert, S. (1993) *The Children's Machine: Rethinking School in the Age of the Computer*, New York, Basic Books, pp. 57–81

In their article Paul Kirschner and colleagues discuss the cognitive need for guidance and teacher support, thereby discussing some of the limitations in arguments for the diminishment of the teacher's role:

- Kirschner, P., Sweller, J. and Clark, R. (2006) 'Why minimal guidance during instruction does not work' *Educational Psychologist*, 41, 2, pp. 75–86

Kenneth Ruthven and his team of researchers from Cambridge University conducted a number of interesting studies during the 2000s on how school teachers use (and do not use) technology in their teaching:

- Deaney, R., Ruthven, K. and Hennessy, S. (2006) 'Teachers' developing "practical theories" of the contribution of information and communication technologies to subject teaching and learning' *British Educational Research Journal*, 32, 3, pp. 459–480

Will Technology Displace the School?

Introduction

As has been argued from Chapter 1 onwards, digital technology is often described as having the potential to support distinctively new and improved ways of doing things. This is especially the case when people talk of technology use within organizations and institutions. Digital technologies are seen to be capable of having a profound impact on the ways that most modern-day organizations and institutions go about their business, from transnational corporations to individual households. As we saw in Chapter 2, many people have welcomed the ways in which digital technologies appear to be 'flattening out' organizational hierarchies and structures. The institutions and organizations of the twenty-first century are often described as operating in more open and 'networked' ways than before – largely driven by the increased use of computerized and telecommunications technology.

Changes such as these would appear to be evident in many different aspects of how contemporary organizations operate – from matters of finance and logistics, through to communication and decision-making structures. This digitally driven 'reorganization' is also seen to influence how individuals engage with and experience the institutions and organizations in their lives. As William Mitchell reasons:

> Once, we had to go places to do things; we went to work, we went home, we went to the theatre, we went to conferences, we went to the local bar – and sometimes we just went out. Now . . . high capacity digital networks . . . deliver information whenever and wherever we want it. These allow us to do many things without going anywhere. So the old gathering places no longer attract us. Organisations fragment and disperse. (2000, p. 4)

Mitchell's analysis would seem to hold true across most organized aspects of everyday life. For example, many people now experience very different ways of interacting with banks, government services, retail organizations and their places of work. As Mitchell implies, the technologically supported provision of entertainment and leisure is also noticeably more fluid and 'client-centred'. Yet it could be argued that the organizations and institutions that relate to education have displayed less obvious evidence of change over the past few decades. As Dan Lortie (2002, p. vii) reflected at the beginning of the 2000s, 'education does not change at a rapid pace – the major structures in public education are much the same today as [30 years ago]'.

Having reached the 2010s, there is little reason to disagree with Lortie's observation of educational inertia. In particular, many people would argue that a slow pace of change is especially evident with the 'traditional' institutions of education – not least the school. In this chapter we shall consider the significance of educational institutions in contemporary education. How can educational institutions such as the school be said to be coping with the demands of digital technology? Is there a continued need for formal institutions in education? Does digital technology in fact render the educational institution obsolete?

The remainder of the chapter will consider these questions in terms of 'compulsory' schooling – that is, the elementary and secondary schooling that is provided free of charge by the state and is generally mandatory for all children and young people. Compulsory schooling is one of the few common experiences for people in the developed world. Nearly all readers of this book will have attended a school for much of their childhood and adolescence.

For better or worse, students and teachers continue to spend upwards of 6 hours per day at school for up to 200 days of the year. Such is the familiarity that stems from this personal experience that most people rarely stop to think about what schools actually are and how they actually work.

Before considering the relationship between digital technology and schools it is important to clearly define our terms of reference. In particular we should distinguish between the concepts of school and schooling. In the most basic sense *schools* can be understood as the institutions where children and young people receive education, usually learning under the guidance of a teacher. *Schooling*, on the other hand, refers to the processes of teaching and/or being taught in a school. While making this distinction may appear to be a little pedantic, it highlights the need to approach schools and digital technology both in terms of structure and in terms of process. For example, with regards to defining the 'structure' of schools, most people would think of the material aspects of schools as places – that is, their buildings, corridors and classrooms. In this sense, schools are physical structures whose architectural design and organization of space influences what goes on inside them. Yet we should also think of the structures of schools in a non-material sense. In particular schools are based around a range of social and cultural structures. These include the hierarchical roles that people assume within the school organization, the hierarchies of knowledge that constitutes the school curriculum, and the organization of time that constitutes the school timetable. All of these structures – although often out-of-sight and rarely talked about – are integral elements of the organization of schools and schooling.

On the other hand, with regards to the 'processes' of schooling most people would immediately think of explicit processes such as teaching, learning, communication and decision-making. However, schooling should also be seen as involving more implicit processes of socialization, regulation and control. Again, all these processes are almost always out-of-sight and rarely acknowledged. Yet they form a core part of the 'business' of schools as organizations. All of these processes and structures highlight the fact that schools should certainly not be seen simply as neutral contexts within which digital technologies are implemented and then used. To extend a theme that emerged during Chapter 6, we need to consider how digital technologies 'fit' with these structures and processes. How do digital technologies complement or challenge the established processes and structures of school organization? In what ways do digital technologies appear to support the 'reconstitution' of schools and schooling?

Technology and the reconstitution of schools and schooling

In exploring the relationship between technology and the structures and processes of schools and schooling we should first consider the ways in which digital technology is being used around the world to reconfigure the nature and form of educational institutions. These efforts tend to take three main forms. The first is the use of digital technology to represent the structures and processes of school – what is often referred to as 'virtual schooling'. Secondly, is the use of digital technology to reconstitute the structures and processes of school – what can be referred to as a digitally driven 'reschooling'. Finally, is the use of digital technology to replace the structures and processes of school altogether – what can be termed a digitally driven 'deschooling'.

Technology and virtual schooling

There is a relatively long history of using technology to set the provision of schooling free from the physical and spatial confines of school buildings, while retaining the major structures and processes of schooling such as curriculum, assessment and certification. In fact we have already discussed some examples of so-called virtual schools in previous chapters. Chapter 3, for example, described the development of radio-based 'Schools of the Air' during the 1940s and 1950s. Similarly, the notion of the 'mega-school' and 'mega-university' outlined in Chapter 5 highlighted the use of technologies such as mobile telephones and computers to deliver schooling to a mass audience regardless of place, geography or distance.

Over the past 20 years the internet has proved to be a particularly powerful technological means of supporting the virtual provision of education. Throughout the 1990s and 2000s a large number of internet-based virtual schools were established to provide online 'out-of-school' schooling. Perhaps the most widespread use of the internet to provide institutional support and provision of teaching and learning has occurred in the United States. One of the first major instances of this was the now defunct Virtual High School programme. This programme was sponsored by $7.4 million of federal funding and, at its peak, boasted students from 10 countries. From these beginnings a large majority of US states now operate online learning programmes for children and young people involved in compulsory schooling. Many states support individual 'cyber schools' as well as having district level online pro-grammes where between 20 and 80 per cent of a student's academic instruc-tion can be delivered via the internet (Watson et al. 2008, Ellis 2008). In this way, it is estimated that over 1 million US school students will take online courses alongside their classroom lessons each year (Means et al. 2009).

These forms of virtual schooling provide online access to conventional schooling that directly replicates the curriculum and culture of traditional 'bricks and mortar' schools but is not delivered in a physical institution. Other forms of virtual schooling include complementary or 'secondary-credit' pro-vision that adds to – rather than replicates – face-to-face schooling. One prominent example was the Australian Virtual School for the Gifted pro-gramme that operated during the 2000s. This programme used remote online tuition to offer supplementary learning opportunities for so-called gifted and talented students who were considered not to be challenged intellectually by their conventional schoolwork. Other prominent instances of complementary virtual schooling include the publically provided and corporately sponsored online 'resource provision' that are now established in many countries. One example of this form of virtual schooling is the British Broadcasting Corpora-tion's highly popular *ByteSize* revision materials in the United Kingdom. A similar commercially provided equivalent is the fast food chain McDonald's provision of subsidized online tutoring programmes to secondary school pupils in Australia (Curtis 2009). As with 'official' virtual school provision, these programmes offer online means of helping school students engage with aspects of their schooling without attending a school.

As we saw in Chapter 5, these forms of virtual schooling are often justified as introducing the benefits of market efficiency and competition into com-pulsory school systems. As these brief examples illustrate, virtual schools tend to be run by a variety of providers – from school districts and universities, to private companies and corporate commercial entities. Growing numbers of commercial companies also act as vendors for the delivery of courses and the licensed use of course materials. This 'learning marketplace' is bolstered by the wealth of content developed by educators and schools themselves. All told, virtual schooling is seen to make school systems more diverse and more competitive.

Besides these system-wide improvements, proponents of virtual schooling also celebrate the benefits of choice and flexibility for the individual learner. For example, virtual schools are seen to provide individual instruction that better meets the specific needs and learning styles of students. Virtual schooling is seen to allow flexibility in terms of scheduling and place, as well as expanding educational access to individuals and groups who would otherwise be unable to engage in high-quality learning in specific subjects. While some students (or their parents) will actively choose virtual schooling, these methods are also seen to play a compensatory role for students who are physically unable to attend 'bricks and mortar' schools. As such virtual schooling is justified as a ready alternative for students who have long-term illness, who have been excluded from school or where schools are considered as unsuitable for them to attend.

Technology and reschooling

Whereas virtual schooling takes place outside of the conventional school, another approach has been the use of technology as an impetus to 'remix' the major structures and process of schooling *within* the physical and spatial confines of the school. This technology-driven reconstitution of the school can be referred to as a digitally driven 'reschooling'. In other words, although the school may look the same from the outside, what goes on within it may be substantially different from before. Of course, efforts have long been made at the margins of educational systems to reconstitute and reconstruct the school. Throughout the twentieth century a number of high-profile 'experimental' and 'free' schools such as Summerhill, Fernwood and the Vancouver New Schools all attempted to reinvent the structures and processes of schooling. Now digital technologies are seen to allow for the wide scale reconstitution of educational institutions across entire school systems – albeit in less radical and overtly political ways.

Many of these proposals for 'digital reschooling' involve the reconfiguration of curriculum and assessment. For example, efforts have been made in many countries to design new forms of digitally driven assessment to support learners – especially in terms of assessing areas of learning such as decision-making, adaptability and co-operation. Attempts have been made to develop technology-based forms of 'peer assessment', as well as collaboratively produced work. Steps are being taken in countries such as Denmark and Norway to allow pupils full access to the internet during school examinations. Similarly, in terms of reconstituting the school curriculum, many educationalists are striving to find ways of foregrounding technology-based practices of collaboration, publication and inquiry within the classroom. Current discussions in the academic educational technology literature will often conclude with

proposals and manifestos for the redefinition of curriculum and pedagogy –
sometimes through radical models of 'mash-up pedagogy' and a 'remix of
learning' (e.g. Fisher and Baird 2009, Mahiri 2011).

Besides issues of curriculum and assessment, attempts are also being made
by some academics to recast education institutions as sites of technological
exploration. An obvious area for change here has been the remodelling of the
physical boundaries of schools to fit with the needs and demands of modern
technology. From William Mitchell's (1995) suggestions for a 'recombinant
architecture' in schools, to proposals for the redesign of the school environment into 'collaboration-friendly' and 'really cool spaces' (e.g. Dittoe 2006) the
idea of redesigning and rebuilding the physical environment of schools to
better accommodate digital technology use continues to gain popularity and
support. For example, it has been suggested that the planning and design of
new schools is less rigidly 'zoned', with schools becoming 'learning spaces' that
are 'blended' in with other spaces and sites within the community (Harrison
2009). All told, the reconstitution of the physical work environment of the
school to accommodate the demands of digital technology use is seen to be
long overdue.

Technology and deschooling

While these ideas of reschooling and virtual schooling have obvious merit,
other academics, educationalists and technologists have chosen to pursue an
even more radical agenda of change – what can be termed the digitally driven
'deschooling' of society. From this perspective, digital technology is seen to
provide an alternative to the physical and spatial confines of the school, as well
as providing an alternative to the major structures and processes of schooling
such as curriculum, assessment and qualifications. These forms of technology-
based deschooling take a variety of guises. For example, a growing number of
online institutions now exist that are based on an ethos of using digital technologies to bypass traditional education institutions. This approach is evident
in online services such as the *School of Everything*. This is a prominent online
space in the United Kingdom designed to put people in the community
who wish to 'teach' with people who wish to 'learn'. This form of teaching and
learning exchange has therefore been described as 'an *eBay* for stuff that does
not get taught in school' (Leadbeater 2008a, p. 26).

Digital technology has also been used to further support and extend the
'home schooling', 'unschooling' and 'self-directed learning' movements where

children and young people are educated by family and community members. For example, the *Free World U* has been developed as an online alternative learning community for home-schooled young children – offering online 'accelerated learning' resources to be shared between communities of parents and learners. The development of online alternative schooling is an increasingly significant part of the efforts of neo-conservative and fundamentalist religious groups in the United States to support alternative forms of home schooling outside of state control of the curriculum (Peters and McDonough 2008). As Michael Apple observed at the beginning of the 2000s, 'there are scores of websites available that give advice, that provide technical and emotional support, that tell the stories of successful home schoolers, and that are more than willing to sell material at a profit' (2000, p. 71).

Reasons for the technology-driven redefinition of schools and schooling

Although all of these examples challenge our traditional concept of 'the school', in a practical sense they remain on the periphery of contemporary educational provision. For the time being, at least, the main significance of such efforts is symbolic rather than substantial. As such it is worth considering the implications of the ideas and arguments that underpin these examples in further detail. All of the examples covered in this chapter certainly reflect a strongly held belief among some academics and educational technologists that profound and significant changes to the organization and arrangements of schools and schooling are imminent. Arguments along these lines are made regularly and forcefully in educational technology discussions and debate – especially by academic commentators. Take, for example, this reaction to the launch of Apple Computer's iPad tablet computer from a prominent 'Professor of New Media Environments' in the United Kingdom:

> This is the beginning of what I like to describe as post-appropriation technology: devices that won't be appropriated by education in the way that calculators, or laptops, or networks were. This device won't be easily banned, won't be 'moulded' to fit education, and will be hugely effective as a web browser, bookshelf, video player, game console and communication device. This time, instead of technology being bent to fit schools (as with the interactive whiteboards for example), schools

must move themselves to meet the new technology. That makes this a significant moment . . . This is a wake-up call for ICT assessment in schools: it's time to move it into the twenty-first century. (Stephen Heppell, in Johnson and Arthur 2010, p. 3)

Of course, Stephen Heppell is not the first commentator to see the educational implications of technology in this way. As we saw in Chapter 3, there is a long tradition of strongly enthusiastic reactions to 'new' technological artefacts and, on occasion, such predictions may well be justified and prescient. Yet statements such as 'schools must move themselves to meet the new technology' and 'it's time to move schools into the twenty-first century' suggest a specific dissatisfaction and distrust of formal educational institutions. In fact some of the discussions and debates about education and technology covered in this book so far have been tinged with an underlying 'down with school' sentiment. We therefore need to ask why this is, and whether such reactions are justified.

Looking back over the arguments covered so far in this book, it would seem that people's enthusiasms for different forms of schooling are usually driven by two interrelated beliefs. First is the widely held assumption among some academics and technologists that digital technology offers a better way of 'doing education' – what could be referred to as a technological 'pull' factor. Secondly, is a general dissatisfaction with current types of schools and schooling – what could be described as an institutional 'push' factor. Together, these beliefs can be seen as underpinning most people's desire for the technology-driven redefinition of schools. In the spirit of all our other discussion up until now, it therefore makes sense to give further consideration to the ideas, beliefs, values and agenda that inform these arguments. Is the school as it currently stands really a dysfunctional institution? Do digital technologies really offer a better way of organizing and providing educational opportunities?

Technology as a better way of 'doing education'

As we have discussed at various points throughout this book, many people see digital technology as a ready means of supporting better forms of teaching and learning than can usually be found in formal educational settings. Technology-based education is seen to provide a more conducive way than 'traditional' schooling to facilitate the informal, collective and communal forms of learning that many educationalists believe to be important. Some people therefore reckon digital technology to be capable of superseding the educational opportunities that can be provided by schools and other formal institutions. This is not to say that technology-driven provision will necessarily replace formal education institutions. Nevertheless, digital technology is certainly seen as able to fulfil many of the same functions and roles. As Allan Collins and Richard Halverson reason:

> We see the question of where education is headed in terms of the separation of schooling and learning. We're not predicting the collapse of your local elementary school. Young people will not be forced to retreat behind computer screens to become educated. Rather, we see the seeds of a new education system forming in the rapid growth of new learning alternatives, such as home schooling, learning centres, workplace learning and distance education. These new alternatives will make us rethink the dominant role of public schools in education as children and adults spend more time learning in new venues. (2009, pp. 3–4)

This enthusiasm for digital technology supporting a set of 'new alternatives' to the school reflects a number of beliefs and values about what education should be. First, many people's interest in the technology-based reconfiguration of schooling reflects a belief in increased individual freedom. As we have seen throughout this book, many people are convinced of the capacity of digital technologies to make education more flexible, fluid and ultimately more empowering for the individual learner. For many commentators it therefore no longer makes sense to retain 'pre-digital' models of organizing learning through institutions that are focused on the rigidly hierarchic mass delivery of static content. Instead, people are now beginning to question how best to develop forms of learning that can be negotiated rather than prescribed and discovered rather than delivered. More often than not, digital technology is seen to provide a powerful means of supporting education that is driven by individual learner needs and based on learners taking control of managing and accessing knowledge for themselves (Facer and Green 2007).

In this sense, growing numbers of authors are now discussing the value of what Jonathan Edson (2007) terms 'user-driven education' – that is, allowing learners to take an active role in what they learn as well as how and when they learn it. Of course, this 'pick and mix approach' to curricular content and form presents a challenge to the professional roles, identities and cultures of teachers and other educators. It also presents a fundamental challenge to the concept of the formal educational establishment as a whole. As McLoughlin and Lee (2008, p. 647) conclude, all of these ideas and arguments depict a

radically different education system – one where 'learners are active participants or co-producers of knowledge rather than passive consumers of content
and learning is seen as a participatory, social process supporting personal life
goals and needs'.

These enthusiasms are often coupled with enthusiasm for the power of
'informal education'. As we discussed in Chapter 1, 'informal' learning that
takes place outside of the control of the formal education system is an
important but often overlooked element of contemporary education. Digital
technologies such as the internet and mobile telephony are seen as especially
conducive to informal learning through their ability to support enhanced connections between people, places, products and services. Above all, technology-
supported informal learning is seen to be more empowering in comparison
to formal schooling. As Nicole Johnson concluded from a study of Australian
teenage 'expert' technology users, with informal learning

> . . . [students] were able to choose what they learned and when they learned.
> They viewed the medium in which they did it as a form of leisure. They were
> also able to choose who and what they learned from – not just what has been
> set up as exclusive and privileged. They were able to both learn and receive
> pleasure from their engagement and not have to be concerned about the
> hierarchisation and failure in relation to how traditional schooling determines
> competence. (2009, p. 70)

This idea of technology users being able to learn in spite (rather than because)
of their schools was also illustrated in Mimi Ito's anthropological study of how
young people engage with digital technologies in their everyday lives. This
study documented how young people across the United States were using
social media to learn in ways that were qualitatively and quantitatively different to the ways that they learned at school. In particular, young people were
found to learn through the processes of what the study described as 'hanging
out, messing around and geeking out' (Ito et al. 2009). This relates to how many
people learn through technology almost without realizing – exploring new
interests, tinkering and 'messing around' with new forms of media. Sometimes,
however, Ito noted how the young people in her study got involved in intense,
'deep' bouts of learning when their interest had been piqued. These instances
were varied in nature – such as young people creating their own online
content, developing a particular talent or researching a particular topic. Ito
described this as using technology to 'geek out' – a highly social activity that
involves engaging with specialized knowledge groups of other people who

share the interest from around the world. As this study concluded, these forms of learning stand in stark opposition to school-based, classroom learning:

> New media allow for a degree of freedom and autonomy for youth that is less apparent in a classroom setting. Youth respect one another's authority online, and they are often more motivated to learn from peers than from adults. Their efforts are also largely self-directed, and the outcome emerges through explora-tion, in contrast to classroom learning that is oriented by set, predefined goals. (Ito et al. 2009)

The school as a dysfunctional technology

As this last quotation implies, much of the enthusiasm for the power of technology-based informal and collective learning is often accompanied by a complementary set of concerns over the failings of formal school systems. Of course 'school-bashing' occurs throughout all aspects of educational debate and is by no means a recent phenomenon. The rise of mass education through-out the twentieth century was accompanied by trenchant critiques of 'the school nightmare' and accusations of schools causing intellectual 'death at an early age' (see Gross and Gross 1969). Many of these critiques centred on fun-damental issues of knowledge, relationships, diversity, community engagement and social justice (e.g. Postman 1996). More recently these long-standing dis-contentments about schools appear to have been amplified and accelerated by the rise of digital technology. In many ways, digital technology now provides a high-profile filter for many long-standing criticisms of formal educational institutions. As the US-based Apple Classrooms of Tomorrow – Today project put it, 'America is caught in the grip of a crisis in education that threatens the ability of an entire generation of Americans to achieve success in life and work' (Apple 2008, p. 4). Support for technology-related changes to education is therefore driven more by the 'push' factor of the supposed inadequacies of the formal educational institution rather than the 'pull' factor of technology's promise.

Criticism of the failings of contemporary forms of schools and schooling is varied. In a technological sense, it is argued that schools as they currently stand do not offer an adequate context for 'doing technology' properly. The conclusion reached by many commentators is that schools, at best, assimilate and incorporate digital technology into their existing practices and processes. As Wilhelm (2004, p. 3) puts it, schools' technology adoption can be seen as being 'largely hewn to established practice'. Many people therefore see schools as unable or even unwilling to change to the more radical demands of digital technology use outlined earlier. Schools are seen to be stuck in a position of lacking what it takes 'to go with the technological flow' (Dale et al. 2004).

As far as many commentators are concerned, the extent of the technological intransience of schools is considerable. For instance, many school buildings have been criticized as being architecturally unsuitable for widespread net-worked and wireless technology use. School leaders and administrators have been accused of lacking the required 'vision' to make the most of the educational potential of digital technology. School curricula have been observed widely as being too rigid and entrenched in 'pre-information age' ways of thinking. School assessment procedures are seen to be overly concerned with the development and assessment of scholastic aptitude rather than 'softer' or creative skills. Indeed, some educational commentators have occasionally expressed a perverse admiration for schools' apparent ability to resist all of the potential disruptions of digital technology. The school is seen to have been preserved as 'normalised and controlled [an] environment' as it has been for over one hundred years (Muffoletto 2001, p. 4).

These criticisms often focus on what is seen as the rigid organizational arrangements and social relations within schools. A perennial concern among many academics, technologists and policymakers relates to the apparent incompatibility between digital technology and what is referred to as the 'Henry Ford model of education' schooling (e.g. Whitney et al. 2007). Such critiques hark back to Alvin Toffler's depictions throughout the 1960s and 1970s of the outmoded 'industrial-era school'. Here Toffler decried schooling as an anachronistic by-product of 'that relic of mass production, the centralised work place' – pointing to the lasting similarities between schools and factories in terms of a reliance on rigid timetables and scheduling, as well as an emphasis on physical presence and ordering of people and knowledge (Toffler 1970, p. 243). Over 40 years on from Toffler's initial observations, many educational technologists continue to denounce the industrial-era school as a profoundly unsuitable setting for the more advanced forms of learning demanded digital technology and the 'knowledge society' (e.g. Miller 2006, Warner 2006). As Frank Kelly and colleagues were led to proclaim in frustration:

> schools must change . . . the world we live in has fundamentally changed. Our students have moved into the Information Age. Meanwhile, our high schools continue to operate on the ideas and assumptions from the Industrial Age. As a result,

there is a fundamental disconnect between students and the schools they attend. (2008, p. 9)

Such criticisms are as diverse as they are damning. At one extreme, very little that takes place within a school is seen to be of particular relevance or use to modern society. In particular, schools' continued reliance on 'broadcast' pedagogies of various kinds, their structured hierarchical relationships and formal systems of regulation are all seen to render them incapable of responding adequately to the challenges posed by digital technology. It is argued that twenty-first-century educators have therefore failed to 'come to terms with the contradictions' that lie between the technological complexities of contemporary learning and the persistence of a model of schooling based on static print culture, competitive individualism and the notion of learning that is 'geographically tied to a desk' (Luke 2003, p. 398). All told, many people simply do not consider schools to be the best places for technology-based learning to take place.

Digital technology and the growing rejection of the school

So far this chapter has outlined a range of arguments, ideas and proposals relating to school change and digital technology. To date much of the established academic thinking has focused on the 'reschooling' view of adjusting and reconfiguring the main structures and processes of schooling along more 'technology-friendly' lines. For example, there is broad agreement within the academic literature, that the educational potential of digital technology is more likely to be realized through a redefinition of the processes and practices of contemporary schooling. Indeed, the need to develop 'school 2.0' is an increasingly common topic of educational technology debate, with digital technology positioned as offering 'a simple, clean approach' to redesigning schools (Apple 2008, p. 4). It is now becoming a fairly orthodox position within educational technology debates to argue that the processes and structures of schools are in need of being updated and rethought in light of digital technology use. However, some of the arguments covered in the last section of this chapter hinted at a creeping frustration among some educational technologists with the general concept of the school altogether. Indeed some commentators are now openly hinting that they consider schools to be beyond salvation. Why then is there a growing rejection of school-based learning within some sections of the educational technology community?

As we saw earlier on in this chapter, powerful arguments are being advanced that children and young people may well be better off learning among themselves through the support of digital technologies. In particular, internet technologies have been promoted as providing a ready basis for young people's circumvention of the traditional structures of their schools and generally 'finding something online that schools are not providing them' as Henry Jenkins (2004, n.p.) has put it. Digital technologies are seen to be able to move schooling away from being 'a special activity that takes place in special places at special times, in which children are instructed in subjects for reasons they little understand' (Leadbeater 2008b, p. 149). In this respect, a great deal of faith continues to be vested in digital technologies as a catalyst for the total discontinuation of twentieth-century forms of schools and schooling.

Indeed, a subtle rejectionist line of thinking can be found in quite a few accounts of educational technology and schools. This can be seen if we think back to the writing of the technologist Seymour Papert – one of the guiding lights of constructionist learning theory, the Logo programming language and One Laptop Per Child programme. It could be argued that Papert has promoted an often overt anti-school agenda throughout all these works. Take, for instance, his contention that schools and schooling are 'relics from an earlier period of knowledge technology' or that new technology will 'overthrow the accepted structure of school, the idea of curriculum, the segregation of children by age and pretty well everything that the education establishment will defend to the bitter end' (Papert 1998, n.p.). Perhaps Papert's most memorable proclamation in this respect was

> the computer will blow up the school. That is, the school defined as something where there are classes, teachers running exams, people structured in groups by age, following a curriculum – all of that. The whole system is based on a set of structural concepts that are incompatible with the presence of the computer. (1984, p. 38)

Such sentiments have implicitly informed the work of many other educational technologists over the past 30 years. More often than not, the rejection of school-based education is presented in a celebratory way that moves education nearer to harnessing the informal learning potential of digital technology. Yet on occasion some educational technologists cannot resist the urge to express their essentially negative view of the school. This sense of terminal incompatibility between technology and school was perhaps best encapsulated in Lewis Perelman's (1992) observation that any attempt to integrate computing into schools 'makes about as much sense as integrating the internal combustion engine into the horse'. Over 20 years later, polemic of this sort continues to be an accepted part of mainstream thinking about education and technology, with many commentators willing to denounce schools as 'anachronistic' relics of the industrial age that are now rendered obsolete by contemporary digital technology. As Juha Suoranta concludes: 'in their current forms it might be that schools not longer belong to the order of things in the late modern era, and are about to vanish from the map of human affairs' (Suoranta and Vadén 2010, p. 16).

In the minds of some commentators, then, the seriousness of the 'school problem' has now passed a point of no return and leaves little choice but to argue for the dissolution of the school as it currently exists. Indeed, there would seem to be an implicit willingness within certain elements of the educational technology community to 'give up' on the notion of the industrial-era school. The idea that technology-based learning could replace the idea of school altogether is becoming an increasingly serious proposition. Yet as with all the debates in this book so far, it is important that we take time to properly consider and challenge these proposals and assumptions. Suggesting that the concept of formal schooling is abandoned altogether is a substantial proposal, and not to be taken lightly. It is worthwhile to therefore consider the roots of these contemporary arguments for the digital 'deschooling' of society – not least their ideological origins.

In particular parallels should be drawn between current calls for a digitally driven deschooling and the work of the philosopher and social critic Ivan Illich. Illich was at the forefront of debates towards the end of the 1960s as educationalists began to consider the emergence of what was being described as 'post-industrial' society. In his 1971 book on *Deschooling Society* Illich challenged the structures, myths and rituals that underpin all of contemporary capitalist society (see Hoinacki 2002), not least educational institutions such as schools, colleges and universities. Above all, much of Illich's work and ideas resonates with – and often informs – present debates over digital technology and education.

At the heart of Illich's thesis was the argument that students become overreliant on educational institutions and quickly become complicit with a 'hidden curriculum' of schooling that is based around perpetuating the commodified consumer society, structurally increasing inequalities, privileging the already privileged, and discouraging individuals 'from taking control of their own learning' (1971, p. 8). In short, Illich contended that individuals in educational institutions are discouraged from taking responsibility for their own self-development, and also from engaging with other potential opportunities for learning within their immediate communities. In making these points Illich's key interest was in finding alternatives to this predicament by drawing upon all the opportunities offered by what he termed the 'technological age'. Yet *Deschooling Society* also acknowledged the ways in which educational technology was often implicated in the perpetuation of the 'tyranny' of institutionalization – and therefore could also be part of the problem rather than the solution. As such, Illich recognized that new forms of educational technology were needed to address the many problems of institutionalized schooling.

In this spirit much of *Deschooling Society* set out proposals for providing learning opportunities along what Illich called 'convivial' rather than 'manipulative' lines – with the purpose of education one of 'facilitating activity' rather than 'organizing production' (1971, p. 53). These proposals recognized the value of what we have referred to earlier as 'informal education' – that is, learning that occurs outside the aegis of a prescribed, compelled curriculum. Following this line of thinking, Illich proposed that co-ordinated efforts could be made by the educational community to facilitate and support forms of 'casual' learning proposing a form of what can be best described as 'planned unplanned learning'. These forms of individually led casual learning could be supported, Illich argued, through the creation of what he termed community-based 'learning webs' or 'opportunity webs' of individuals, resources and tools that may be drawn upon to learn. In this sense education was conceived as a mutual process, involving all members of a community matching their skills and interests with each other as appropriate. Illich encapsulated this view in the memorable phrase 'education for all means education by all' (1971, p. 22).

Even in 1971, new technology was seen to play a key role in Illich's proposals for the reconstruction of education along convivial and communal lines. *Deschooling Society* outlined alternative arrangements where technologies were not merely technologies of mass consumption of instruction. Instead, Illich argued for the development of new technologies with new values. He talked, for example, of individuals being matched with opportunities to learn that best suited their needs through 'computer systems' and 'computer arranged meetings' and peer-matching networks. Of course, Illich's imagination was bounded within the technologies of his time. While some of his examples were decidedly low-tech (such as the connection of rural hamlets with a 'spider web' of trails and communal three-wheeled mechanical donkeys), other examples anticipated the digital practices of the 2010s. This can be seen, for example, in Illich's notion of a sophisticated 'read/write' network of tape recorders:

> The money now tied up in TV installations throughout Latin America could have provided every fifth adult with a tape recorder. In addition, the money would have sufficed to provide an almost unlimited library of pre-recorded tapes, with outlets even in remote villages, as well as an ample supply of empty tapes. This network of tape recorders, of course, would be radically different from the present network of TV. It would provide opportunity for free expression: literate and illiterate alike could record, preserve, disseminate, and repeat their opinions. (1971, p. 77)

Even in these crude terms, Illich's faith in the notion of placing new technology at the heart of communities is clear. Technology was therefore seen as a ready way to give people the opportunity to access a range of educational objects, skill exchanges, peer-matching and 'educators-at-large'. Indeed, many of Illich's suggestions for establishing 'educational webs' (1971, p. 77) within communities were remarkably prescient to current debates over education and technology. Throughout *Deschooling Society*, for example, Illich stressed the value of learning through games or distributed 'educational artefacts' throughout community settings including 'storefront learning centres', jukeboxes and museum-based centres. These are all ideas that continue to be proposed in one form or another over 40 years later.

Reconsidering the ideology of digital deschooling

It is evident that many of the twenty-first-century arguments outlined earlier in this chapter for the discontinuation of schooling in favour of technological means (un)consciously update the arguments of Ivan Illich. At first glance, Illich's thinking fits well with many of the issues raised throughout the chapter. Take, for example, his condemnation of institutionalized learning as inhibiting individual growth due to its emphasis on 'progress' through mass production and consumption. This reading of school and schooling fits well with contemporary discussion of digital technologies and education. As Charles Leadbeater (2008b, p. 44) reasoned, 'in 1971 [deschooling] must have sounded mad. In the era of *eBay* and *MySpace* it sounds like self-evident wisdom'. As Leadbeater then goes on to admit, 'the self-help' philosophy of his own thinking on social media and education 'is an attempt to realize some of Illich's ideals' (2008b, p. 45). Similarly, as Juan Suoranta concludes:

> Illich's utopia is turning out to be more of a topical scenario for our so-called information age than anyone imagined. Illich's learning web metaphor is in itself interesting. Its represents nicely the current trend that it is as if all the best minds in education are found in the virtual world of the worldwide web. (Suoranta and Vadén 2010, p. 19)

The linkages between current educational technology thinking and the arguments advanced by writers such as Illich 40 years earlier reflect the highly ideological nature of debate over the schools and digital technology. Illich himself was a politically fluid but essentially anarchistic thinker who in later years argued against the entire notion of 'education' altogether. Indeed, he reasoned that as people have historically always known many things without enforced and compulsory forms of education, then current generations therefore would do better to learn outside the aegis of the state altogether. Of course, the intentions of many commentators on education and technology may well be rooted in similar counter-cultural sensibilities – especially among more idealistic elements of the computer programming community. Yet one of the key differences between the original deschooling debates of the 1970s and those in the 2010s is the diversity of often conflicting ideological standpoints that are currently arguing for such change. As such, the people arguing for the digitally driven deschooling of society in the 2010s are doing so for a variety of reasons and rationales – not all counter-cultural or anarchic in intention.

Many of these ideological agendas relate back to Chapter 5's discussion of the ideological foundations of people's efforts to use technology to make education fairer. In particular, the prospect of the digital replacement of the school has been used to support neo-liberal arguments for the 'end of school' and the realization of the 'dream of education without the state' (Tooley 2006). Here digital technology is valorized in decidedly different terms than with Illich – that is, as an ideal vehicle for the establishment of 'a genuine market in education, where there was no state intervention of any kind, in funding, provision or regulation' (Tooley 2006, p. 26). From this perspective digital technology is celebrated as a means to reposition education around the power of radical individualism, market forces and the rational pursuit of self-interest.

So while the general premise of technology being used to replace the school may be seductive, it should be remembered such arguments are also used to support a number of more 'laissez-faire' arguments for the dismantling of the state and public sector. Of course, we are not suggesting that these neo-liberal arguments should be rejected out-of-hand any more than Illich's arguments should be agreed with. It may well be that the convenience of digital techno-logy allows the 'privilege and convenience' of education to be provided through the power of the market and 'without the unsightly mess' of state provision (Dean 2002). Yet, if these terms are accepted as the basis for the (re)organiza-tion of contemporary education, then it could be argued that a number of important principles of mass schooling in society are weakened – in particular the principles of collective responsibility and empowerment. Indeed, the counter-argument could be made that there are a number of very good reasons to argue for the continuation – rather than dismantling – of the school in the twenty-first century.

Above all, it could be said that digital technologies should not be allowed to overshadow the basic social importance of formal schooling. From a social justice perspective alone, the argument could be advanced that educational technologists (however well-intentioned) have no right to legitimize calls for the alteration or dismantling of the publically provided 'industrial-era' school. It could be argued that, for all their faults, current forms of mass schooling play a significant role in the improvement of life chances for all children and young people. As Michael Young has argued, academic commentators should remain mindful that schools fulfil a societal purpose as a valuable source of 'powerful knowledge' and social mobility for all children and young people – not just the technologically privileged few (Young and Muller 2009).

This concept of 'powerful knowledge' provides an important argument for the continuation of school-based education. It refers to specialist knowledge that can lead to powerful outcomes, such as new ways of thinking about the world, new abilities to act in society, and so on. Michael Young argues that these kinds of knowledge and learning are varied – from the high-status knowledge that leads to qualifications and jobs (e.g. formal maths, science and English), through to matters of citizenship and even high-status digital technology use (Young 2007). These are all forms of knowledge that many children and young people cannot acquire easily at home or in the community.

Crucially, this is often knowledge that is not accessible through informal education and that can only be transmitted through the school. In the case of these forms of powerful knowledge, it could be argued that the school plays a crucial enabling and supporting role. These are not things that learners can discover or explore for themselves – not least because learners 'cannot know what they do not know' (Young and Muller 2009, p. 7). To reiterate one of the arguments made towards the end of Chapter 6, there may well be a 'time for telling' as well as a 'time for discovering' knowledge. In this sense the formal school is one of the most appropriate means of providing a place, as well as a time, for 'telling' and instruction.

Conclusions

All of these discussions and arguments highlight the complex nature of the question 'will technology displace the school?' Doubts over the continuation of schools and schooling have endured for many decades, and will undoubtedly endure for many more decades. As this chapter has illustrated, these debates are often ideological in nature and are driven by wider arguments over what education is for and how society should be arranged. As Levinson and Sadovnik (2002, p. 2) observe, 'schools are a Pandora's box for visualising a number of conundrums currently facing liberal democratic societies'.

In particular, while the idea of a digitally driven displacement of schools may be justified on technical grounds of increasing the efficiency, economy and even conviviality of education, there are a number of other socially focused arguments for not radically altering schools and schooling. Although it is easy to denounce the many technological frustrations of the 'industrial-era' school, we should be wary of setting a precedent where the interests of technology outweigh all other social, cultural and political concerns. It could be argued that there are actually few compelling reasons to assume that formal schooling is set to lose significance and status in contemporary society. In fact, the continued persistence of a top-down, hierarchal configuration of formal schooling could be seen as testament to what Steven Kerr identified as the 'historical flexibility of schools as organisations, and of the strong social pressures that militate for preservation of the existing institutional structure' (1996, p. 7). Whether we like it or not, there is little historical reason to anticipate the imminent institutional decline of the 'industrial-era' school in the near future.

That said, many of the issues raised in this chapter would seem to point towards the need for *some* degree of change in order for educational institutions to make the most of digital technology and, indeed, to get the most from digital technology-using learners. It could well be that these changes can be achieved through relatively modest 'readjustments' to technological practices that do not disrupt existing institutional structures and boundaries. We should be wary of giving-up on the entire notion of the industrial-era school or university as it currently exists. Instead, it may be more productive – and certainly more practical – to set about addressing the 'problem' of formal education and technology in subtler and less disruptive ways than radically altering educational institutions or even disposing of them altogether. In this sense, we need to think carefully about the future shape and forms of the educational landscape in term of its formal *and* informal elements. These issues are now addressed in the final chapter.

Further questions to consider

- Which digital technologies help individuals learn through the processes of 'hanging out', 'messing around' and 'geeking out'? Could it be said that people have always learnt like this? If so, what is new or different about technology-based informal learning and 'geeking out'? Can these forms of learning only take place outside of an educational institution?
- Are we heading towards a digital deschooling of society? If so, how can learning be provided to all individuals regardless of circumstance? Are ideas of deschooling simply too idealistic to come to fruition in the twenty-first century?
- What changes could (or should) be made to existing forms of school curriculum and assessment to help realize the potential of digital technology? Think in particular about the nature of digital information and knowledge. What implications would these changes have for what is learnt in schools and how this learning is assessed?

Further reading

This book offers an interesting argument for the decreased significance of formal schooling in twenty-first-century society:

- Collins, A. and Halverson, R. (2009) *Rethinking Education in the Age of Technology: The Digital Revolution and Schooling in America*, New York, Teachers College Press

Following our discussion of reschooling, this book uses the example of social media and web 2.0 applications to discuss how the structures and processes of contemporary schooling could change:

- Solomon, G. and Schrum, L. (2007) *Web 2.0: New Tools, New Schools*, Washington DC, International Society for Technology in Education

These two articles provide a thorough overview of the nature of school organization and culture. Although written over 15 years ago, the piece by Steven Hodas develops a powerful analysis of why schools appear to 'resist' technological change:

- Hodas, S. (1996) 'Technology refusal and the organizational culture of schools' in Kling, R. (ed.) *Computerization and Controversy: Value Conflicts and Social Choices*, San Diego, Academic Press
- Tyack, D. and Tobin, W. (1995) 'The "grammar" of schooling: why has it been so hard to change?' *American Educational Research Journal*, 31, 3, pp. 453–479

This book provides an interesting – if provocative – account of how web-based participatory media may lead to a 'deschooled' form of university and adult education for the twenty-first century:

- Suoranta, J. and Vadén, T. (2010) *Wikiworld*, London, Pluto Press

Education and Technology – Looking to the Future

Introduction

This book has considered a wide range of issues and debates that underpin the ever-changing field of education and technology. Of course, the scope of our discussions has been determined in part by the limits of being fitted into eight chapters. As such, no book can provide a totally exhaustive analysis of every aspect of education and technology. In narrowing the scope of this book down to eight substantive areas of debate, there are inevitable gaps and issues that would merit further consideration if we had the time. For example, the book has not addressed many of the educational psychology debates on topics such as 'techno-phobia' or 'learning styles'. There is certainly more that could be said on the topics of the 'new literacies' and 'multimodalities' of digital technology use. The book has also shied away from some of the high-profile issues that have dominated recent discussions of 'technology-based practice' in education, such as e-assessment, internet safety, and so on. The book has also had relatively little to say on the matter of the production, development and design of educational technologies.

Some of these omissions have been deliberate. Many current 'hot topics' have only been mentioned in passing in order to give our discussions some longevity and relevance in years to come. Readers in the early 2010s may be surprised to see relatively little mention of 'serious gaming', 'tangible computing', 'mobile learning', and so on. However, readers in the late 2010s may struggle to remember what these concepts were. Similarly, in order to engage as wide a range of readers as possible there has been relatively little reference to debates that are predominantly of academic concern. In sociological terms, for example, the perennial theoretical preoccupations of identity, power, modernity, and so on have only been addressed on occasion. There has been relatively little attention given to the role of 'grand' theory in explaining some of the fundamental issues covered in this book. All of these deficits can be addressed by engaging with the specialist academic literature on technology, new media and society.

These omissions and silences notwithstanding, this book has certainly addressed many of the fundamental issues and tensions that lie at the heart of technology use in education. We have been interested in the recent history as well as current realities of technology use in education. In particular we have developed a framework for looking at education and technology that accounts for the 'wider picture' beyond the immediate concerns of the technological devices and artefacts themselves. Armed with this more 'holistic' understanding, it should now be possible to make more sense of why technologies are used (and not used) in the ways that they are in education. More importantly, it should also be possible to make sense of how technologies may be 'better' used in the future.

The previous seven chapters of this book have covered a great deal of ground. First, we established that technological devices, tools and gadgets are perhaps the least important aspects of education and technology to think about. While it is understandable that people who are interested in technology tend to devote most of their attention to the 'artefacts' of educational technology (i.e. hardware devices, software applications and services), it is equally important to understand educational technology in terms of what people do with technologies (i.e. the activities and practices). It is also important to understand educational technology in terms of the wider contexts, social structures and relationships that surround these activities and practices. To fully understand educational technology one has to consider a multitude of issues – what has been termed 'the milieu' of education and technology. This way of thinking encompasses issues ranging from the specific instance of an individual learner using a digital technology to the wider economic, political and commercial structures that underpin this use.

Of course, such an approach to conceptualizing education and technology goes against many of the common-sense ways that people tend to think about technology. For instance, we have deliberately attempted to look beyond the widely presumed 'transformative' qualities of digital technologies – that is, the idea that the 'digital' relates unproblematically with more efficient or more elegant ways of doing things than was previously possible in 'pre-digital' times. We have also tried to move beyond conceiving of educational technology only in terms of the presumed benefits to learners and learning. Hopefully, anyone having read this book will now be ready and able to think about education and technology in ways that look well 'beyond learning'.

Many of this book's chapters have reached the conclusion that technology use does not inevitably involve a 'change for the better'. We have seen how many of the changes associated with digital technologies are not intrinsic to the technology. Instead we have seen how the changes associated with educational technology are socially shaped as well as technologically driven. While this observation can be made of all aspects of technology and society, this seems to be an issue that is especially relevant to educational contexts. Many of the 'outcomes' and 'effects' of technologies in education have been shaped heavily by the characteristics of the educational contexts and settings these technologies have been used in. In this sense, the outcomes of technology use in education are certainly not predictable, but often involve a range of unintended consequences and subtle side-effects. The complicated and often compromised picture is highlighted in the long history of inconsistent technology use in educational contexts across the ages – not least throughout the rapid technological developments of the twentieth century.

This book has spent a great deal of time attempting to account for the gap between the 'clean' rhetoric and the 'messy' realities of technology use in education. One recurring conclusion over the previous seven chapters has been that the straightforward claims that are often made on behalf of educational technology belie a host of complex issues and wider tensions relating to the wider politics of education. For example, Chapter 4 discussed in detail how digital technologies have the potential to be used to support different forms

and types of learning. Yet we also saw that using technology to support different forms of learning often does not necessarily equate with 'better' forms
of learning. In fact we concluded that it is difficult – if not impossible – to
'prove' with any degree of certainty or rigour that technology leads to any
enhancements in learning.

As mentioned earlier, many of the chapters in the book have looked deliberately beyond matters of learning in order to fully understand the wider
politics of education and technology. In particular many of the chapters have
attempted to situate educational technology within the sets of social relations
and various social contexts that constitute 'education'. For example, Chapter 7
described in detail how educational institutions – such as schools, colleges and
universities – are key social contexts where the characteristics of education
technology are embedded, shaped and given meaning. We saw in Chapter 6
how the structures and processes of formal education have a profound bearing
on how teachers use technology. Matters of curriculum, assessment and the
monitoring of performance mean that some technological practices 'fit' better
than others with the 'job' of being a teacher. In a similar vein, Chapter 5 explored
how many of the efforts to use technology to make education a more equitable
process are also shaped by non-technological issues – again highlighting the
notion of 'goodness of fit' between an educational technology and its wider
social contexts.

All of these issues contribute to the emerging sense that technology – in
and of itself – does not provide a ready panacea for educational problems.
As we also saw in Chapter 5, technological interventions are often less likely
to help those who need help most, and are more likely to advantage those who
are already advantaged. Like many things in life, educational technologies
often tend to benefit people who are already more able, competent and
confident. Similarly, in Chapters 6 and 7 we saw how technology does not
simply overcome the perceived shortcomings of teachers and their educational institutions or, indeed, displace or even replace them. Of course, there
is a clear need to continue to adjust and reassess the formal provision of
education. Yet educational institutions and individual teachers look set to
remain to have an integral role in education for many years to come. If
anything, new digital technologies should be seen as involving *more* – rather
than less – work and responsibility for educational institutions and those
who work within them.

These issues, debates and arguments are all well and good, but it is now time
to give some thought to the future. While there are few sensible grounds for

any educational technologist to refute this book's analysis of the present 'messy realities' of education and technology, many people would contend that we should not be too hasty in reaching definite conclusions. It *could* be argued that the full effects of digital technologies are now only beginning to be felt. In fact many academic commentators and educational technologists would consider it simply too early to judge the use of digital technology in education. While the history of educational technology has undoubtedly been fraught with difficulty and disappointment, many people would contend that the next 10 to 20 years look set to finally witness the fundamental transformation of educational arrangements and relations after the past 50 years of unfulfilled predictions and potential. In this respect, many people would anticipate and expect the near future of education and technology to be very different to its current state-of-affairs. So before we conclude the book it is perhaps worth thinking back to one of the issues that emerged from our discussion of technological convergence towards the end of Chapter 3. Could it be that there will be something intrinsically different about the new educational technologies that will emerge during the 2010s and 2020s? If so, what are the likely future forms of education and technology? Now that we have considered all that has come before, what is likely to be coming next?

Looking towards the future of education and technology

As was implied at the beginning of this book, the academic study of educational technology is often drawn inexorably towards a forward-looking, 'leading-edge' perspective. Much of the educational technology literature focuses on what could be termed 'state-of-the-art' issues – asking questions of what *could* happen, and what *should* happen once the latest technologies and digital media are placed into educational settings. A great deal of excitement tends to be reserved for the short-term, imminent changes in educational technology (the 'next big thing' that is 'just around the corner'). Moreover, there is also considerable interest in the speculative forecasting of the medium- to long-term future of education and technology.

Of course, commenting on the possible future of either education or technology can be a perilous pastime. Chapter 3's overview of the history of educational technology showed how even the most informed and articulate of commentators find technological forecasting to be a tricky business.

Take, for instance, the assertion in 1943 that there only would ever be 'a world market for maybe five computers' (a quotation attributed to Thomas J Watson – then Chairman of IBM). Or 50 years later when the internet was dismissed by Bill Gates as 'a passing fad'. It seems that even those at the sharp end of technological change are reduced to guessing games when it comes to predicting the future. In the same vein, the nature of educational change has proved to be just as difficult to forecast accurately – as was evident in the many extravagant depictions of the 'classroom of 2000' offered throughout the second half of the twentieth century. All told, predicting the possible new shapes and forms of educational technology is fraught with difficulty.

Although making predictions remains a risky business, the need to assess accurately the potential impacts of technology on society is an important part of attempting to manage and control technology. The twentieth century saw a rise in 'technological forecasting' by many different people and organizations, not least a popularist strand of technology assessment that became known as 'futurology' or 'future studies'. This area of study is based on the scrutiny of past and present trends in order to forecast future developments. While often speculative and descriptive in nature, it is nevertheless important to consider the ways in which writers working in the area of Future Studies are envisaging the main issues for education and technology over the next 10 to 30 years – what is often referred to by futurologists as the 'near future'.

Reconsidering future visions from the past

Futurology and future studies rose to prominence during the 1960s and 1970s. In particular, the concept of futurology first came to mainstream attention through the work of authors such as Alvin and Heidi Toffler, John Naisbitt and others. Throughout the Cold War and economic-crisis ridden 1970s and 1980s various best-selling books offered optimistic visions of technology-led new eras – a trend repeated though a similar rash of writings in the internet-obsessed 1990s and the social media fixated 2000s. While it is easy to dismiss these accounts of new technology-based societies as fanciful and popularist, early examples of futurology such as Toffler's *Future Shock* and Naisbitt's *Megatrends* introduced many of the key aspects of how we now think about contemporary society to wider audiences. In particular, Toffler highlighted many issues that later came to be important elements of debates over the information society, such as 'telecommuters', 'prosumers' and the 'crack-up of the nation'.

One of the more prescient 'past' future portrayals of education and technology came from a competition held by Apple Computers in 1988 asking some of the top US universities to forecast the state of education, technology and society in the year 2000. The winners of the 'Project 2000' competition took a twofold approach to considering the technologies that could be produced and, perhaps more importantly, what they described as 'how this technology can be used meaningfully by people' (Young et al. 1988, p. 62). In terms of technology devices and artefacts, Project 2000 foresaw the widespread use of a touch screen tablet with handwriting and speech recognition, infra-red network connections, built-in GPS and portable one gigabyte 'Laser Card Mass Storage Units'. Even looking back 25 years, these predictions of the technological artefacts of the future are remarkably accurate.

However the Project 2000 descriptions of the educational activities and practices that tablet computing would be used for were less accurate. Here, the winning experts foresaw a form of 'tele-university' education where learners no longer specialized in arts or sciences but took a variety of subjects that were learnt through simulated exploration and experimentation. Individual children and adults were imagined as accessing simulated learning in a time-shifted, 'on-demand' basis, dipping in and out of face-to-face exchanges as they saw fit, and communicating with peers and tutors via video email and bulletin boards. Of course, while much of this 'imagineering' certainly mirrors how educational technologists continued to talk about the potential of education and technology throughout the 1990s and 2000s, it did not turn out to be an especially accurate portrayal of actual mainstream uses of the technology. On-demand simulated 'tele-education' remains as much of a peripheral educational activity now as it was in 1988.

Similar 'successes' and 'failures' are apparent throughout the forecasts of future forms of education and technology that were made throughout the 1970s, 1980s and 1990s. Tom Stonier and Cathy Conlin's (1985) *Interlude in the Year 2010* displayed a particularly imaginative take on the technological and social aspects of life in the future – forecasting the ubiquitous use of household robots, holographic video-boxes and wrist-computers. These authors also predicted that 12-year-old students would be going on six-month cultural exchanges and study visits to Pakistan and Russia sustained by computer-phone contact with their families. In particular, Stonier and Conlin saw education as being profoundly de-institutionalized. Technology was used to support home-based education for school students, built around the provision of daily programmes of work that young learners experienced as games or stories. Similarly, adult education was seen to take place through expert systems, with the teacher offering 'the human touch ... a kind of fatherly reassurance that the students were really clever enough to handle the system' (1985, p. 177).

Similarly, the UK technologist Christopher Evans was 'particularly confident' that 'the printed word would be virtually obsolete' by the year 2000 and that 'computer education would have made great inroads' (1979, p. 201). Evans gained many plaudits at the time for his predictions that ultra-intelligent machines would soon be underpinning most of human activity. In line with other futurologists of the 1970s and 1980s, Evans also foresaw a profoundly de-institutionalized version of education. As he put it, 'the average child [will] own a portable teaching computer of great power, more knowledgeable and, in certain aspects, more intelligent than any human teacher' (Evans 1979, p. 205). As with many of these futurologists, Evans was convinced of the technological capacity for change but less clear of the human commitment of realizing technology's potential. As Evans concluded in his book *The Mighty Micro*, the 'most potent limiting factor of all could be Man himself' (1979, p. 204).

Reconsidering future visions from the present day

As all these 'future visions' from the past demonstrate, the popularity of such writing does not necessarily derive from its ability to provide an accurate or balanced view of the technological future. Criticism of futurology has long centred on the limitations of its models and the subjective nature of its projections. In particular, many futurology accounts of the 'inevitability' of technological 'progress' reflect an implicit technological determinism. Whereas many of the predictions outlined above proved in hindsight to be reasonably accurate in their imagining of the possible technological artefacts and devices of the future, they proved less successful in imagining the social activities and arrangements that accompanied the technologies. With this caveat in mind, we should perhaps consider briefly some of the present-day attempts to forecast the near future of education and technology across the first half of the twenty-first century.

Whereas many of the writers of the 1970s and 1980s adopted the year 2000 as the most appropriate 'event space' to imagine the future, current future-orientated writing has tended to focus on the years 2020, 2025 and 2030. One such example was the recent UK government-sponsored Beyond Current Horizons programme. Beyond Current Horizons tasked over 100 academic experts to consider potential socio-technical futures for education in 2025. In terms of technological development, these experts identified a number of fairly certain short-term trends such as the continued increase in computing power available to individuals and organizations, coupled with a shift over the 2010s from networked to ubiquitous computing. The programme also highlighted a number of less obvious longer-term trends including the rise of pharmacological technologies such as smart drugs. Other predictions included the migration of cognitive functions to external devices – the development of biotechnological devices that will literally think on behalf of their users (see Facer and Sandford 2010).

In terms of predicting the socio-technical futures for education, many of the Beyond Current Horizons reports expanded upon some of the main themes that have emerged throughout this book. For example, great care was taken to re-imagine the role of education in a society where the amount of available information has become 'denser, deeper and more diverse' as well as personally owned by individuals rather than managed through institutions. The reports also foresaw people as becoming comfortable with working and living alongside machines and other technologies. As Keri Facer concluded:

> Over the coming two decades, people are likely to become increasingly accustomed to machines taking on more roles previously occupied by humans across both professional and manual occupations and in homes and workplaces. Whether through devolving simple tasks or outsourcing the management of complex systems, such devolution of responsibility potentially brings a number of adjustments in our understanding of the respective roles of machines and humans. (2009, p. 231)

In terms of addressing the key issues and questions raised in this book, the Beyond Current Horizons programme foresaw a continued weakening of boundaries between institutions that have traditionally been seen as separate – especially the boundaries between workplaces, homes, entertainment venues and educational establishments. As Facer and Sandford (2010, p. 86) contended, 'over the coming twenty years, the monopoly of the "school" or the "university" as the sole sites of education may be profoundly challenged, leading to an examination of what it means to be an educational institution and of how to enable learners to navigate a significantly more complex landscape of educational provision'. The reports also foresaw the reorientation of teaching as a profession towards becoming 'a mentoring and networking workforce'. Perhaps most significantly, the role of curriculum was highlighted as being a key site of change. Here the experts recommended the (re)design of 'curricula for networked learning' that would enable individuals to learn to work effectively within social networks for educational, social and civic purposes.

Many of these predications and forecasts seem remarkably familiar to the issues raised by the forecasts of the 1970s and 1980s, perhaps reflecting the cyclical nature of such exercises. These similarities can also be seen in the Futurelab 2020 project – a precursor to Beyond Current Horizons that was also tasked with considering the educational implications of a fast changing, personalized and ubiquitous technological landscape. As far as this project was concerned, 2020 looked set to be characterized by increasingly networked and connected modes of interacting with other people and accessing information and knowledge:

> Interaction with digital technologies will be more pervasive, seamless and invisible than today and will facilitate much of our everyday lives – enabling ongoing interactions with people, buildings and materials and with a constantly connected network. We will be able to tap into unimaginable computing power and reliable storage capacity on the network, which will enable us to interact with more intelligent (and responsive) technologies, to 'outsource' memory, and to use simulations and visualisation tools to solve problems, experience alternative realities and prepare for new experiences. (Daanen and Facer 2007, p. 27)

As the Futurelab 2020 report then went on to reason, the artefacts, activities and contexts associated with these modes of technology use will undoubtedly provide challenges to the 'fundamentals of teaching and learning, curriculum and institutions' (Daanen and Facer 2007, p. 27). These challenges were seen to include issues of what is taught, the skills that are developed and how knowledge and competences are tested and assessed. For example, returning to notions of 'connectivist' learning outlined in Chapter 4, the report challenged the continued importance and relevance of instruction and memorization in a world where information is constantly accessible to any individual. The report also highlighted the need to redesign educational environments as 'intelligent environments' that are able to meet the needs of different occupants of the space.

Recognizing the contested nature of the future

As our earlier overview of the predications of the 1970s and 1980s suggested, these 'current' future scenarios and trends are by no means assured. We should remain mindful that such forms of 'future' forecasting are usually informed by a politically-driven desire to see 'better' forms of society. Of course, it is understandable that futurologists will use education and technology as a means through which idealized societies can be proposed. Yet it is important to see these future scenarios and forecasts as prescriptive rather than predictive in nature. As David Nye (2007, p. 35) reflects, 'all technological predictions and forecasts are in essence little narratives about the future. They are not full-scale narratives of utopia, but they are usually presented as stories about a better world to come.'

Following this line of thinking, Nick Zepke (2008) suggests three conceptual categories for characterizing portrayals of the future of technology and society. These include 'the science of the probable' (based on the rigorous forecasting of preceding trends), 'the art of the possible' (the creative imagination of alternative futures) and 'the politics of the preferable' (based on the values, assumptions and preferences of specific groups of people). Clearly many of the technological predictions outlined so far in this chapter fall into the category of 'the science of the probable'. However, predictions of the socio-technical arrangements of technology-based education fall more readily into either the creative imagination of the possible or, more often than not, the value-led 'politics of the preferable'.

Indeed, many of the present-day visions of education and technology of 2020, 2025 or 2030 are largely driven by matters of ideology rather than objective forecasting. In other words, much of what is said and much of what is believed about the education and technology of the future relates to what is believed about the education and society of today. It therefore makes little sense to search for definitive answers of what the future of education and technology will definitely look like. Instead, it makes more sense to recognize the contested nature of these future-orientated debates. Above all, it is important to treat any claims made on behalf of the future of education and technology with a degree of caution and scepticism. With these thoughts in mind, we can now conclude by turning our attention away from the vagaries of futurology and predictions of the near future. Instead we should look towards the present-day realities of education and technology. What have we learnt about education and technology from the previous seven chapters and what bearing do these lessons have for educators and education provision? Most importantly, how can the wide range of people who are involved in education develop 'better' forms of technology use that draw upon – rather than clash with – their own 'local' experiences and practices?

Lessons learnt about education and technology

The questions posed at the beginning of each chapter of this book were written to be deliberately polemic in nature. It should now be clear that a question such as 'will technology displace the teacher?' does not have a single 'yes' or 'no' answer. Instead, the question acts as a starting-point to challenge existing assumptions and to think about education and technology from a slightly different perspective than one might be used to. These are all questions intended to help us 'make the familiar strange' – in other words to gain a little distance and see things from a new perspective. As such, most of the questions contained within the book's chapter titles are not meant to be statements that one can either agree whole-heartedly with *or* dismiss out-of-hand. Instead, they are intended to offer a 'way in' to considering some of the key non-technological elements of the practices, activities and contexts of educational technology use. These are all questions that hopefully have helped us to see things from the perspective of the learner, the teacher and the educational institution. These are all questions that hopefully have helped us to also consider the political, commercial and societal aspects of education and technology.

Although these chapter titles were not intended to be taken at face value, it would seem that many popular perceptions of education and technology often *do* actually concur with their rather bold and provocative implications. For example, many of the enthusiasms for technology in education over the past 50 years would certainly appear to have been driven by a strong belief that technology is capable of enhancing learning in particular ways. It would seem that some commentators on education and technology would quite like to replace 'industrial-era' educational institutions and the people who work within them. In a general sense, many proponents of technology do actually appear to be driven by the belief that technology can lead to a better set of social arrangements of education – however, one may choose to define 'better'.

One of the main conclusions that has emerged from this book is that to continue to cling to these 'black' and 'white' conceptions of education and technology is to somewhat misunderstand the complex nature of the topic. All of these popular reactions run the risk of overlooking or wilfully ignoring many of the crucial issues that shape education and technology. We have seen from Chapter 1 onwards how digital technologies are often instinctively associated with expectations of the significant improvement of existing educational processes and the transformation of education into new forms. Yet we have also seen how digital technologies, more often than not, are linked to the continuation and perpetuation of many existing and deeply entrenched patterns. In fact, educational technology usually appears to be a case of 'more of the same' rather than distinct change or improvement. Despite all the excitement and hyperbole that surrounds it, there is often little that is truly 'new' about new technology. The really important questions about education and technology are not what people think may happen but what is actually happening. One of the key questions that should always be asked of education and technology is the simple question of 'what is new here?' In other words, what is technology making possible that was not possible before?

Developing a rich understanding of education and technology therefore relies upon developing a more critical sense of what concepts such as 'new' and 'change' actually mean. Here it is useful to return to the notion of 'remediation' that was introduced in Chapter 1. From this perspective, we would not expect technology to completely change pre-existing circumstances and situations. Although digitally based activities may well borrow from, refashion and occasionally surpass their earlier pre-digital equivalents, it is highly unlikely that there will ever be a complete break with what came before. In fact, it could be argued that the notion of the 'totally new' is an impossible concept. As Kelli Fuery argues 'the old media is embedded in the new, twisting it, informing it, shaping its future . . . there are joint versions, varieties, and movements from the old into something else. In this sense all new media contains old media' (2009, pp. 22–23). Extending this logic, it could also be said that all 'new' educational practices and activities using technology contain old educational practices and activities.

So why then is the idea of 'new' digital technology still associated with a sense of exoticism and excitement in twenty-first-century discussions of education? On one hand, digital technology is often described as being 'new' for commercial reasons (i.e. to add value to the latest product), or in technical terms to denote an innovative configuration or design. Yet when educationalists get excited about digital technologies the idea of 'new' tends to be used in a discursive rather than descriptive sense. The concept of 'new' digital technology in education is usually employed to suggest a set of substantial social and cultural discontinuities and variations from what went before. As Kelli Fuery suggests, on some occasions we may expect a 'new' digital technology to prompt a significant disruption or corruption of the social and cultural arrangements that went before. On other occasions we may expect 'new' digital technologies to bring together different areas of life that were previously unconnected. In all instances, the idea of the 'new' carries a symbolic value of significant changes to come.

Yet while these ideas of 'the new' continue to have symbolic currency and value in twenty-first-century education, the actual social differences and improvements in practice are almost always very subtle and often imperceptible. As Fuery reasons, in many ways the differences between watching a television programme on a 'new' high definition TV set and a now 'old-fashioned' digital TV set are negligible – especially in terms of the social and cultural practices, activities and contexts of television watching. To make an educational comparison, the differences between teaching with a 'new' electronic smart-board and an old-fashioned 'dumb' whiteboard often do not constitute a substantial change to the social and cultural practices of the classroom or the activities and contexts of teaching and learning. Nevertheless, the idea of these new technologies continues to feel significant, innovative and life changing. In short, these new technologies are symbols of progress rather than guaranteed harbingers of change and improvement.

This reappraisal of the 'new' corresponds with one of the main conclusions that has emerged throughout this book – that is, that the claims made for educational technologies are highly symbolic and often ideologically driven in nature. It would be naive to see debates over education and technology as somehow neutral and disinterested accounts of an inevitable future. It would be foolhardy to ignore the fact that many of the enthusiasms and many of the concerns expressed for digital technology in education are driven by people's wider beliefs, values and agendas. Indeed, most of the chapters in this book have reached the conclusion that the idea of 'educational technology' is used as a site for wider debates, contests and struggles over education. In this sense, much of what is said and believed about education and technology relates to what is said and believed about education and society.

For example, how technology is seen to relate to learning depends very much on what assumptions we make about the nature of desirable learning. Here a number of values and positions are apparent – that is, a belief in the value of learner-centred learning as opposed to teacher-led instruction, a belief in the relative value of free discovery and exploration as opposed to instruction, or a belief in the value of social and communal learning as opposed to individual learning. Similarly, much of the debate over the continued relevance of the teacher relates to the assumptions that we make about authority and expertise in contemporary society. Much of the debate over the continued relevance of the school relates to the assumptions that we make about role of the state in providing services to all, as opposed to the role of market forces. How technology is used to make education fairer depends on what conception we hold of 'fairness' and 'equality'. As we have seen throughout this book, people's enthusiasms for technology in education are often based around combinations of these values and beliefs. It would certainly be fair to conclude that many of the claims made for educational technology are often more of a matter of faith than a matter of fact. As this current chapter has just illustrated, this is certainly the case with visions of education, technology and society in the near future.

There is a pressing need, therefore, to develop and promote more sophisticated present-day understandings of education and technology. Of course, it would be churlish to deny the educational potentials of digital technologies altogether – technology is obviously having a major influence in a range of educational contexts. Yet as we have seen throughout this book, any changes, improvements or even 'transformations' are never consistent or straightforward and rarely turn out to be the inevitable and holistic improvements that some people would have us believe. In this sense we need to develop and promote a better understanding of the realities of education and technology. Why is it that digital technology has not yet made a radical difference to the quality and reach of education in the ways that we are always being told that it will?

In order to address this question we have learnt that there is a clear need to develop a greater sense of realism when approaching issues relating to education and technology. This sense of realism involves paying more attention to the social, cultural, political, economic and historical aspects of education and technology. Of course, we should not lose sight of the fact that the current wave of digital technologies has obvious educational potentials and 'advantages'. Undoubtedly, the next 'new wave' of digital technologies will also have obvious educational potentials and advantages. Yet any understanding of the potential of these technologies must be seen in relation to the long history of gradual and often unpredictable changes in education associated with technology implementation and use. There is a need to be relentlessly realistic as well as occasionally optimistic about the relationship between education and technology.

In particular, it would seem important to develop a greater understanding of the 'here-and-now' realities rather than future possibilities and potentials of educational technology. The practical significance of an avowedly forward-looking perspective on education and technology is limited – tending to underplay social influences and relations, and offering little useful insight into how present arrangements may be improved or adjusted. Instead of focusing on the 'state-of-the-art', more effort should be made to ask questions concerning what is *actually* taking place when a digital technology meets an educational setting and how this compares to what has taken place in the past. These questions fall broadly into three basic forms, that is: What is the use of technology in educational settings actually like? Why is technology use in educational settings the way it is? What are the consequences of technology use in educational settings?

As these deceptively simple questions imply, educational technology is best seen as a site of ongoing negotiation and, often, intense social conflict and struggle. Addressing these questions therefore requires a deliberate focus on what has been referred to throughout this book as the 'messy realities' of education technology use. This involves showing a particular interest in instances where technologies are *not* being used, or where technologies are being used in ways that suppress and disadvantage. In this sense, we need to pose questions that are perhaps more challenging and awkward than is usually found in the academic literature and popular discussions on educational technology. We need to develop lines of enquiry that may be less forward-looking and undoubtedly less 'high-tech' than is usually the case with the study of educational technology, but are certainly no less important.

All of these conclusions and contentions point to the need to stimulate and sustain proper debates over education and technology – debates that are not confined to academic circles but are driven by all of the actors and interests involved in education. Indeed, many of the dominant academic understandings of education and technology are notable for their lack of consideration for the 'voice' of the learner, the teacher or the educational institution. As best academics and educational technologists tend to speak on behalf of these interests, rather than allowing them to speak for themselves. This is clearly the case with many of the assumptions made about education and technology in the ICT4D literature. It is very rare for the educational technology literature to feature the 'voices' of the 1.3 billion people in the developing world who exist on less than a dollar a day, and for whom any kind of schooling is a privilege rather than a problem. Educational technology is often something that is 'done to' learners, teachers, educational institutions and the less privileged and less affluent – rather than 'done by' them.

As Hans Daanen and Keri Facer have argued, one of the key issues that therefore underpins any use of technology in education is the simple question of 'who decides?' At present it is clear that technology is usually something that is 'handed down' to those involved in education as a *fait accompli* rather than something that is negotiable and malleable. As we discussed in Chapter 2, technology is often 'handed down' to educators under a number of wider imperatives of economic efficiency, future employment needs or vague notions of modernization and effectiveness. In all these instances, technology is presented to those in education as a 'black box' that must be responded to as best as they can. Yet as Daanen and Facer contend, technology is too more important and significant a thing to be simply 'handed down' to education in a reactive manner:

> When we look at the capacity emerging technologies may offer to reorganise the institutions, practices and people of education, the issues raised are broader than those raised by the needs of future employers. The challenges raised are more significant than can simply be addressed by educators harnessing the second-hand off casts of the business world for education. As such, we cannot leave discussions of the future role of technology in education only to the technology industry, or indeed, only to educators. Instead, we need to develop the mechanisms for an open and public debate on the nature and purpose of education in the digital age which goes beyond safe slogans such as 'meeting the needs of every child' (who can disagree with that?). Instead, we need to confront the fact that longstanding assumptions about what education is for, who conducts it, and how it is assessed, may need to be challenged. And this challenge will need to take place in the public spaces of the media, not the confines of the education community – with families, children, businesses, technologists, religious leaders and scientists all making their case for how education may need to change to meet the social, environmental, spiritual and human needs of the future. (Daanen and Facer 2007)

As this quotation implies, one of the most important steps towards realizing the potential of educational technology is stimulating debates that involve all of the 'publics' of education and technology – not least teachers, learners, parents and other people in the 'silent majority' of end users. At the moment it appears that few people are overly concerned or involved with the topic of education and technology beyond a vague notion that digital tools and applications are a desirable feature of contemporary society. Despite the increased tendency of parents, employers and other 'end users' of education to exert their 'consumer rights' on all manner of other matters, there is often a distinct agnosticism and apathy when it comes to the issue of improving digital technology use in educational settings. Education and technology is simply not a topic that many people talk openly about, let alone get impassioned or angry about. In this sense it is high time that there is an increased public and professional engagement with the politics of educational technology.

Conclusions – turning informed debate into informed action

Of course, the whole point of stimulating serious and sustained public debate about education and technology is to provoke action and change. Many of the chapters in this book have concluded that educational technology is a contested area – a struggle over ideas, values and beliefs of what education should and could be like. At present these struggles involve a variety of largely 'high-level' interests from politicians to industrialists, learning scientists to academics. It now seems essential that learners, teachers and other people involved in the day-to-day realities of education are also allowed to play a major part of these negotiations and struggles – getting *their* voice heard, arguing for *their* demands for change, and then being centrally involved in initiating these changes. Learners, teachers and other 'grass-roots' educators have a key role to play in developing plausible suggestions as to how current inequalities, inefficiencies and inconsistencies may be countered. They also have a key role to play in deciding how digital technology use in educational settings may be reshaped along 'better', fairer and more equitable lines.

A number of potential ways in which this involvement could take place have been highlighted throughout this book. One obvious area is the increased involvement of learners, teachers and other educators in producing digital technologies for education. This could entail teachers getting more involved in the commercial production and development of technologies, tools and applications – letting software developers and hardware developers know exactly what technologies are required to 'fit' with the day-to-day demands of the educational settings. There are also opportunities for more 'bottom-up' involvement in the shaping of technology production. It could be that 'open source' style communities of teachers and learners can take more responsibility for developing, sharing and refining their own digital resources for learning and teaching. The 'open courseware' and 'open knowledge' models reviewed in Chapter 5 suggest a number of ways that educators-as-producers can be involved in taking responsibility and control for shaping the technologies that they use.

There are also clear opportunities for teachers and other educators to re-emphasize the role of the 'pre-digital' elements of education that are seen to be challenged by 'digital' education. For example, present debates over the future of educational institutions and the relevance of the teacher appear to have been captured by the views and opinions of technologists and those seeking the radical reform of public services. Very rarely are the alternative opinions of disinterested teachers, schools or even learners heard in these re-imaginings of the education system. Even the language that is used to discuss education and technology is often overly technicist and far removed from the language used by teachers and learners to discuss their education. We therefore need a change of emphasis *and* a change in vocabulary in the ways that education and technology are discussed. Policymakers and those responsible for the future shaping of education tend to take debates over such nebulous concepts such as 'school 2.0' and 'edgeless' education very seriously. It is crucial that those people who are directly involved in the consequences of these changes have a greater say in the nature and form of these debates.

This is not to naïvely imagine the restorative power of a unified 'learner voice' or 'teacher lobby' as a neatly packaged counterweight to the opinions and actions of the powerful. Instead it is simply a call for individual teachers, learners, educators, parents and everyone else with a stake in education to get engaged actively in the shaping of 'their' educational technology. Of course, any 'bottom-up' suggestions and interventions will be as value-driven and ideologically led as the current 'top-down' debates and development of educational technology. It is likely that learners, teachers and other educational interests will be no more coherent than anyone else at agreeing on what constitutes making learning 'better', more 'effective' or 'fairer'. It is likely that any such interventions and actions would be very local in their nature and very specific in their influence. As such there is no easy way to completely transform or overhaul education and technology.

Yet the lack of any easy solutions is no reason to give up on the democratization of educational technology. It is important that the alternative perspectives, beliefs and values of those involved at the grass roots of education are more prominently included in the development and implementation of educational technologies. As we have stated throughout this book, technology does not have – and never has had – an inevitable impact on education. As Daanen and Facer conclude, the educational changes associated with technology 'are not inevitable – they happen if society wants them to happen (or simply looks the other way and hopes they go away)' (2007, p. 28). It is therefore crucial that everyone working in and around education realizes that they are as much capable of shaping technology as technology is capable of shaping them. Hopefully, the ideas and debates raised in this book can act as a starting-point for better things to come.

Further questions to consider

- Why should the future of education and technology be any different to how it is now? What changes in technology-based *activities* and *practices* have taken place over the past 20 years? What equivalent changes may be reasonably expected over the next 20 years? How might the *contexts* of educational technology use have changed in 20-years time?
- How might those people involved in education have more of an influence on the nature of educational technology? In terms of the production of technology, for example, what might an educationally designed search engine look like? What might a learner-designed virtual learning environment differ from the ones currently in use? How might educators and learners be more involved in the popular debates that surround education and technology? How might educators and learners be more involved in the political decisions that are made about education and technology?
- Is the idea of stimulating and supporting public awareness and debate about educational technology simply too idealistic? Think of the educational issues that are currently at the forefront of public contentiousness and news media attention. Is the issue of educational technology as important as these issues? How can educational technology become a topic that is widely discussed and debated?

Further reading

The book provides a fascinating overview of the role of 'futures thinking' in understanding educational change:

- Facer, K. (2011) *Learning Futures: Education, Technology and Social Change*, London, Routledge

This article provides a good overview of the UK Beyond Current Horizons programme:

- Facer, K. and Sandford, R. (2010) 'The next twenty-five years: future scenarios and future directions for education and technology' *Journal of Computer Assisted Learning*, 26, 1, pp. 18–27

Finally, here are some authors who continue many of the discussions pursued throughout the eight chapters of this book and offer a social science perspective on education and technology. All these books expand on the key ideas and debates outlined in this current book at all levels of educational provision from preschool children to adult learners:

- Plowman, L., Stephen, C. and Peake, J. (2010) *Growing Up with Technology: Young Children Learning in a Digital World*, London, Routledge
- Buckingham, D. (2007) *Beyond Technology*, Cambridge, Polity Press
- Monahan, T. (2005) *Globalization, Technological Change, and Public Education*, London, Routledge
- Robins, K. and Webster, F. (2002) *The Virtual University?*, Oxford, Oxford University Press
- Selwyn, N., Gorard, S. and Furlong, J. (2005) *Adult Learning in the Digital Age*, London, Routledge

References

Allen, M. (2008) 'Web 2.0: an argument against convergence' *First Monday*, 13, 3 [http://firstmonday.org] Last accessed 1 Sept. 2010.

Allen, W. (1956) 'Audio-visual materials' *Review of Educational Research*, 26, 2, pp. 125–156.

Anderson, C. (2009) *Free: The Future of a Radical Price*, New York, Hyperion.

Angrist, J. and Lavy, V. (2002) 'New evidence on classroom computers and pupil learning' *The Economic Journal*, 112, pp. 735–765.

Apple (2008) *Apple Classrooms of Tomorrow – Today: Learning in the Twenty-First Century*, Cupertino CA, Apple Corporation.

Apple, M. (1991) 'The culture and the commerce of the textbook' in Apple, M. and Christian-Smith, L. (eds) *The Politics of the Textbook*, London, Routledge.

Apple, M. (2000) 'Away with all teachers' *International Studies in Sociology of Education*, 10, pp. 61–80.

Apple, M. and Jungck, S. (1990) 'You don't have to be a teacher to teach this unit' *American Educational Research Journal*, 27, 2, pp. 227–251.

Arthur, C. (2006) 'What is the one per cent rule?' *The Guardian*, 20 July, Technology supplement, p. 2.

Atkinson, C. (1938) *Education by Radio in American Schools*, Edinboro PA, Edinboro Educational Press.

Barrera-Osorio, F. and Linden, L. (2009) *The Use and Misuse of Computers in Education*, Washington DC, World Bank.

Bates, A. (1988) 'Television, learning and distance education' *Journal of Educational Television*, 14, 3, pp. 213–225.

Bates, A. (2004) *Why Education Must Change*, 14 December – keynote speech to Open University of Hong Kong.

BBC News (2008) 'Dell joins cut-down laptop market' *BBC News Online*, 29 May [http://news.bbc.co.uk/1/hi/7425099.stm] Last accessed 1 Sept. 2010.

Becker, H. (1994) *Analysis of Trends of School Use of New Information Technology*, Irvine CA, Office of Technology Assessment, University of California.

Beck-Gernsheim, E. (1996) 'Life as a planning project' in Lash, S., Szerszynski, B. and Wynne, B. (eds) *Risk, Environment and Modernity*, London, Sage.

Beer, D. and Burrows, R. (2007) 'Sociology of and in web 2.0' *Sociological Research Online*, 12, 5 [www.socresonline.org.uk/12/5/17.html] Last accessed 1 Sept. 2010.

Ben-David Kolikant, Y. (2011) 'Digital natives, better learners? Students' beliefs about how the internet influenced their ability to learn' *Computers in Human Behaviour*.

Bentley, T. (2000) 'Learning beyond the classroom' *Educational Management, Administration and Leadership*, 28, pp. 353–364.

Bereiter, C. (2002) *Education and the Mind in the Knowledge Age*, London, Lawrence Erlbaum.

Besser, H. (1993) 'Education as marketplace' in Muffoletto, R. and Knupfer, N. (eds) *Computers in Education*, Cresskill NJ, Hampton Press.

Bianchi, W. (2008) 'Education by radio' *TechTrends*, 52, 2, pp. 36–44.

Biesta, G. (2006) *Beyond Learning*, Boulder CO, Paradigm.

Bijker, W., Hughes, T. and Pinch, T. (eds) (1987) *The Social Construction of Technological Systems*, Cambridge MA, MIT Press.

Bloom, B. (1956) *Taxonomy of Educational Objectives*, London, Longman.

Bolter, J. and Grusin, R. (1999) *Remediation: Understanding New Media*, Cambridge MA, MIT Press.

Bonk, C. (2009) *The World is Open*, New York, Jossey-Bass.

Boody, R. (2001) 'On the relationships of education and technology' in Muffoletto, R. (ed.) *Education and Technology: Critical and Reflective Practices*, Cresskill NJ, Hampton Press.

Bracken, C. and Lombard, M. (2004) 'Social presence and children' *Journal of Communication*, 54, 1, pp. 22–37.

Braverman, H. (1974) *Labour and Monopoly Capital*, New York, Monthly Review Press.

Bruner, J. (1996) *The Culture of Education*, Cambridge MA, Harvard University Press.

Bruns, A. (2008) *Blogs, Wikipedia, Second Life and Beyond*, New York, Peter Lang.

Buckingham, D. (2007) *Beyond Technology's Promise*, Cambridge, Polity.

Buckingham, D. and Scanlon, M. (2005) 'Selling learning: towards a political economy of edutainment media' *Media, Culture and Society*, 27, 1, pp. 41–58.

Bugeja, M. (2006) 'Facing the Facebook' *The Chronicle of Higher Education*, 52, 21, 27 January, section C, p. 1.

Bush, V. (1945) 'As we may think' *Life*, 10 September, pp. 112–124.

Carmichael, P. and Honour, L. (2002) 'Open source as appropriate technology for global education' *International Journal of Educational Development*, 22, 1, pp. 47–53.

Carr, D. and Oliver, M. (2010) 'Second Life, immersion and learning' in Zaphiris, P. and Ang, C. (eds) *Social Computing and Virtual Communities*, London, Taylor and Francis.

Carr, N. (2008) 'Is Google making us stupid?' *The Atlantic*, July/August [www.theatlantic.com/magazine/archive/2008/07/is-google-making-us-stupid/6868/] Last accessed 1 Sept. 2010.

Carter, M. (1979) 'Microelectronics in education' *Educational Media International*, 16, 2, pp. 13–14.

Cascio, J. (2009) 'Get smarter' *The Atlantic*, July/August [www.theatlantic.com/doc/200907/intelligence] Last accessed 1 Sept. 2010.

Cassidy, M. (1998) 'Historical perspectives on teaching with technology in K-12 schools' *New Jersey Journal of Communication*, 6, 2, pp. 170–184.

Castells, M. (1996) *The Rise of the Network Society*, Oxford, Blackwell.

Chatfield, T. (2010) 'Why computer games can teach youngsters valuable life lessons' *The Observer*, 10 January, p. 28.

Chatti, M., Amine, J. and Quix, C. (2010) 'Connectivism: the network metaphor of learning' *International Journal of Learning Technology*, 5, 1, pp. 80–99.

Cigman, R. and Davis, A. (2008) 'ICT and learning: an introduction' *Journal of Philosophy of Education*, 42, 3–4, pp. 501–503.

Clark, R. (1983) 'Reconsidering research on learning from media' *Review of Educational Research*, 43, 4, pp. 445–459.

Cohen, M. (1993) 'Machines for thinking: the computer's role in schools' *Innovations in Education and Teaching International*, 30, 1, pp. 57–59.

Colle, R. and Roman, R. (2003) 'ICT4D: a frontier for higher education in developing nations' *African and Asian Studies*, 2, 4, pp. 381–420.

Collins, A. and Halverson, R. (2009) *Rethinking Education in the Age of Technology*, New York, Teachers College Press.

Collis, B. and Gommer, E. (2001) 'Stretching the mould or a new economy?' *Educational Technology*, 41, 3, pp. 5–18.

Collis, B. and van der Wende, M. (2002) *Models of Technology and Change in Higher Education*, University of Twente, Centre for Higher Education Policy Studies.

Conrad, L. (1954) 'Schools can start using TV now' *Educational Leadership*, 11, 6, pp. 373–374.

Conte, C. (1997) *The Learning Connection*, Washington DC, Benton Foundation [www.benton.org/Library/Schools] Last accessed 1 Sept. 2010.

Convery, A. (2009) 'The pedagogy of the impressed: how teachers become victims of technological vision' *Teachers and Teaching*, 15, 1, pp. 25–41.

Crook, C. (2002) 'The social character of knowing and learning' *Journal of Information Technology in Teacher Education*, 10, pp. 19–36.

Crook, C. (2008) 'Theories of formal and informal learning in the world of web 2.0' in Livingstone, S. (ed.) *Theorising the Benefits of New Technology for Youth*, University of Oxford/London School of Economics.

Cuban, L. (1986) *Teachers and Machines: The Classroom Use of Technology since 1920*, New York, Teachers College Press.

Curtis, P. (2009) 'McDonald's to sponsor Australian maths lessons' *The Guardian*, 20 March, p. 23.

Daanen, H. and Facer, K. (2007) *2020 and Beyond: Educational Futures*, Bristol, Futurelab.

Dale, R., Robertson, S. and Shortis, T. (2004) 'You can't not go with the technological flow, can you?' *Journal of Computer Assisted Learning*, 20, pp. 456–470.

Daniel, J. (2010) *Mega-Schools, Technology and Teachers*, London, Routledge.

Darrow, B. (1932) *Radio: The Assistant Teacher*, Columbus OH, RG Adams.

De Botton, A. (2009) 'My week' *The Observer*, 21 June, p. 36.

Dean, J. (2002) *Publicity's Secret*, Ithaca NY, Cornell University Press.

Dittoe, W. (2006) 'Seriously cool places' in Oblinger, D. (ed.) *Learning Spaces*, Washington DC, Educause.

Dreyfus, H. (2001) *On the Internet*, London, Routledge.

Dutton, W. (2008) 'Discussant comments' in Livingstone, S. (ed.) *Theorising the Benefits of New Technology for Youth: Controversies of Learning and Development*, University of Oxford/London School of Economics.

Dutton, W. and Helsper, E. (2009) *Oxford Internet Survey: The Internet in Britain 2009*, Oxford, OXiS.

Edson, J. (2007) 'Curriculum 2.0: user-driven education' *The Huffington Post*, 25 June [www.huffingtonpost.com/jonathan-edson/curriculum-20-userdri_b_53690.html] Last accessed 1 Sept. 2010.

Eisner, E. (2005) *Reimagining Schools: The Selected Works of Elliot W. Eisner*, London, Routledge.

Ellis, K. (2008) 'Cyber charter schools: evolution, issues, and opportunities in funding and localized oversight' *Educational Horizons*, 86, 3, pp. 142–152.

Evans, C. (1979) *The Mighty Micro*, London, Coronet.

Facer, K. (2009) *Beyond Current Horizons: Final Report*, London, Department for Children, Schools and Families.

Facer, K. and Green, H. (2007) 'Curriculum 2.0: educating the digital generation' *Demos Collection*, no. 24, pp. 47–58.

Facer, K. and Sandford, R. (2010) 'The next twenty-five years: future scenarios and future directions for education and technology' *Journal of Computer Assisted Learning*, 26, 1, pp. 18–27.

Farooq, U., Schank, P., Harris, A., Fusco, J. and Schlager, M. (2007) 'Sustaining a community computing infrastructure for online teacher professional development' *Computer Supported Cooperative Work*, 16, 4–5, pp. 397–429.

Feenberg, A. (2003) 'Modernity theory and technology studies: reflections on bridging the gap' in Misa, T., Brey, P. and Feenberg, A. (eds) *Modernity and Technology*, Cambridge, MIT Press.

Fisher, M. and Baird, D. (2009) 'Pedagogical mashup: Gen Y, social media, and digital learning styles' in Hin, L. and Subramaniam, R. (eds) *Handbook of Research on New Media Literacy at the K-12 Level*, Hershey PA, IGI Global.

Friedman, T. (2007) *The World is Flat* [Release 3.0] New York, Farrar, Straus and Giroux.

Fuchs, T. and Woessmann, L. (2004) 'What accounts for international differences in student performance?' *Econometric Society 2004 Australasian Meetings* paper 274.

Fuery, K. (2009) *New Media: Culture and Image*, Basingstoke, Palgrave Macmillan.

Fullan, M. (2007) *The New Meaning of Educational Change*, New York, Teachers College Press.

Gage, N. (1978) *The Scientific Basis for the Art of Teaching*, New York, Teachers College Press.

Gane, N. (2005) 'An information age without technology' *Information, Communication and Society*, 8, 4, pp. 471–476.

Garrison, D. and Kanuka, H. (2004) 'Blended learning: uncovering its transformative potential in higher education' *Internet and Higher Education*, 7, pp. 95–105.

Garrison, M. and Bromley, H. (2004) 'Social contexts, defensive pedagogies and the (mis)uses of educational technology' *Educational Policy*, 18, pp. 589–613.

Gauntlett, D. (2008) *Participation Culture, Creativity, and Social Change*, Inaugural lecture to the University of Westminster, 12 November.

Gee, J. (2005) 'Semiotic social spaces and affinity spaces' in Barton, D. and Tusting, K. (eds) *Beyond Communities of Practice*, Cambridge, Cambridge University Press.

Gere, C. (2008) *Digital Culture*, [second edition] London, Reaktion.

Gertner, A. and van Lehn, K. (2000) 'Andes: a coached problem-solving environment for physics' *Lecture Notes in Computer Science*, volume 1839/2000, pp. 133–142.

Goyder, J. (1997) *Technology and Society: A Canadian Perspective*, Toronto, University of Toronto Press.

Grabinger, S. and Dunlap, J. (1996) 'Rich environments for active learning' in Kommers, P., Grabinger, S. and Dunlap, J. (eds) *Hypermedia Learning Environments*, Mawah NJ, Lawrence Erlbaum.

Graham, S. (2002) 'Bridging urban divides?' *Urban Studies*, 39, 1, pp. 33–56.

Grant, L. and Villabos, G. (2008) *Designing Educational Technologies for Social Justice*, Bristol, Futurelab.

Greenfield, S. reported in Lords Hansard (2009) 'Children: social networking sites: debate' *Lords Hansard*, vol. 707, no. 33 (12 February) columns 1290–1293 [www.publications.parliament.uk/pa/ld200809/ldhansrd/index/090212.html] Last accessed 1 Sept. 2010.

Gross, R. and Gross, B. (1969) *Radical School Reform*, London, Penguin.

Haigh, G. (2007) *Inspirational and Cautionary Tales for Would-Be School Leaders*, London, Taylor and Francis.

Harrison, A. (2009) 'Changing spaces, changing places' paper for the *Beyond Current Horizons Project* London, Department for Children, Schools and Families.

Hawkridge, D. (1983) *New Information Technology in Education*, Beckenham, Croom Helm.

Haythornthwaite, C. (2005) 'Social networks and internet connectivity effects' *Information, Communication and Society*, 8, 2, pp. 125–147.

Healy, J. (1999) *Endangered Minds*, New York, Simon & Schuster.

Heeks, R. (2008) 'ICT4D 2.0: the next phase of applying ICT for international development' *Computer*, June, pp. 26–33.

Hezel, R. (1980) 'Public broadcasting: can it teach?' *Journal of Communication*, 30, 3, pp. 173–178.

Himanen, P. (2001) *The Hacker Ethic and the Spirit of the Information Age*, London, Martin Secker & Warburg.

Hirschheim, R. (2005) 'The internet-based education bandwagon' *Communications of the ACM*, 48, 7, pp. 97–101.

Hoban, C., Hoban, C. and Zisman, S. (1937) *Visualising the Curriculum*, New York, Dryden Press.

Hodkinson, P. and Macleod, F. (2010) 'Contrasting concepts of learning and contrasting research methodologies: affinities and bias' *British Educational Research Journal*, 36, 2, pp. 173–189.

Hoinacki, L. (2002) 'Reading Ivan Illich' in Hoinacki, L. and Mitcham, C. (eds) *The Challenges of Ivan Illich*, New York, State University of New York Press.

Hornbostel, V. (1955) 'Audio-visual education in urban school systems' *Educational Technology Research and Development*, 3, 3, pp. 206–212.

Illich, I. (1971) *Deschooling Society* London, Marion Boyars.

Illich, I. (1973) *Tools for Conviviality*, London, Marion Boyars.

The Instructor (1928) 'Nature study by radio' *The Instructor*, 7, 6, p. 287.

Ito, M., Horst, H., Bittanti, M., Boyd, D., Herr-Stephenson, R., Lange, P., Pascoe, C. and Robinson, L. (2008) *Living and Learning with New Media*, Chicago, MacArthur Foundation.

Ito, M., Baumer, S., Bittanti, M. and Boyd, D. (2009) *Hanging Out, Messing Around, Geeking Out*, Cambridge MA, MIT Press.

Jenkins, H. (2004) 'Why Heather can write' *Technology Review* [BizTech], 6 February [www.technologyreview.com] Last accessed 1 Sept. 2010.

Jenkins, H. (2005) *Confronting the Challenges of Participatory Culture*, Chicago, MacArthur Foundation.

Jensen, B. (2001) *Simplicity: The New Competitive Advantage in a World of More, Better, Faster*, Cambridge MA, Perseus.

Jewitt, C. (2005) 'Multimodality, reading and writing for the twenty-first century' *Discourse: Studies in the Cultural Politics of Education*, 26, 3, pp. 315–331.

John, P. and La Velle, L. (2004) 'Devices and desires' *Technology, Pedagogy and Education*, 13, 3, pp. 307–326.

Johnson, B. (2009) '1980s computing for the twenty-first century' *The Guardian*, Technology supplement, 4 November, p. 5.

Johnson, B. and Arthur, C. (2010) 'Wait is over – but is it the future of media or oversized phone?' *The Guardian*, 28 January, pp. 2–3.

Johnson, N. (2009) 'Teenage technological experts' views of schooling' *Australian Educational Researcher*, 36, 1, pp. 59–72.

Jonassen, D. (1994) 'Evaluating constructivist learning' in Duffy, T. and Jonassen, D. (eds) *Constructivism and the Technology of Instruction*, New York, Lawrence Erlbaum Associates.

Jones, G. (2010) *Cyberschools: An Education Renaissance*, [second edition] Centennial CO, JIU Books.

Jones, S. and Fox, S. (2009) *Generations Online in 2009*, Washington DC, Pew Internet and American Life Project.

Jones, S., Johnson-Yale, C., Millermaier, S. and Seoane Perez, F. (2009) 'U.S. college students' internet use' *Journal of Computer-Mediated Communication*, 14, pp. 244–264.

Kay, A. and Goldberg, A. (1977) 'Personal dynamic media' *Computer*, 10, 3, pp. 31–42.

Keen, A. (2007) *The Cult of the Amateur*, London, Nicholas Brealey.

Keller, F. (1968) 'Goodbye teacher' *Journal of Applied Behaviour Analysis*, 1, pp. 78–89.

Kelly, F., McCain, T. and Jukes, I. (2008) *Teaching the Digital Generation: No More Cookie-Cutter High Schools*, Thousand Oaks CA, Corwin Press.

Kelly, K. (1995) *Out of Control*, New York, Basic.

Kerr, S. (1996) 'Toward a sociology of educational technology' in Jonassen, D. (ed.) *Handbook of Research on Educational Communications and Technology*, New York, Macmillan.

King, W. (1954) 'What teachers expect from educational television' *The Instructor*, 63, 10, pp. 19–20.

Klopfer, E. (2008) *Augmented Learning*, Cambridge MA, MIT Press.

Kozma, R. (2003) *Technology, Innovation, and Educational Change*, Eugene OR, International Society for Technology in Education.

Lanier, J. (2010) *You are Not a Gadget*, London, Allen Lane.

Lankshear, C. and Bigum, C. (1999) 'Literacies and new technologies in school settings' *Pedagogy, Culture and Society*, 7, 3, pp. 445–465.

Lash, S. (2002) *Critique of Information*, London, Sage.

Laurillard, D. (2008) *Digital Technologies and Their Role in Achieving Our Ambitions for Education*, London, Institute of Education.

Lauven, E., Lindahl, M., Oosterbeek, H. and Webbink, D. (2003) *The Effect of Extra Funding for Disadvantaged Students on Achievement*, Department of Economics, University of Amsterdam.

Lave, J. and Wenger, E. (1991) *Situated Learning: Legitimate Peripheral Participation*, Cambridge, Cambridge University Press.

Leadbeater, C. (2008a) 'People power transforms the web in next online revolution' *The Observer*, 9 March, p. 26.

Leadbeater, C. (2008b) *We-Think*, London, Profile.

Leadbeater, C. (2010) *Cloud Culture*, London, Counterpoint.

Leask, M. and Younie, S. (2001) 'Communal constructivist theory' *Technology, Pedagogy and Education*, 10, 1, pp. 117–134.

Levinson, D. and Sadovnik, A. (2002) 'Education and society: an introduction' in Levinson, D., Cookson, P. and Sadovnik, A. (eds) *Education and Sociology*, London, Taylor & Francis.

Levy, P. (1997/1999) *Collective Intelligence: Mankind's Emerging World in Cyberspace* (trans. Bononno, R.) London, Perseus.

Lewis, R. (1962) 'TV or not TV? That is the question' *Teachers College Record*, 63, 7, pp. 564–569.

Lievrouw, L. and Livingstone, S. (2002) *Handbook of New Media: Social Shaping and Social Consequences*, London, Sage.

Light, A. and Luckin, R. (2008) *Social Justice and User-Centred Design*, Bristol, Futurelab.

Livingstone, D. (2000) 'Researching expanded notions of learning and work and underemployment' *International Review of Education*, 46, 6, pp. 491–514.

Lockee B., Burton J. and Cross L. (1999) 'No comparison: distance education finds a new use for "no significant difference"' *Educational Technology Research and Development*, 47, 3, pp. 33–42.

Lortie, D. (1975) *Schoolteacher: A Sociological Study*, Chicago, University of Chicago Press.

Lortie, D. (2002) *Schoolteacher: A Sociological Study* [second edition] Chicago, University of Chicago Press.

Luckin, R. (2010) *Re-Designing Learning Contexts: Technology-Rich, Learner-Centred Ecologies*, London, Routledge.

Luke, C. (2003) 'Pedagogy, connectivity, multimodality, and interdisciplinarity' *Reading Research Quarterly*, 38, 3, pp. 397–413.

Luyt, B. (2008) 'The One Laptop Per Child project and the negotiation of technological meaning' *First Monday*, 13, 6 [http://firstmonday.org] Last accessed 1 Sept. 2010.

Mably, C. (1980) 'The microelectronics revolution and teacher education' *European Journal of Teacher Education*, 3, 1, pp. 25–35.

MacKenzie, D. and Wajcman, J. (1985) *The Social Shaping of Technology*, Milton Keynes, Open University Press.

McKinney, D., Dycka, J. and Lubera, E. (2009) 'iTunes University and the classroom: can podcasts replace professors?' *Computers & Education*, 52, 3, pp. 617–623.

McLoughlin, C. and Lee, M. (2008) 'Mapping the digital terrain' in Proceedings ascilite Melbourne 2008 [www.ascilite.org.au/conferences/melbourne08/procs/mcloughlin.pdf] Last accessed 1 Sept. 2010.

McWilliam, E. and Taylor, P. (1998) 'Teacher im/material: challenging the new pedagogies of instructional design' *Educational Researcher*, 27, 8, pp. 29–35.

Mahiri, J. (2011) *Digital Tools in Urban Schools: Mediating a Remix of Learning*, Ann Arbor MI, University of Michigan Press.

Markoff, J. (2006) 'For $150, third-world laptop stirs big debate' *New York Times*, 30 November [www.nytimes.com/2006/11/30/technology/30laptop.html] Last accessed 1 Sept. 2010.

Marsick, V. and Watkins, K. (1990) *Informal and Incidental Learning in the Workplace*, London, Routledge.

Martin, J. and Norman, A. (1970) *The Computerised Society*, Englewood Cliffs NJ, Prentice Hall.

Masschelein, J. and Quaghebeur, K. (2005) 'Participation for better or for worse?' *Journal of Philosophy of Education*, 39, 1, pp. 52–65.

Mathews, N. (1932) 'Social-science broadcasts for Cleveland schools' *Education on the Air*, 3, pp. 177–180.

Mayes, T. (1995) 'Learning technologies and Groundhog Day' in Strang, W., Simpson, V. and Slater, D. (eds) *Hypermedia at Work*, Canterbury, University of Kent.

Mayes, T. (2007) 'Groundhog Day again?' Keynote speech to JISC Conference, Innovating e-Learning 2007: Institutional Transformation and Supporting Lifelong Learning online conference, June.

Means, B., Toyama, Y., Murphy, R., Bakia, M. and Jones, K. (2009) *Evaluation of Evidence-Based Practice in Online Learning*, Washington DC, U.S. Department of Education.

Miller, R. (2006) 'Equity in a twenty-first century learning intensive society' *Foresight*, 8, 4, pp. 13–22.

Mitchell, W. (1995) *City of Bits*, Cambridge MA, MIT Press.

Mitchell, W. (2000) *E-Topia*, Cambridge MA, MIT Press.

Monahan, T. (2005) *Globalization, Technological Change and Public Education*, London, Routledge.

Morehead, H. (1955) 'Television and learning' *Educational Leadership*, 13, 3, pp. 167–179.

Morgan, J. (1931) 'National committee on education by radio' *Education on the Air*, 2, pp. 3–14.

Moss, R., Jones, C. and Gunter, B. (1991) *Television in Schools*, London, Independent Television Commission.

Muffoletto, R. (2001) *Education and Technology: Critical and Reflective Practices*, Cresskill NJ, Hampton Press.

Mumford, L. (1964) 'The automation of knowledge' *Current Issues in Higher Education*, 19, pp. 11–21.

Murdock, G. (2004) 'Past the posts: rethinking change, retrieving critique' *European Journal of Communication*, 19, 1, pp. 19–38.

Naughton, J. (2005) 'The $100 laptop question' *The Observer*, Business supplement 4 December, p. 6.

Negroponte, N. (1995) *Being Digital*, London, Coronet.

Nielsen, J. (2006) *Participation Inequality: Encouraging More Users to Contribute*, [www.useit.com/alertbox/participation_inequality.html] Last accessed 1 Sept. 2010.

Njenga, J. and Fourie, L. (2010) 'The myths about e-learning in higher education' *British Journal of Educational Technology*, 41, 2, pp. 199–212.

Noble, D. (2002) *Digital Diploma Mills*, New York, New York University Press.

Nunes, M. (2006) *Cyberspaces of Everyday Life*, Minneapolis, University of Minneapolis Press.

Nye, D. (2007) *Technology Matters: Questions to Live With*, Cambridge MA, MIT Press.

O'Reilly, T. (2005) 'What is web 2.0? Design patterns and business models for the next generation of software' [www.oreillynet.com] Last accessed 1 Sept. 2010.

OLPC [One Laptop Per Child] (2010) *One Laptop Per Child – Mission Statement* [www.laptop.org/vision] Last accessed 1 Sept. 2010.

Oppenheimer, T. (1997) 'The Computer Delusion' *The Atlantic Monthly*, 280, 1, pp. 45–62.

Palfrey, J. and Gasser, U. (2008) *Born Digital*, New York, Basic.

Papert, S. (1983) 'Seymour Papert's 'Microworld': an educational utopia – interview with Charles Euchner' *Education Week* 18 May [www.edweek.org] Last accessed 1 Sept. 2010.

Papert, S. (1984) 'Trying to predict the future' *Popular Computing*, 3, 13, pp. 30–44.

Papert, S. (1996) 'Schools out? Interview of Seymour Papert by David S. Bennahum' [http://memex.org/meme2-13.html] Last accessed 1 Sept. 2010.

Papert, S. (1998) 'Does easy do it? Children, games, and learning' *Game Developer* June/September, pp. 88–92 [www.papert.org/articles/Doeseasydoit.html] Last accessed 1 Sept. 2010.

Perelman, L. (1992) *School's Out*, New York, Avon.

Peters, M. and McDonough, T. (2008) 'Editorial' *Critical Studies in Education*, 49, 1, pp. 127–142.

Petrina, S. (2005) 'How (and why) digital diploma mills (don't) work' *Workplace*, 7, 1, pp. 38–59.

Pew Internet and American Life Project (2003) *The Ever-Shifting Internet Population: A New Look at Internet Access and the Digital Divide*' Washington DC, Pew Internet and American Life Project.

Plowman, L., Stephen, C. and Peake, J. (2010) *Growing Up with Technology: Young Children Learning in a Digital World*, London, Routledge.

Postman, N. (1996) *The End of Education: Redefining the Value of School*, New York, Vintage.

Prensky, M. (2001) 'Digital natives, digital immigrants' *On the Horizon*, 9, 5, pp. 1–6.

Prensky, M. (2005) 'Listen to the natives' *Educational Leadership*, 63, 4, pp. 8–13.

Prensky, M. (2008) 'The role of technology in teaching and the classroom' *Educational Technology*, 48, 6, November/December [www.marcprensky.com/writing/] Last accessed 1 Sept. 2010.

Prensky, M. (2009) 'H. Sapiens Digital: from digital natives and digital immigrants to digital wisdom' *Innovate*, 5, 3, February/March [www.marcprensky.com/writing/] Last accessed 1 Sept. 2010.

Reedy, G. (2008) 'PowerPoint, interactive whiteboards, and the visual culture of technology in schools' *Technology, Pedagogy and Education*, 17, 2, pp. 143–162.

Reiser, R. (2001) 'A history of instructional design and technology' *Educational Technology Research and Development*, 49, 1, pp. 53–64.

Reynolds, D., Treharne, D. and Tripp, H. (2003) 'ICT – the hopes and the reality' *British Journal of Educational Technology*, 34, 2, pp. 151–167.

Richmond, S. (1974) 'Man= the rational hunter' *Philosophy of the Social Sciences*, 4, 2, pp. 279–291.

Rifkin, J. (2000) *The Age of Access*, Harmondsworth, Penguin.

Rigney, D. (2010) *The Matthew Effect*, New York, Columbia University Press.

Robins, K. and Webster, F. (1989) *The Technical Fix: Education, Computers and Industry*, London, Macmillan.

Rogers, A. (2003) *What is the Difference?* Leicester, National Institute for Adult Continuing Education.

Russell, T. (2001) *The No Significant Difference Phenomenon*, Montgomery AL, International Distance Education Certification Centre.

Saettler, P. (1990) *The Evolution of American Educational Technology*, Englewood CO, Libraries Unlimited.

Säljö, R. (1979) 'Learning in the learner's perspective' *Reports from the Institute of Education*, University of Gothenburg, report no.76.

Sarason, S. (1990) *The Predictable Failure of Educational Reform*, San Francisco, Jossey Bass.

Sawchuk, P. (2003) 'The 'unionization effect' among adult computer learners' *British Journal of Sociology of Education*, 24, 5, pp. 639–648.

Scardamalia, M. and Bereiter, C. (1994) 'Computer support for knowledge-building communities' *The Journal of the Learning Sciences*, 3, 3, pp. 265–283.

Schultz, N. (2009) 'Time to banish the neuromyths in education?' *The New Scientist*, 203, 2726, 16 September, pp. 8–9.

Schwartz, D. and Bransford, J. (1998) 'A time for telling' *Cognition and Instruction*, 16, 4, pp. 475–522.

Sellen, A. and Harper, R. (2001) *The Myth of the Paperless Office*, Cambridge, MIT Press.

Sellinger, M. (2009) 'ICT for education: catalyst for development' in Unwin, T. (ed.) *ICT4D: Information and Communication Technology for Development*, Cambridge, Cambridge University Press.

Selwood, I. (2005) 'Primary school teachers' use of ICT for administration and management' in Tatnall, A., Osorio, J. and Visscher, A. (eds) *Information Technology and Educational Management in the Knowledge Society*, Berlin, Springer.

Sfard, A. (1998) 'On two metaphors for learning and the dangers of choosing just one' *Educational Researcher*, 27, 2, pp. 4–13.

Shirky, C. (2008) *Here Comes Everybody*, London, Allen Lane.

Siemens, G. (2004) 'Connectivism: a learning theory for the digital age' [www.elearnspace.org/Articles/connectivism.htm] Last accessed 1 Sept. 2010.

Sigman, A. (2009) 'Well connected' *The Biologist*, 56, 1, pp. 14–20.

Skinner, B. (1958) 'Teaching machines' *Science*, 128, 3330, pp. 969–977.

Sleeman, D. and Brown, J. (1982) *Intelligent Tutoring Systems*, London, Academic Press.

Small, G. and Vorgon, G. (2008) *iBRAIN: Surviving the Technological Alteration of the Modern Mind*, London, Collins.

Smith, M. (1962) 'Using television in the classroom' *Teachers College Record*, 63, 7, pp. 564–564.

Solomon, G. and Schrum, L. (2007) *Web 2.0: New Tools, New Schools*, Washington DC, International Society for Technology in Education.

Somekh, B. (2007) *Pedagogy and Learning with ICT*, London, Routledge.

Standish, P. (2008) 'Preface' *Journal of Philosophy of Education*, 42, 3–4, pp. 349–353.

Stonier, T. and Conlin, C. (1985) *The Three Cs: Children, Computers and Communication*, London, Wiley.

Suoranta, J. and Vadén, T. (2010) *Wikiworld*, London, Pluto Press.

Suppes, P. (1966) 'The uses of computers in education' *Scientific American*, 215, pp. 206–220.

Suppes, P. (1984) 'Observations about the application of artificial intelligence research to education' in Walker, D. and Hess, R. (eds) *Instructional Software: Principles and Perspectives for Design and Use*, Belmont CA, Wadsworth.

Sutherland, R., Robertson, S. and John, P. (2008) *Improving Classroom Learning with ICT*, London, Routledge.

Swain, H. (2009) 'Look! No fees' *The Guardian*, Education supplement, Tuesday 6 October, p. 7.

Tapscott, D. (1999) 'Educating the net generation' *Educational Leadership*, 56, 5, pp. 6–11.

Teich, A. (1997) *Technology and the Future*, New York, St. Martin's.

Tiagert, J. (1923) 'Film and education' *Addresses and Proceedings – National Education Association of the United States, Volume 1*, Washington DC, National Education Association of the United States.

Toffler, A. (1970) *Future Shock*, London, Bodley Head.

Tondeur, J., van Braak, J. and Valcke, M. (2007) 'Towards a typology of computer use in primary education' *Journal of Computer Assisted Learning*, 23, pp. 197–206.

Tooley, J. (2006) 'Education reclaimed' in Booth, P. (ed.) *Towards a Liberal Utopia?* London, Continuum.

Trilling, B. and Fadel, C. (2009) *Twenty-First Century Skills: Learning for Life in Our Times*, New York, Jossey-Bass.

Tufekci, Z. (2008) 'Grooming, gossip, Facebook and MySpace' *Information, Communication and Society*, 11, 4, pp. 544–564.

Tyack, D. and Hansot, E. (1985) 'Futures that never happened: technology and the classroom' *Education Week*, 4 September, p. 40.

Tyack, D. and Tobin, W. (1995) 'The 'grammar' of schooling: why has it been so hard to change?' *American Educational Research Journal*, 31, 3, pp. 453–479.

van Dijk, J. (2005) *The Deepening Divide*, London, Sage.

Van Loon, J. (2008) *Media Technology: Critical Perspectives*, New York, McGraw Hill.

Volti, R. (1992) *Society and Technological Change*, New York, St. Martin's Press.

Volungeviciene, A. and Leduc, L. (2006) 'Variations in transnational tutoring in distance learning' *International Journal of Technologies in Higher Education*, 3, 2, pp. 19–27.

von Hippel, E. (2005) *Democratising Innovation*, Cambridge MA, MIT Press.

Warner, D. (2006) *Schooling in the Knowledge Era*, Victoria, Australian Council for Education Research.

Warschauer, M. (2003) *Technology and Social Inclusion*, Cambridge MA, MIT Press.

Watson, J., Gemin, B. and Ryan, J. (2008) *Keeping Pace with K–12 Online Learning 2008: A Review of State-Level Policy and Practice*, Philadelphia PA, Evergreen Consulting Associates.

Weber, S. (2000) '*The Political Economy of Open Source Software*' 'Berkeley Roundtable on the International Economy' – Economy Project Working Paper 15.

Weber, S. and Bussell, J. (2005) 'Will information technology reshape the north-south asymmetry of power in the global political economy? *Studies in Comparative International Development*, 40, 2, pp. 62–84.

Weinberg, A. (1966/ 1997) 'Can technology replace social engineering?' in Hawisher, G. and Selfe, C. (eds) *Literacy, Technology and Society*, New York, Prentice Hall.

Wellman, B., Haase, A., Witte, J. and Hampton, K. (2001) 'Does the internet increase, decrease, or supplement social capital?' *American Behavioural Scientist*, 45, 3, pp. 436–455.

Wessels, B. (2010) *Understanding the Internet*, Basingstoke, Palgrave-Macmillan.

Whitney, P., Grimes, J. and Kumar, V. (2007) *Schools in the Digital Age*, Chicago, MacArthur Foundation.

Whitworth, A. (2009) *Information Obesity*, Oxford, Chandros.

Wilhelm, A. (2004) *Digital Nation*, Cambridge MA, MIT Press.

Williams, P. (2008) 'Leading schooling in the digital age' *School Leadership and Management*, 28, 3, pp. 213–228.

Windschitl, M. and Sahl, K. (2002) 'Tracing teachers' use of technology in a laptop computer school: the interplay of teacher beliefs, social dynamics, and institutional culture' *American Educational Research Journal*, 39, 1, pp. 165–205.

Winner, L. (1986) *The Whale and the Reactor*, Chicago, University of Chicago Press.

Witchalls, C. (2005) 'Bridging the digital divide' *The Guardian*, 'Online' supplement, 17 February, p. 23.

Withers, K. with Sheldon, R. (2008) *Behind the Screen*, London, Institute for Public Policy Research.

Woelfel, N. and Tyler, K. (1945) *Radio and the School*, New York, World Book Company.

Woolgar, S. (2002) *Virtual Society? Technology, Cyberbole, Reality*, Oxford, Oxford University Press.

Young, L., Thearling, K., Skiena, S., Robison, A., Omohundro, S., Mel, B. and Wolfram, S. (1988) 'Academic computing in the year 2000' *Academic Computing*, 2, 8–12, pp. 62–65.

Young, M. (2007) *Bringing Knowledge Back In*, London, Routledge.

Young, M. and Muller, J. (2009) '*Three Scenarios for the Future*' Paper for Beyond Current Horizons programme London, Department for Children, Schools and Families.

Zepke, N. (2008) 'Futures thinking' *Computers in New Zealand Schools*, 20, 3, pp. 4–12.

Ziegler, S. (2007) 'The (mis)education of Generation M' *Learning, Media and Technology*, 32, 1, pp. 69–81.

Index